Talk about Faith

How do people of faith use language to position themselves, and their beliefs and practices, in the contemporary world? This pioneering and original study looks closely at how Christians and Muslims talk to people inside and outside of their own communities about what they think are the right things to believe and do. From debates to podcasts and YouTube videos, the book covers a range of engaging texts and contexts, showing how doctrine and beliefs are not nearly as fixed and static as we might think, and that people are prone to change what they say they believe, depending on whom they are talking to. From abortion, to hell, to whether it's okay to sell alcohol, Pihlaja investigates how Christians and Muslims struggle with different elements of their own faith and try to make decisions about what to do when there are so many different voices to believe.

STEPHEN PIHLAJA is Reader in Stylistics at Newman University. Recent publications include *Religious Talk Online* (Cambridge University Press, 2018).

T0384605

Talk about Faith

How Debate and Conversation Shape Belief

Stephen Pihlaja

Newman University

CAMBRIDGE
UNIVERSITY PRESS

CAMBRIDGE
UNIVERSITY PRESS

Shaftesbury Road, Cambridge CB2 8EA, United Kingdom

One Liberty Plaza, 20th Floor, New York, NY 10006, USA

477 Williamstown Road, Port Melbourne, VIC 3207, Australia

314–321, 3rd Floor, Plot 3, Splendor Forum, Jasola District Centre, New Delhi – 110025, India

103 Penang Road, #05–06/07, Visioncrest Commercial, Singapore 238467

Cambridge University Press is part of Cambridge University Press & Assessment, a department of the University of Cambridge.

We share the University's mission to contribute to society through the pursuit of education, learning and research at the highest international levels of excellence.

www.cambridge.org
Information on this title: www.cambridge.org/9781108469333

DOI: 10.1017/9781108629881

First published 2021
First paperback edition 2023

A catalogue record for this publication is available from the British Library

Library of Congress Cataloging-in-Publication data
Names: Pihlaja, Stephen, author.
Title: Talk about faith : how debate and conversation shape belief / Stephen Pihlaja, Newman University.
Description: Cambridge, United Kingdom ; New York, NY, USA : Cambridge University Press, 2021. | Includes bibliographical references and index.
Identifiers: LCCN 2020031356 (print) | LCCN 2020031357 (ebook) | ISBN 9781108475990 (hardback) | ISBN 9781108629881 (epub)
Subjects: LCSH: Faith. | Christianity. | Islam. | Communication – Religious aspects. | Language and languages – Religious aspects.
Classification: LCC BT771.3 .P54 2020 (print) | LCC BT771.3 (ebook) | DDC 234/.23–dc23
LC record available at https://lccn.loc.gov/2020031356
LC ebook record available at https://lccn.loc.gov/2020031357

ISBN   978-1-108-47599-0   Hardback
ISBN   978-1-108-46933-3   Paperback

Contents

Acknowledgements

Support from the Linnaeus University Centre for Concurrences in Colonial and Postcolonial Studies (Växjö, Sweden) made this book possible.

1   Talk about Faith in Context

Important moments in religions often come wrapped in epic stories: Moses coming down from the mountain with tablets in his hands, Mohammad returning to Mecca in 629 CE, Jesus riding into Jerusalem on a donkey. These stories are etched in the minds of religious believers because they represent ways of understanding how the supernatural interacts with humans. They become parts of sacred texts and doctrinal statements that define how people think about right beliefs and practices. They involve prophets and theologians and priests and religious leaders speaking the very word of God to people who listen and act on it.

At the same time, the day-to-day experiences of religious believers include both the mundane and the sacred. Prayers might be chanted in ancient languages but also muttered under the breath in moments of frustration. Talk about religious faith does, of course, happen within religious institutions, but it also occurs in the daily interaction of believers, whose conversations might include subtle references to sacred texts or prayers or hymns. Believers might look to one another for advice and support, making decisions about what they should or shouldn't do depending on what those in their own faith community say. Sacred texts and doctrine about right practice and belief can come and go in these conversations, as people work to live out the ideals of their faith in the messy contexts of real life.

The importance of interaction within religious communities was clearest to me as a university student when I was very involved in an Evangelical Christian campus ministry. The ministry was student-led, with a loose affiliation to a national association; as a student leader, I organised a variety of events throughout the week – prayer meetings, mentorship programmes, and large group meetings where we met for collective worship on Friday nights. One weekly meeting of an accountability group met late on Wednesday nights. This particular meeting was for men only, with a women's group meeting at another time in the week, and was organised around eleven questions all the members would memorise and which we would all answer in turn. The questions ranged in topics from health and fitness to personal devotion to sexual purity, that topic often taking the most time in the meeting. These meetings became very important for the participants, where we laughed together and did practical theology and ethics, attempting to put into practice our faith and challenge one another.

An institution did not sanction the meetings – there was no instruction or Bible study. There was no explicit hierarchy or leadership; although there were some members who were more consistent attenders, or older, or more pious, the conversations were those of friends, taking bits of theology, scripture, practical advice, and experience to piece together our Christian lives in the challenging university context, with alcohol, sex, and drugs constantly tempting us away from a pure life. The meetings grounded us in a community that supported and encouraged in a way that prayer meetings or sermons or collective worship didn't. In the accountability group, the real questions of faith were hashed out in the back and forth of our discussions about what we were facing in our lives and how we might live in light of the commitments we had made.

Over the years, long after leaving Christianity as a faith system, I've often thought about the conversations that occurred in the accountability group and how important they had been for my own formation and how I thought about myself as a person of faith in the world. The dynamics of the group interaction included irreverent in-jokes and code words but also group prayer and scripture reading. Members of the group would appeal to what they had heard pastors say or things they had read in books, all while interacting with others who would agree with them or challenge them or offer slightly differing views on any number of topics, views which might evolve over weeks or semesters or years, as the group members grew or changed or experienced new things.

My men's accountability group at Knox College is not likely to come to mind when you think of *religious discourse* – it simply doesn't have the authority or publicity that the Pope's declaration about the immorality of the death penalty does, for example. The conversations in open-air food courts that follow Friday prayer in Malaysia are not seen as important as the prayers themselves. Real talk in real contexts challenges a foregrounding of institutional religious discourse. If we are going to understand how religion and theology are developing in the contemporary world, we need to look beyond what pastors and priests, theologians and imams, are teaching in formal contexts, and we need to engage seriously with informal religious discourse, what people who interact with one another every day are saying in contexts where faith is a developing, emerging part of a broader social world. This real world does, of course, include the rules of sacred texts about what is or is not acceptable, and the words and teachings of people with authority. However, everyday interaction also includes the bending of rules for specific situations or times when a faith practice needs to be adapted for a new context. The discourse processes by which people put their faith into action in the real world and how sacred texts, teachings, and institutional discourses interact may very well be the real locus for religious development.

1.1   Discourse

To begin a study of *religious discourse*, we need to define what we mean by both 'discourse' and 'religion', two terms that have historically been used to describe a variety of very different things. The Foucauldian (Foucault, 1971) concept of discourse as describing larger social systems of ordering knowledge and power is a useful starting point for thinking about how language is not just the words we use and how we order them but exists within certain societal structures that restrict how people communicate. In this sense, discourse comes to encompass more than just the language in use in a particular context, but the practices and beliefs underpinning that language usf. Understanding discourse as embedded in cultural practice helps analysts describe how meaning emerges in interaction because ways of speaking differ depending on cultural and contextual constraints. From a Foucauldian perspective, describing the 'Discourse of Islam' may well be a useful category to distinguish between how Islam could be ordered as a social system compared and contrasted with the 'Discourse of Christianity'. The work of the analyst, from this perspective, is a kind of archaeology, to work through written and spoken language to make sense of the larger social structures.

Foucault's description of discourse highlights that individuals do not speak or write in a void. There are, as Foucault (1971, p. 7) writes, 'no beginnings' and the speaker is merely standing in the path of the 'nameless speaking voice' and entering into something that already exists. The individual speaks within a larger system of language and thought, one that is constrained by social and linguistic systems. The Bakhtinian (1981) *heteroglossia* resonates in this understanding of discourse; *heteroglossia* describes how the individual speaks within the constraints of an ordered system of language, but with the creative potential – Foucault refers to the 'slender gap' (1971, p. 7) – to do something novel. Analysts, then, interested in making sense of what people say and write at any given time, need to understand not only the history of the thing that is being spoken about, whether it be a religious belief or a sport or a popular TV show, but how that thing has been spoken about in the past and the ways in which it is spoken about in the present.

Foucault further differentiates among different kinds of discourse, describing first-order and second-order discourses, a concept which is particularly useful in analysis of interaction around religion and belief. Foucault shows how first-order, or fundamental, discourses occupy a primary position, and subsequent second-order discourses 'reiterate, expound, and comment' (Foucault, 1971, pp. 12–13) on the fundamental discourse. The fundamental discourse can give rise to any number of new discourses and become 'blurred and disappear' (p. 13) in the commentary and retelling. Foucault gives the example of Homer's *Odyssey* from which other commentaries and retellings emerge (perhaps most famously, James Joyce's *Ulysses*). The texts which are subsequently based on the *Odyssey* are, to varying degrees, distinct from the original, and any individual reader's interaction with a retelling of the story will include varying degrees of knowledge of the original.

Considering the category of religion, the fundamental discourses of sacred texts can be seen in this same way, and the residue of the fundamental discourse can be seen in interaction, with speakers aware, again to varying degrees, of the presence of the fundamental discourse in their own talk. A Christian may have varying levels of biblical knowledge when, for example, speaking about their actions 'bearing fruit'. The extent to which this is a deliberate reference to John 15, where Jesus tells the parable of the vine and the branches, or Galatians 5:22–23 which describes the Fruits of the Spirit, might be hard to see in a discourse context, but Foucault's point is that the speaker need not be explicitly aware of the reference for the foundational discourse to be relevant. These discourses are baked into cultural knowledge. You don't need to be aware of where they come from exactly to use them effectively, in the same way that you don't need to know the origins of the idiom 'kick the bucket' to use it in conversation.

For analysts interested in describing the specifics of interaction, however, the Foucauldian use of discourse can become problematic because although it is helpful in understanding how institutions and foundational texts exert influence on interaction, Foucauldian discourse analysis is not an inductive process. Rather, Foucault starts with the assertion that there is a system to uncover and then works to uncover it through analysis. For researchers looking at the empirical effects of language on belief and how order emerges in interaction, the focus is the opposite. 'Discourse' might then, in a narrower description, be simply a way of describing language 'above the sentence' (Cameron, 2001), capturing the idea that language is not just individual words, but how they are used in particular texts in particular contexts. This definition focuses on language in use and builds on Saussure's (2011 [1916]) distinction between *langue* and *parole* – language as a system vs. language in use – by differentiating between the constitutional elements of the sentence and the use of those elements in complex social interaction. Of course, the individual lexico-grammatical elements of language can and should be of interest in how analysts understand concrete utterances (Bakhtin, 1986), but discourse describes the level beyond that, where language has meaning and accomplishes certain actions because of the context in which it is used. To understand, as a classic example goes (Austin, 1975), the consequences of someone saying the phrase 'I now pronounce you husband and wife', the analyst needs to know if the speaker is at a wedding ceremony or in a bar on a Friday night. The meaning exists beyond the words and how they are ordered.

Importantly, the understanding of discourse as language above the sentence is conceptual and does not see it as something that can be counted and quantified. The analyst needs further empirical categories, like an academic lecture or a conversation, or, perhaps more generically, a discourse event to segment-specific instances of discourse in the world. This kind of discourse, however, cannot be used to describe a 'Discourse of Muslims' in the way that we might in a Foucauldian sense because the analyst might immediately ask, which Muslims and where and in what context? Is it the discourse of Muslims shopping for fruit in Indonesia, or Muslims attending an *Iftar* meal during Ramadan in Detroit? The specific context will be much more important in making sense of what is being said and whether being Muslim is even particularly relevant to the analysis.

I introduce both conceptions of discourse not to force a choice between how the term is understood, but to recognise that the challenge for discourse analysts is balancing the empirical analysis of individual elements of interaction, be they pauses, or overlaps, or laughter, in any exchange, with attempts to understand these observations and analyses in the light of larger cultural and societal structures. The close analysis of interaction, as conversation analysts like Sacks, Jefferson, and Schegloff have shown, the regularities of conversation result in patterns that can be observed with surprising regularity in day-to-day interaction (see Schegloff, 1972; Sacks, Schegloff, & Jefferson, 1974; Sacks, 1992). These regularities and learned ways of speaking have consequences for meaning making and identity construction, as foundational sociolinguistic work by Labov (Labov & Waletzky, 1967; Labov, 1972) has also shown. Any pattern, belief, or regularity observed in social interaction exists in a feedback loop where individual utterances reflect, as Bakhtin (1986, p. 60) writes, 'the specific conditions and goals of each' area of human activity, and then feedback into genres of interaction with varying degrees of stability.

To describe the tension of stability and dynamism, Larsen-Freeman and Cameron (2008) use Complex Systems Theory, which has as a key principle the concept of emergence of phenomena on different scales over time. This means that outcomes in discourse are not the result of central planning but emerge from the interaction of components within a system. These factors might include central planning or institutional pressures from powerful people and organisations, but these factors are not necessarily determinative. Complex systems are open systems – the outcomes change as the components in the system change. The outcomes are also scalable. Phenomena that emerge in individual interactions can also emerge as consistent discourse practices on larger scales, the way a neologism might be taken up by more and more speakers over time and eventually enter the standard lexicon.

The interaction of different components in a system and interconnection among scales of discourse can then account for patterns and regularities in interaction in a variety of contexts, but particularly for faith and religion. As a complex system, religious discourse can be regular and predictable, but also dynamic and open for change, with a range of possibilities in between. The regular call to prayer in a Muslim community, the impromptu prayer of a Bible study group, and an encounter between a Muslim street preacher and a drunk person on a city street – each of these examples of religious discourse will feature varying levels of predictability and dynamism. Each exists within what we might say is a genre of interaction, but with incredible heterogeneity in the material conditions of that interaction, how each person might sound, the words that an individual might use, how long a prayer may last. There is always a range of possibilities for how any particular instance of prayer, for example, might occur and the extent to which it follows or doesn't follow a particular pattern will depend on a number of factors.

In a practical sense, the Discourse Dynamics Approach (Cameron, 2015) isolates five levels at which discourse, and particularly spoken interaction, might be analysed. Level 0 is the precondition of any interaction, the starting point of a conversation or a lecture or a prayer group meeting. This includes all the factors – social, cultural, personal, and so on – that exist before an interaction takes place. Once an interaction begins, a timescale of milliseconds (Level 1) could be analysed to follow the micro aspects of interaction that can affect how a conversation develops. This might include changes in intonation, a change in facial expression, or the start of an interruption, all of which can be observed on close analysis. The next scale, Level 2, includes the minute-by-minute engagement of speakers. These interactions can be seen as units in themselves, Level 3, single discourse events. Finally, Level 4 is where the patterns and regularities in individual interactions accumulate to become the preconditions for new interactions. Importantly, the Discourse Dynamics Approach insists on an empirical basis for identifying patterns and regularities and argues, if not for a consideration of all levels of discourse equally, the necessity of keeping them in mind when considering how and why certain interactions follow the course they do, and the need to do so without relying on deductive, common-sense understandings.

Still, the extent to which cultural and social systems are at work in the production of discourse may be difficult to empirically observe. Relevance theorists (e.g. Sperber & Wilson, 1986; Clark, 2013) have shown a complex interaction between communicative and cognitive contexts, with implicit practices – situated, cultural, personal – leading to different outcomes. Beyond the empirical evidence which can be captured in a systematic study of interaction, the stuff of context requires some 'native' knowledge, knowledge that is often hidden as common sense for speakers. The focus placed on patterns in interaction by Conversation Analysts, for example, reveals how everyday life creates and maintains norms and values in society and is regularly enacted by speakers living in the same broader cultural context. Work can be done, of course, to make this knowledge explicit: in Linguistic Ethnography, for example, the context of interaction can be understood through longitudinal observation and even just talking to people about what they are doing, making explicit how insider and outsider perspectives might offer insight into social life (Rampton et al., 2004; Creese, 2008). Speakers can also explicitly be asked in systematic ways about meanings they intended in any particular utterance, as in Interactional Sociolinguistics (Gumperz, 1982).

In short, linguists have developed a range of tools to observe what occurs 'beyond the sentence' in language in interaction. These methods require robust, reflexive processes, ones that pick apart which components of any given system are exerting influence at any given time to understand why people say the things they do and why they have the effect that they do on the world around them. The analyst must work their way up and down from the minutia of interaction in particular places in particular times to the larger structures that might be at play to make sense of what people say and use that information to understand its place in the social world.

1.2 Religion

Like discourse, religion, as a category, can also be difficult to define, particularly given its common use in everyday conversation – an academic might well do away with the category if it weren't so prevalent. A classic definition sees religion as a 'unified system of beliefs and practices' (Durkheim, 2008 [1915]: 47). Hjarvard's similar definition – 'human actions, beliefs and symbols related to supernatural agencies' (2008; translated by and quoted in Lövheim, 2011, p. 154) – adds the important element of symbols and their relationship to the supernatural, the 'ineffable' qualities of religion and religious experience (McNamara & Giordano, 2018), which have also been a focus of research into religious language. Religion often includes some belief that one can know and interact with something beyond this natural world, something transcendent, and that this interaction is reflected in religious practices and beliefs.

Implicit in Durkheim's conception of religion (its inclusion of 'belief') is a bias towards confessional faiths, particularly Christianity, which would have been prevalent in the early twentieth century. Christianity, Judaism, and Islam are all faiths that include some clear statement of belief or creed to which adherents affirm with intent. However, as Harrison (2006, p. 148) shows in a useful review of the topic, religion is never 'one thing', and essentialist approaches to the category are unlikely to capture the diversity of the ways people believe and act within religions or create useful boundaries between what should or shouldn't be included. Instead, Harrison (2006) categorises three approaches to religion: intellectual, focusing on belief; affective, focusing on emotions; and functional, focusing on practice. Each of these approaches foregrounds particular religions over others and has implicit strengths and weaknesses. A 'beliefs plus practices' model of religion, for example, describes Christianity and Islam well. However, they are less useful in describing Jainism, Hinduism, Buddhism, Shintoism – any number of other religions where belief might be backgrounded or absent and practices are not clearly delineated from other community or cultural functions.

Understanding religion also need not necessarily foreground belief in the supernatural, and it might be more useful to focus on the empirical elements of religious practice to understand how a religion functions within a particular cultural context. Analysts might instead employ a community of practice model (Lave & Wenger, 1991) to describe how religious communities work, focusing on the things the people *do* in religious communities and the ways in which people learn how to do those things. Religious identity might also be seen as one part of a larger social identity and be described using social identity models (Tajfel, Billig, Bundy, & Flament, 1971; Tajfel, 1983) which describe the various ways in which humans understand themselves in relation to those around them and in terms of in-groups and out-groups. Membership Categorisation Analysis (Sacks, 1992; Housley & Fitzgerald, 2002), which describes how people talk about and potentially think about each other as members of different categories, may also be a fruitful way of understanding religious distinctions while taking an agnostic position on the existence or non-existence of the supernatural. Being a Christian or being a Muslim is then not necessarily a static identity, but one with different incumbent beliefs and practices that depend on the interactional context and how categories are being defined, something my own work has shown in relation to the categorisation of 'Christians' in online interaction (Pihlaja, 2014b).

Beliefs and practices about the supernatural are, of course, not limited to named religions with clear doctrinal statements and practices. For example, a 'spiritual, not religious' distinction has grown in prevalence since the 1960s (Ammerman, 2013), implying a suspicion of ordered, organised religious practice while still accepting the importance of recognising the role of spirituality in day-to-day life. To be spiritual but not religious suggests a differentiation between internal and external processes – the spiritual is internal and focused on belief, whereas the religious is external and focused on organised practice. The spiritual might be conceived of as personal, experiential, and free, whereas the religious is institutional, confessional, and organised. To be spiritual but not religious may also suggest rejecting membership in a larger structure of institutional beliefs and rules, and establishing an identity to free oneself from the prejudices of the organisational and institutional and to be 'unchurched' (Fuller, 2001).

However, for many people, even for members of confessional faiths for whom a beliefs and practices model might describe their use of religion, the definition creates a false dichotomy. Durkheim's description holds – the beliefs an individual has motivate and affect their practices, in both the religions in which they participate and the moral decisions they make. Ammerman's (2013) research showed this point precisely – seventy-five of ninety-five respondents included 'Identifying with or participating in a religious tradition' as a part of their understanding of being spiritual (p. 263). The belief, and the practices associated with it, connects the individual to a larger community of fellow adherents and a history of practice and belief, one that is not necessarily orthodox but like any other category provides a sense of shared identity. Like faith and practice, the interaction between the internal and the external experiences of a religion cannot be separated. Instead, the religious practices – and the discourse which emerges in those practices – are a natural outworking of an internal, spiritual experience. Discourse around religious belief and practice goes hand-in-hand with the experience of those beliefs and practices; in them, individuals come to claim their own unique religious identity.

Despite variation in individual religious experience, institutional religious categories are often controlled by organisations with their own explicit hierarchies (Yandell, 2002). What the organisational structures sanction and prohibit frames the way religion is seen in particular cultural contexts. These institutions also produce first-order and second-order discourses that govern both the doctrine of the religion and the individual faith of adherents. An inevitable connection exists between power structures and the possible religious identities that people can claim for themselves. That control may be explicit, as with the authority to allow or disallow membership in a group – one cannot be a member of the Church of Jesus Christ of the Latter Day Saints without taking part in rituals and practices which only the church can administer. Control can also be exerted more implicitly in, for example, decisions about who is chosen for leadership, with people of particular backgrounds being favoured and championed over others. Institutional religious structures are inevitably and unavoidably foundational to how religious categories are conceived of in particular cultural contexts.

What interaction should and shouldn't be included in analysis of religious practice and belief is difficult to delineate. Indeed, what counts as religious for any individual will differ depending on their experiences, and what beliefs are considered central and which are seen as more periphery may look like those of other non-religious communities of practice, with the engagement of the members of the religion, what they do together, and how they talk about their beliefs and practices affecting how one might be seen and see oneself within a particular context. The negotiation of membership, beliefs, and practices may be, in institutional contexts, top-down as in the Catholic liturgy or Islamic calls to prayer, which are the same across a wide variety of different local contexts. They will, however, also be negotiated in particular local contexts, with individuals exerting influence as central members in each community. Like discourse, there will be a tension between the universal, the unity of the named belief, and the individual, the person claiming the belief for themselves.

The categorical label of any particular belief, when it is taken up by an individual, can be a part of identity work, but the label has different functions for different people – ticking the 'Muslim' box in a questionnaire form for, say, your child's primary school application may foreground certain practices and beliefs and signal those beliefs and practices to a particular audience. At the same time, the category is not a complete descriptor. Simply knowing that a child is a Muslim is unlikely to give the primary school information about what could be expected of any particular student and, indeed, the particular beliefs and practices that any individual Muslim keeps. Importantly, again as Ammerman's (2013) work shows, individuals can do discursive work to hide and highlight different elements of their own faith, dependent on how they view themselves; in what context they are speaking about their belief; and the larger political and cultural pressures, either real or perceived.

For each person, religious categorisations, to the extent that they are useful, are elements of different identities, where class, ethnicity, gender, sexuality, personal history, and any number of other factors come together to make any individual who they are. The intersectional nature of identity has been particularly important in showing how discrimination does not occur on a single-categorical axis (Crenshaw, 1989), and that conceptions of race and sex 'become grounded in the experiences that actually represent only a subset of a much more complex phenomenon' (Crenshaw, 1989, p. 140). For members of marginalised groups, the intersection of faith and ethnicity can be observed, for example, in the labelling of 'black' churches in the United States. This label shows the implicit bias towards the dominant power structures in that race must be marked for a minority congregation, but a similar Evangelical church with a largely white population would unlikely be described as a 'white' church. The cultural and sociopolitical contexts produce categories and limit individuals' ability to claim their preferred identity and how they may be seen by others.

To that end, any analysis of religious discourse must also take into account other elements of identity, particularly when considering marginalised and oppressed communities. Discourse analysis can provide empirical descriptions of how categories are negotiated in interaction and how different elements in categorisation are worked out. As mentioned earlier, Membership Categorisation Analysis as conceived by Sacks (1992), but particularly its more recent applications (Eglin & Hester, 2003; Housley & Fitzgerald, 2009), focuses on the situated nature of categorisation, looking at, for example, how a racial category like 'Asian' can be used in creative ways to meet institutional goals (Shrikant, 2018) or how religious categories can be used to differentiate among different beliefs and religious piety (Pihlaja, 2014b). Although categories of faith and ethnicity are considered relatively stable (the person describing themselves as a Christian today is likely to describe themselves the same way tomorrow), in practice, the situated nature of categorisation might mean that an individual use of a category like Christian or Muslim may mean very different things even for the same person. The contextual discursive work can be done to include or exclude individuals, be it the maintenance of a narrow set of beliefs and practices or in ecumenical movements which attempt to include potentially disparate groups to accomplish particular goals.

From a practical sense, the religions which are the focus of my analysis – Christianity and Islam – can be broadly defined as following the main tenants of the two faiths. For the Muslims, this begins with a statement of belief, the *Shahada*, where one professes in Arabic: 'There is no god but God (*Allah*), and Mohammad is his messenger.' The other four pillars of Islam – the giving of tithes (*Zakat*), fasting at Ramadan (*Sawm*), pilgrimage to Mecca (*Hadj*), and daily prayer (*Salat*) – also are expected of practising Muslims. For Christians, the basic belief in the death and resurrection of Jesus Christ and the need to accept this as a sacrifice for one's own sins are the central tenets, with faith and trust in Jesus an important indicator of one's faith. What that belief entails can change depending on the denomination of Christianity – Anglicans, for example, believe that Jesus was God, while Jehovah Witnesses do not. Other concerns, such as belief in the infallibility of the Bible and the exclusive nature of Christian faith as a means of salvation are also considered more or less central, depending on the particular belief system of an individual or denomination.

The specifics of each belief, in settings where they are the topic of argument (as in the debates between Muslims and Christians), are often not discussed in situations where there is an implicit agreement about what categories mean. Speakers rarely, if ever, make attempts to define what makes someone a Christian or Muslim, despite numerous examples of questions about whether or not certain actions should be done by adherents of each faith and if doing a particular action meant that an individual was not either a Christian or a Muslim. This in-and-of-itself is an important finding and one that is worth considering in light of the literature that we have so far reviewed. The categories of Christian and Muslim are used as unproblematic labels. However, although broad definitions work pragmatically in describing the range of beliefs and practices that fall into these categories, how exactly they are worked out in the interaction among religious believers and in oppositional settings, who gets to define what the categories entail, and the effect of different forces on those categorisations will be one of the focuses of the analysis.

1.3   Language and Religion

The relationship between language and religion has long been essential to philosophical and theological discussions about God and the supernatural. However, analysis of interaction about religion and within religious context has been less prevalent, with some notable exceptions. Crystal's (1965) early work on religious language looked specifically at sacred texts and institutional (Christian) settings, here again seeing religious language as something special and set apart from other kinds of human interaction. Within this tradition, the concept of 'religious language' has been important. McNamara and Giordano (2018) state, 'Use of language in religious contexts is unlike any other domain of language use' (p. 116), arguing that religious language is not primarily used for communication, with some exceptions, perhaps, including communication with 'supernatural agents' (p. 116). Religious language in this understanding relates to the ways humans attempt to express the ineffable qualities of religious experience and ultimate reality including, for example, when talking about the very concept of 'God' (Wierzbicka, 2018) or praying (Downes, 2018). This study of religious language has then looked to cognitive explanations for how and why we talk about religious experiences and concepts, with frameworks built on Lakoff and Johnson's (1980; Lakoff, 1987) work on Conceptual Metaphor Theory, and other cognitive and neurological explanations (see, for example, Downes, 2011; McNamara & Giordano, 2018).

Van Noppen's (1981, 2011, 2006) work on and use of the term *theolinguistics* potentially broadens the concept of 'religious language'. Crystal (2008) describes theolinguistics as 'the study of the relationship between language and religious thought and practice, as illustrated by ritual, sacred texts, preaching, doctrinal statements and private affirmations of belief' (p. 484), and van Noppen's work has subsequently developed as a 'critical theolinguistics' (van Noppen, 2006), which importantly begins to think and talk about religious language in terms of its social contexts and consequences, rather than treating it as a special category. Van Noppen (2006) points out that speech acts are particularly powerful in religious, particularly Christian, contexts, where 'praying, hymn-singing, meditating, preaching, praising, blessing, forgiving, confessing one's belief, excommunicating, theologising and many other practices are, first and foremost, forms of linguistic behaviour' (p. 1).

Within particular religious traditions, discussion of language use has also played an important role in understanding the meaning of sacred texts. Sider's (1995) work. as an example, uses linguistic analysis of metaphor in biblical parables as a tool in hermeneutic activity. Similarly, Keach's (1975) work looks at the nature of metaphor in preaching and teaching, with a clear theological purpose for its analysis. Within Islam, close studies of language in the Qur'an are used to argue that it is a 'linguistic miracle' (see, for example, Bentrcia,

Zidat, & Marir, 2018). These analyses focus on understanding the meaning of the sacred texts for the purpose of edifying religious believers or making an argument for a particular text's uniqueness and often assume a belief about a text (i.e. it is 'sacred').

Language and religion have come again to the forefront in recent years, particularly interest in cognition, religion, and language with several significant collections of research on the topic (Omoniyi & Fishman, 2006; Rosowsky, 2017; Chilton & Kopytowska, 2018; Yelle, Handman, & Lehrich, 2019) and looking at how language engaging with religious concepts is uniquely human and can (or cannot) be integrated across different cultures, languages, and religions – if there is, indeed, a kind of 'God-talk' (van Noppen, 2006) and what study of the mind and the brain can bring to the understanding of religion. This work follows the interest taken by early research into conceptual metaphor (Lakoff & Johnson, 1980, 1999; Lakoff, 1987) and how language is processed in the mind (Fauconnier, 1984; Gibbs, 1994; Turner & Fauconnier, 1995). From this perspective, language processing affects how people speak and how people speak subsequently affects how people think. The topics and focus highlighted in van Noppen's description of contexts for looking at religious language (praying, hymn singing, meditating, preaching, praising, blessing, forgiving, confessing one's belief, excommunicating, theologising) continue to be the focus of research in language and religion.

Metaphor has consistently remained an important focus in analysis of religious language, dating back to van Noppen's (1983) work on theolinguistics (and how speakers attempt to express the ineffable of religious experience using language) to current research on metaphor in institutional, historical, and naturally occurring discourse (see Charteris-Black, 2016; Koller, 2017; Neary, 2017; Richardson, 2017). In one sense, this reflects an interest in how language is used to represent the supernatural; however, at the same time, it has tracked with research into metaphor studies that have moved beyond a conceptual understanding of metaphor to an embodied view (Gibbs & Franks, 2002; Casasanto, 2009). As Richardson's (2012) work has shown, the use of metaphor need not only be about representing unspeakable religious truths but is a key way in which speakers communicate their own development in life, drawing on conceptual metaphors that are not necessarily the exclusive domain of the religion, such as LIFE IS A JOURNEY. Ringrow (2020) shows a similar pattern in religious fashion blogs, where LIFE IS A JOURNEY is used to conceive of spiritual and ethical life, as well as conceiving of God in metaphorical ways such as GOD IS AN ARTIST.

Legitimising political power (van Noppen, 2006) and establishing authority structures (Spolsky, 2003) are also functions of religious language that go beyond traditional domains of institutional religious contexts. Van Noppen's work, for example, shows the connection between industrial capitalist ideology and the Methodist work ethic. The connections can be drawn between the language of hymns, ostensibly intended for worship, and the teaching of work as a 'calling'. This same concept of 'calling', van Noppen also shows, is present in the language of George W. Bush, who viewed himself as being called by God to be president of the United States. Connecting the implicit language of the Christian Evangelical mission with the language of political power, van Noppen (2012) shows how small phrases like 'wonder-working power' in Bush's description of the 'goodness and idealism and faith of the American people' echoed the language of a Christian hymn which uses the phrase 'wonder-working power' to refer to the power of Jesus. Although van Noppen refers to this as a 'complete misuse' of the hymn, the re-voicing of the lyrics allowed Bush to show affiliation with Christian belief without explicitly making reference to his own faith.

Moving away from analysis of religious language as a unique category of talk, work within sociolinguistics has also taken an interest in interaction in and around religious experience and contexts (see research in Omoniyi & Fishman, 2006; Darquennes & Vandenbussche, 2011). Sociolinguistic approaches often assume a humanistic understanding of language about religion as a social practice, rather than as an attempt to communicate about an 'ultimate reality'. Splosky (2006), in this tradition, suggests four dimensions for studying religion and language: the effects of religion on language; the mutuality of language and religion; the effects of language on religion; and language, religion, and literacy. From a sociolinguistic perspective, perhaps unsurprisingly, the focus of research is on the social contexts and consequences for the interaction of language and religion – the effects of religion on language, and vice versa (Mukherjee, 2013).

There has been some growth in the study of religion and language as it relates to other elements of identity, including research on literacy, religion, and education (Lytra, Volk, & Gregory, 2016; Souza, 2016), online spaces (Rosowsky, 2017), and my own work on social media (Pihlaja, 2014a, 2016, 2018) that looks at how language, religion, and identity interact. Lytra and colleagues' (2016) edited collection investigates the rich and diverse ways in which language relates to religious practice in religious institutions, families, and communities. In these contexts, religion, ethnicity, and other social identities cannot be extracted from one another, with religion being isolated as a single factor that be analysed apart from the other identities. Discussing linguistic practices of speakers always requires some engagement with their ethnic and national identities. Souza's (2016) work offers a clear case study of how language, ethnicity, and religion interact in the experiences of Brazilian migrants in London, showing how Brazilian mothers felt the need to 'keep cultural and linguistic links with their place of origin' (146). This complex interaction between culture, language, and religion included either catechising children into the Catholic faith or converting them to a Pentecostal faith, with consequences for how individuals understood themselves and others within their communities.

My own work (Pihlaja, 2018) investigating religious, Evangelical discourse has shown how the identities of individuals can become backgrounded in interaction in social media contexts, where, for example, atheists might argue that Evangelical Christian theology is always wrong and cannot be a positive force in any individual's life, regardless of their identity or local context. I've also shown how Christians might also seek to impose the universality of their own beliefs for all Christians, without taking into account their own local contexts (Pihlaja, 2014a, 2017b) and how the things they believe or practice might not be applicable for others in other contexts, for example, with Evangelical Christians in the southern parts of the United States making arguments that take for granted their own white, capitalist identities. Although identity is not always foregrounded in the interaction, it is always a factor in how speakers understand themselves and others.

The complexity of religious language in everyday interaction is revealed in empirical studies of everyday talk, but an orientation to religion in language use from a discourse analysis perspective, although not the main focus of much research, has not been entirely absent. Ferguson (1985), for example, showed how the language of ritual prayer could be used in day-to-day interaction as a way of indexing belief, which he referred to as a 'metaphorical extension of discourse structure' (p. 212). Szuchewycz (1994) analysed Irish Catholic charismatic prayer meetings to show the ways that structure and spontaneity interacted to create meaning which could be recognised as evidence of being 'spirit led'. What Szuchewycz's work shows, importantly, is how structured ways of speaking in religious settings take on meaning in emergent ways. The participants in the meeting draw explicitly on the ritual language of the church but also employ religious language at key moments to mark religiosity, something I have observed in my own work with the use of the word 'doth', for example, rather than 'does' in certain contexts (Pihlaja, 2017b). There is discursive work done in collective and public prayer which is empirically observable – it is structured and affective and has social consequences for the participants. The use of Arabic phrases invoking Allah (*inshallah*, if Allah wills it; *mashallah*, Allah has willed it; *supanallah*, praise be to Allah; etc.) in English conversation can also be seen as the integration of religious language in the everyday, as speakers use these invocations as discourse markers that implicitly show religiosity (Clift & Helani, 2010; Pihlaja, 2018). The phrases serve important, interpersonal, communicative purposes.

Despite the breadth of work that has been done on the topic of language and religion, several limitations remain. First, although there has certainly been interest in the language of religion in non-Western or non-Christian contexts (exemplar research includes Clift & Helani, 2010; Dorst & Klop, 2017; Silvestre-López & Ferrando, 2017; El-Sharif, 2018; Gao & Lan, 2018), the analysis of language and religion in the West has historically been on 'English in Christianity' and in institutional religious contexts. This is particularly dangerous when, as we have shown, understandings of 'religion' can be varied across cultures and may not include a clear belief in gods or God (Wierzbicka, 2018). Moreover, cultural and religious practices are often deeply integrated, making the role of belief in talk about religion and in religious contexts particularly problematic. Ritual prayer, for example, may be a useful category in some contexts but significantly less useful and potentially reductive in other contexts.

Second, discourse analysis of specific interaction between religious believers has not been fully explored, particularly with the current interest in cognition and religion. However, rich evidence from discourse analytic studies suggests that the interactional context has determinative effects on how people make and navigate meaning. For example, if analysis of reading groups and reading in communal contexts (Allington & Swann, 2009; Peplow, 2011, 2016; Peplow, Swann, Trimarco, & Whiteley, 2015) has shown how meanings of texts are negotiated among speakers, studying real interaction around religious texts is imperative for understanding how meaning is also discursively constructed. Analysts must account for what occurs in these complex contexts – wherein reading practices interact with belief about the interpretation of sacred texts – and unpick the range of factors that lead to particular readings in particular places at particular times.

Finally, studies of religious discourse have not always recognised the importance of individual identity and the intersections of different identities in the development of belief structures and practices (Lytra et al., 2016; Souza, 2016). If religious practices are, fundamentally, social practices, embedded in social structures, understanding religious language requires understanding these structures. Researchers also must recognise how analysis of institutional discourse, theology, and sacred texts gives preference and deference to powerful individuals within powerful institutions, often to the exclusion of traditionally marginalised writers and speakers – minorities, women, children, and LBGTQ+ individuals. Looking at language use occurring outside the institution carries the possibility of new perspectives on how members of religious communities understand their own beliefs and practices. This interaction occurs both in and outside of devotional contexts of collective worship, prayer, and teaching within religious institutions.

Religious discourse is any use of language in religious belief and practice, including in sacred texts, religious teaching, prayer, and any other religious rituals. It includes language use around and about these beliefs and practices. Analysis of religious discourse aims to provide empirical descriptions for how discourse creates and sustains religious belief and practice in the social world. Religious discourse does not view talk about religious experience or indeed the use of language within religious rituals as any more or less unique than any other area of human experience. Instead, it sees religious belief and practice as contextual, and what someone believes and how they speak about their own belief may change on a variety of different scales. Analysing religious discourse requires making sense of language in context and focusing on the confluence of different factors to understand what any individual says in any instance and why.

1.4   Mediatisation and Secularisation

The development of technology and particularly the spread of the Internet continue to shape how religion develops. From a historical perspective, this interdependent relationship between technological progress and religious belief is not novel – the printing press, for example, revolutionised how knowledge was disseminated and with it, how people responded to that knowledge. The printing press, and the ability to disseminate the Bible in a common vernacular meant that individuals were able to read the text for themselves and depend less on its presentation in institutional contexts. The consequence of this technology was, of course, a proliferation of new readings of the Bible, resulting in the landscape of different churches and beliefs that are present in the contemporary world (Eisenstein, 1980). The Protestant Reformation was itself arguably the result of this technology.

The interdependent relationship of technological, cultural, and societal development has been theorised by Hjarvard (2013) as 'mediatisation'. For Hjarvard, shifts in communication over new technologies change not only how messages are sent and received but also how the messages themselves come to be produced and consumed in contemporary social processes, including politics, religion, and play. What has been valued in the past can lose its social currency, and novel ideas and figures can emerge. The presidency of Donald Trump serves as a particularly startling example of how mediatisation can change what is seen as normal practice. The confluence of factors, including not only the exploitation of media but also the nature of the media itself resulted in the election of a man who, by any measure, did not fit the historical model of president. To describe Trump's rise to power as only the result of effective use of media is misleading – his successful candidacy was also the result of a process in which he was used by various media organisations to provide consumers with a product they were willing to consume.

Mediatisation has historically had many different effects on religious belief and practice, but the most recent technological developments in personal and personalised devices and media have had particularly important consequences how religious belief and practice are understood. Lövheim (2011) points out that personalisation has a dialectic property, one that both supports and hinders the development of religion:

[M]ediatisation can support a certain kind of religion in modern society, but it is a volatile religion that has limited power to define, maintain and reproduce a social world on an individual as well as social level. As it is built on sensitivity to a plurality of individual interests and preferences, its authority is undermined by the same processes that make it possible – the plurality of individually accustomed life worlds made visible and accessible through the media. (p. 157)

Lövheim's comment on mediatisation highlights the consequences for religion in creating a context where each individual lives their own unique life but is at the same time immersed in an increasingly complex reality of possible worlds made accessible through media channels. The individual experiences these different possibilities and must maintain a stable understanding of the world.

Along with mediatisation, globalisation has had a profound impact on how religious belief and practice develop. In a basic sense, 'globalisation' is the development of integrated markets across national borders (Steger, 2017), but it has come to describe how other human systems and markets have become increasingly integrated. Research into globalisation and religion shows how physical space can affect faith, particularly when those spaces are changed (Knott, 2015), and can lead to complex social identities mixing ethnic, national, and religious characteristics, like, for example, 'Pakistani British Muslim' (Jacobson, 2006). Globalisation can also lead to the spread of certain forms of religious expression that carry with them social and political ideologies, such as a form of market capitalism embedded in Pentecostal Christianity (Coleman, 2000), akin to the spread of empire and Christian missionary endeavours (Neill, 1964; Yates, 1996). Works by both Lytra and colleagues (2016) and Souza (2016) cited earlier engage with the effects of globalisation on the development of individual identities in relation to larger sociopolitical and socio-economic forces, and the role of religion in these exchanges.

The intertwining of markets in globalisation also carries with it the implicit concept that products and services can be sold in similar ways in different markets, the physical representation of this being clearly evident in the proliferation of a McDonald's Big Mac in diverse markets such as Tokyo, Paris, and New York. For religion, similar effects can be seen on the ways in which beliefs and practices are presented as applicable around the world, without necessarily taking into account local communities. Both Christianity and Islam have long histories in a variety of physical contexts among diverse adherents from a variety of different backgrounds, and both are, therefore, well suited for a global market. At the same time, global evangelism implies the global applicability of beliefs and ethics, and the implicit message that the core beliefs of any religion can and should work in any cultural context. The belief in the universal applicability of world views can be seen particularly in evangelistic endeavours on social media, where users make arguments and share their faith – or lack of faith – without caveats about their own social context (Pihlaja, 2018).

The confluence of these different factors has also had effects on how religious institutions and authorities are regarded. In some spaces, institutions like churches can be reconstituted, with the *affordances*, or the perceived action possibilities (McGrenere & Ho, 2000), of the online spaces changing in subtle ways how religious practices develop and communities grow (Hutchings, 2007, 2017). Although much attention has been paid to 'digital religion' (Campbell, 2017), the development of technology has had effects beyond digital contexts. Discussing religious interaction without considering the role of technology either explicitly or implicitly in those interactions is impossible – the changes are embedded in the practices. These changes can be intertwined with media and technological developments linked to consumer patterns, like the 'Jesus Calling' app which produces devotional information based on user preferences (Trammell, 2015). Churches like Lifechurch.tv discussed in Hutchings's (2017) analysis, often seen as an online church, actually mix different forms of mediated interaction, leading to a diversity of formal and informal contexts wherein religious belief and practice might be discussed.

These changes to how religious experience is mediated by technology shape how people come to experience faith in contemporary contexts, for example, in the 'meme-ing' of the religious other, where genres of online engagement are used to negatively represent religious belief (Campbell, Joiner, & Lawrence, 2018) or the prevalence of 'trolling' in 'post-truth' politics (Hannan, 2018). They are not novelties but affect the ecology of faith systems beyond what is happening online. In contexts where social media services like Facebook are hubs for social interaction and sharing news, churches attempting to 'reach out' to their communities and engage their members must have Facebook pages. The marketisation forces and commodification of social interaction in social media spaces apply also to the religious users and institutions. The effect is not merely on a subset of people who use social media – the presence of social media affects how institutions constitute themselves, how they choose topics to address in teaching, and how they communicate.

Furthermore, the late twentieth- and early twenty-first centuries have seen a decline in the authority of religious organisations in political and social life. Lee (2015) maps the different ways in which these changes might be conceived as alternatives to religion – non-religion, irreligion, anti-religion, non-theism, atheism (p. 39). These are, however, separate from the concept of the 'secular', which rather than signifying belief or non-belief differentiates between a religious world and an 'alternative world that [is] not governed' by religious principles (p. 40). Seeing secularity – and the processes of secularisation – in this way then allows for a reframing of social change around religious belief and practice. Although there is an increase in the number of individuals rejecting religious belief and taking up categorical distinctions which explicitly reject religion (Cimino & Smith, 2011), the presence of the secular in contemporary life does not preclude the existence of religion. For example, secularism also has given rise to new conceptualisations of confessional faiths like Islam, with categories like secular Muslim (Fernando, 2009) taking into account the complexity of religion in individual lived experience.

Still, atheism and an explicit rejection of faith in God and supernatural powers more generally have emerged as an important part of the discussion of religion, both in how public life and policy are determined and in individual belief and practice. The rise of so-called New Atheism can be attributed to a shift in the perception of organised religion made possible in key ways by social media and internet technology (Cimino & Smith, 2011). The increased visibility of atheism has also been a flashpoint for moral panic, like the case of the 'Atheist Bus' in the United Kingdom, where advertisements with an atheist message on public transport evidenced a 'material' presence of atheism, something that became a part of the everyday lived experience of the average person living in London, for example (Lee, 2017). The presence of atheism in public spaces and the media coverage surrounding it then contributed to a sense of its rising prominence, even if individuals themselves might not have been interacting with more atheists in their daily lives.

At the same time, atheism is not simply the emergence of a new, popular categorisation of (dis)belief but is also the product of the social context in which it has emerged. Cimino and Smith's (2007, 2014) work has shown how demographic shifts can result in individual aversion to religious authority and institutions and that movements like New Atheism are embedded in historical sociopolitical contexts from which they cannot simply disconnect. If, as is the case in the United Kingdom and the United States in particular, Christianity is the dominant faith system, then 'new' movements inevitably have some discursive relationship with those faiths. This is particularly true of humanism and Christianity, sometimes leading to a messy relationship between the two where some elements of Christianity are preserved, while others are rejected (Engelke, 2014). These complicated relationships lead to new expressions of belief and practice, as in the Sunday Assembly, a non-religious gathering dubbed an 'atheist church' (Pigott, 2013) which rethinks religious structures within a 'post-Christian' lens (Bullock, 2018). Humanism, New Atheism, and any other movement born in a historically Christian context will inevitably find itself interacting with Christianity.

Change, however, does not occur unilaterally and the presence of new humanist movements and the popularisation of New Atheism also have consequences for religious belief and practice. The response of religious adherents, particularly in the United States, has meant that the emergence and visibility of atheism can lead to a conservative reaction with complicated relationships among faith, nationalism, and ethnic identity (Parker & Barreto, 2014; Wong, 2018). Reactions to a push towards secularisation in public institutions – in government and education, for example – may embolden religious believers and further entrench conservative ways of thinking and being (Robin, 2011). Like the complexity of discourse, changes in culture and context, in technology, in politics, and in any of several other areas can have unforeseen and novel consequences for how religious beliefs and practices emerge over time. Ignoring these changes and still surviving as a belief system are simply not possible.

The importance of technology in contemporary religious life is difficult to overstate, although certainly not without precedent. As noted earlier, the printing press is a good reference point for thinking about the importance of technological change in the development of religion, as it had profound influence on how knowledge was disseminated, standardised, and preserved (Eisenstein, 1980) – religious change and technological change came hand in hand. In a similar way, the socio-historical context coupled with the technological advancements from 1990 through 2010 have provided opportunities for new authorities to emerge. These changes have been numerous, particularly in terms of accessibility to people with different beliefs (Pihlaja, 2018) and can have influence on not only how beliefs are presented but also on the focus and practice of belief.

Another consequence of technology on the development of faith has been the rise of religious authorities whose influence comes from their popularity. These figures, particularly when they emerge on social or new media platforms, have been described as 'micro-celebrities' for what they are or as 'influencers' for what they do. The concepts of 'influencer' and 'self-branding' have gained currency in marketing and media channels as ordinary users have been able to monetise their popularity (Khamis, Ang, & Welling, 2017). Users are now able to not only have advertising sold for their content by the platform provider but can also seek out or be sought out for endorsement of products on their own platforms. In these cases, users' popularity, and in particular the number of followers they have on a given platform and how those followers interact with their content, acts as a measure of their influence, with sites like socialbluebook.com allowing users to assess their own value in these terms.

The rise of the influencer as a cultural figure has consequences for all elements of social life, including religion and religious discourse, whereby a person's visibility on a particular social media platform may give them a unique authority. This authority grows in a recursive cycle between being recognised as an influencer which in turn then increases the ability of the user to further develop their influence through the acquisition of both monetary capital and social capital that comes from being identified as an influencer. Users like traditional celebrities can then become famous for being famous, using their categorisation as an influencer to gain further prominence as sites promote them and their content as exemplar users of the site.

In challenging authority, the new and social media can have consequences beyond the religious sphere, particularly in contexts where political and religious power is explicitly linked and new media channels can effectively challenge these authorities (Eickelman & Anderson, 2003). At the same time, the convergence of traditional media and new/social media now means that broadcast media may cover news that is unfolding on social media channels, or that audiences are more likely to watch broadcast news or television show clips on YouTube rather than when they are broadcast. Rather than a complete revolution in media content, changes to distribution channels and access to global audiences have led to far fewer radical changes, with traditional media figures simply adopting social media strategies.

Making a clear delineation between traditional and new/social media celebrity and influence is likewise becoming more difficult. The emergence of Donald Trump through traditional media channels, while also making use of Twitter to spread his message and influence, highlights how different forms of media now interact. Attributing Trump's success to any simple narrative in terms of media exposure is unlikely to capture the essence of his rise to power. At the same time, Trump's access to traditional sources of power is well documented and while a changing media landscape offered him novel approaches to publicising and distributing his message, this message and his political positions are arguably less radical than their messaging suggests.

The change to the messaging, the immediacy and informality of this public discourse, is, potentially, new. The discussions and confessions of my men's accountability group which I presented at the beginning of this chapter are now more likely to occur in public, technologically mediated spaces. Moreover, changes to distribution and mass communication enabled by technology also have the potential for new voices to emerge that are not necessarily supported by traditional institutions, religious or otherwise. Reaching a large audience is now a potential possibility for anyone with an internet connection. New media affordances mean that new authorities can and do emerge, following expectations of these new contexts, while still connected to the traditions from which they are developing.

The radical changes in technology, media channels, and technologically mediated communication continue to create contexts where unexpected outcomes can emerge. For religious discourse in the contemporary world, the consequences of new forms of distribution and social media mean that while there has been, in some ways, a democratisation of access to audiences, the long histories of religious belief, sacred texts, and models for interaction among religious believers persist. These histories are never eliminated in new contexts – they are new components in the complex system of religious belief and practice.

Religious discourse outside of traditional institutions has proliferated in public spaces, without clear markers of authority to guide who should be trusted. Considering the contemporary context in which religious discourse occurs, several key questions emerge about how religious belief and practice develop in a world where technology has created an unavoidable orientation towards public audiences. Understanding how religion is developing in these spaces requires looking closely at the interaction between people of religious belief and the resources they draw on in discursive settings to make decisions about what they should believe and do. Several specific questions follow:

- How are right practice and belief represented and constructed in interaction among religious believers?
- How do religious believers address perceived challenges to their practices and beliefs by changing social norms?
- How does the presence of diverse audiences affect the presentation of faith in public contexts?

Answering these questions requires looking closely at religious discourse in a variety of contexts where religious belief and practice are the focus of discussion. It also requires stepping beyond the devotional contexts of religious institutions and investigating places where religious discourse occurs both formally and informally, in discourse explicitly oriented towards religious belief and practice, and in discourse oriented towards the lived experience of religious practitioners.

2 Religious Discourse as Data

Doing religious discourse analysis in the contemporary world begins with deciding what exactly should be analysed. Analysis of language and religion has often focused on the nature of faith as the experience of the ineffable (McNamara & Giordano, 2018) – you don't need to read much to get the sense that many scholars believe something special is happening when people pray, for example. The struggle is the extent to which religious language, and language about religion, should take into account the belief of the individuals speaking in religious contexts. If someone or something is genuinely communicating with the religious believer when they pray – or if the person praying experiences someone or something communicating with them – the analyst should of course take this into account. The internal processes of the individual praying, what mental models they have built for the supernatural and how it might be interacting in their lives are without a doubt very real, and ignoring or downplaying them can have serious effects in the ability to understand what is happening when people pray.

At the same time, the study of religious language should not be focused entirely on these internal states; the social function of prayer, for example, and how it changes the social world deserves equal attention. Setting aside what the individual experiences internally in prayer, their talk about that experience is not limited to their internal state, and saying, for example, 'I'm praying for you' in a social setting will have observable effects. Religious language can appear in any part of the day-to-day experience of individuals, in discussions about whether a young Muslim woman should sell alcohol as a part of her job, or how white Christians should respond to police killings of black men in America. Theology and faith are a part of these discussions to be sure, but the interactants are working to apply their beliefs and the structure of their faith to their everyday lives. Their experience of God, or the ineffable, though present in the conversations is often not the focus. They are, instead, attempting to *do* religion, to act out their faith in their daily lives.

Religious discourse is the use of language in religious belief and practice, including language use around and about these beliefs and practices. This approach to the role of language in religion insists on understanding religious discourse as something that permeates day-to-day experience, rather than a special language that can be relegated to spaces and texts thought to be sacred. Religion is a part of the lived experiences of individuals, and understanding the role language plays in the development of religion requires that attention be paid beyond the contexts which have been traditionally seen as exclusively the domain of religious language. To truly understand religious discourse, analysts must also consider spaces where the position of religious belief and practice is simply a part of contemporary, daily life.

2.1   Approaches to Religious Discourse

Theolinguistics, and particularly van Noppen's (2006) introduction of Critical Theolinguistics, has highlighted the cultural position of religious language more broadly and has shown, for example, how religious language creeps into political discourse as a means of showing particular ideological affiliations. To understand how language and religion are operating in these contexts – theology as a part of the lived experience of ethical choice making – theory for studying the complexity of everyday social interaction is needed. To that end, analysis should focus on tracing and describing the role of religion in discourse as it unfolds in the moment-by-moment interaction of the real speakers – how they talk about their faith and actions in regard to themselves and others, both those who profess the same confessional faith as they do and those who don't. What happens, for example, when a religious believer tells a colleague that they are praying for the colleague's ill partner? How do the positions of each, their relationships, their shared or differing beliefs, affect what happens next?

To answer these questions, analysis of *positioning* can be useful. Positioning Theory describes the dynamic ways people talk about themselves and others in particular contexts, oriented towards specific categories or roles (Davies & Harré, 1990; Harré & van Langenhove, 1998; Harré, 2000). Instead of viewing categories or roles like mother or boss or politician as fixed, Positioning Theory sees social positions as fluid and contextual – a person's position changes depending on where they are, whom they're with, and what they're doing. Positions are socially constructed and require more than a person claiming a position for themselves; others in a specific social context must also accept a positioning as valid. Harré & van Langenhove (1998) use the example of one person telling another to iron their shirts. For the command to be effective, the positioning of each person must be accepted by both people in that context – the person being told to iron the shirts must accept that the person telling them to iron the shirts is in a social position where such a command is morally acceptable.

Positioning includes different levels of autonomy and privilege depending again on the context. An individual's own positioning may or may not be a conscious choice. People may not necessarily desire or choose for themselves a specific positioning, and positionings can be the result of ideological patterns of belief about who one should or shouldn't be. Harré and van Langenhove's example of a person doing the ironing at the request of another doesn't require that the person doing the ironing enjoys or desires the positioning, simply that their doing of the task is not out of the ordinary and unreasonable. However, because positionings are not always accepted, Harré and van Langenhove do distinguish between first-order and second-order positionings: in first-order positionings, the interactants accept, often implicitly, the positionings they've been given. In second-order positioning, however, a person might reject the positioning and, in the example of the ironing, reject the positioning of another.

The concept of first-order and second-order positioning is potentially problematic from a discourse dynamics perspective, because it describes one positioning as primary, as coming first. Although this might be the case within particular discourse events – we might be able to identify the first instance of one person positioning another – the preconditions of any interaction, the Level 0 of discourse events (Cameron, 2015), include positionings of individuals. The example given by Harré and van Langenhove may be the first explicit evidence of a positioning within social interaction, but it is unlikely that the two people in the example would not have had a tacit understanding of how they would be positioned before the interaction began. The interconnected nature of discourse requires considering the state of the system before any interaction or explicit positioning occurs.

This model of positioning is useful in conceptualising how people interact in simple social contexts, but it also requires some further critical evaluation, particularly considering the dominant ideological power structures at work in social interactions, a key component of Critical Discourse Analysis (Fairclough, 1995). Power relations are discursive and ideological and constitute society and culture (Fairclough & Wodak, 1997), and positionings occur within these power structures. Not all speakers have the same level of autonomy, and institutions, categories, and the experiences of each speaker often limit the positionings that are available to individuals. The socio-historical, sociopolitical context can create stable positionings for individuals, particularly within religious institutions which are fundamentally conservative.

Harré and van Langenhove's (1998) Positioning Theory further suggests that larger structures called 'storylines' emerge to make sense of how positionings of people fit together in coherent ways. Positioning is then a part of larger common sense models of how people can and should operate in the social world and includes moral reasoning about what actions are acceptable. This moral reasoning can be understood in light of the discursive power structures that Fairclough's (1995) work has highlighted – while positioning is always local and locally realised, the resources people draw on to position themselves and others are those that are already available to them in the social context. These positionings are regularly employed in specific situations, but how people are expected to act can be understood with abstract models. In the example of the command to iron shirts, we might recognise a storyline we know well, where a boss commands a worker to do a task. We not only recognise that this is a common occurrence in our lived experience, but we also accept it as a *moral* request. The positionings of both the boss and worker mean that the command is ethical, and the worker *should* do what they have been commanded to do.

De Fina and Georgakopoulou (2012) have further argued that these larger structures can't necessarily be extracted from local storytelling contexts but rather emerge when speakers engage in back-and-forth interaction. They suggest that positionings should not be treated as 'independent, pre-discursive entities that exist out there ready to be taken off the shelf and to be reproduced and revealed in discursive action' (De Fina & Georgakopoulou, 2012: 163). Instead, positionings and storylines show the properties of *heteroglossia* (Bakhtin, 1981), that each instance of language use is both unique and produced in the moment to meet the needs of particular contexts and also part and parcel to the larger unified language, where words and patterns reoccur with regularity and truly novel expression is rare.

Positioning can also be approached from a narrative perspective (Bamberg, 1997, 2004). Narrative has been used in a variety of contexts and frameworks (De Fina & Georgakopoulou, 2012), but Bamberg's (1997) model for positioning analysis starts with Labov's (Labov & Waletzky, 1997) concept of 'narrative' as both the recounting of personal experience and accomplishing 'sense-making' (p. 335) in interaction. Although Labov's narrative focused on 'small stories', and how they 'are often employed as heuristics for the inquiry into tellers' representations of past events and how the tellers make sense of themselves in light of these past events' (Bamberg & Georgakopoulou, 2008, p. 378), Bamberg and Georgakopoulou's (2008) later work on positioning also includes 'narratives-in-interaction' and looks at the importance of these narratives in identity work (see also De Fina & Georgakopoulou, 2012). In this sense, narratives are not only about sense-making and representation of events but do important relational work in interaction. Bamberg and Georgakopoulou (2008) write, 'We are interested in the social actions/functions that narratives perform in the lives of people: how people actually use stories in everyday, mundane situations in order to create (and perpetuate) a sense of who they are' (pp. 378–9). Narrative positioning can occur in any interaction where speakers are talking about their experience in the world and responding to the positionings of others in a process of storytelling (Ochs & Capps, 2011).

Positioning can also be used in negative ways, including in discourse about minority communities. *Malignant positioning* describes positioning wherein certain rights – and the ability to position oneself – are deleted (Sabat, 2003). Malignant positioning is particularly important in racist narratives or stereotyping where the voice of the positioned must necessarily be excluded to maintain an incomplete or false narrative. This can be seen in reporting on terrorism and the positioning of Muslims. Baker et al. (2013), for example, show how media portrayals of Muslims can position commitment to Islam in a negative way, forcing Muslims into categories such as moderate or fundamentalist. This positioning does not allow for a storyline in which devout religious expression by Muslims is positioned positively and has the potential to create incongruity in young Muslims' lives, as they may aspire to greater piety in their religious expression but are forced into negative positions by dominant storylines about themselves.

The stories people tell about themselves and the stories people tell together are part of the process of making sense of actions and beliefs, and the construction of one's identity, something Labov and Waletzky (1967) argued more than fifty years ago. At the same time, the stories that people tell are often not novel or original, and generic stories and ways of talking about particular topics and themes reoccur in interaction. These regularities have been conceived of and described in different ways, including master narratives (Bamberg, 1997); constituent parts of larger discourses (Foucault, 1971); and storylines (Harré & van Langenhove, 1998); or, even more basically, cognitive analyses of language use. These stories might be considered parts of dynamic embodied patterns called *image schemas* (Johnson, 1987; Lakoff, 1987). In the Harré and van Langenhove example, the positions of boss and worker include generic stories of how bosses and workers interact in cultural contexts. The stories that people tell follow recognisable patterns for interaction that are told and retold in different contexts.

The stories that people tell about their lives can be abstracted as storylines at different levels, starting from a specific instance in one's life (e.g. Last Tuesday, I spilled coffee on myself), to a recurring instance in one's life (e.g. I'm always spilling coffee on myself), to generalisations (e.g. Busy people like me are always making clumsy mistakes), with the actions and beliefs of the particular individuals first based in their embodied experience, then being recognised as patterns of actions, and finally being understood on higher levels of abstraction, with categories taking the place of individuals and particular actions as they become more abstract. The storylines include reasoning for the actions of individuals and can, as they are abstracted, provide heuristics for moral judgements. In the example given by Harré and van Langenhove (1998), the story not only implies what workers and bosses do but also the telling of the story, and how one represents the interaction between the individuals also reveals beliefs about what workers and bosses *should* do. The actions and reactions of the people in a story and how those actions are represented show the attitudes of the storyteller and the audience, an observation made by Bamberg (1997) in an analysis of narrative positioning.

Adapting Harré and van Langenhove's example of positionings and the storyline from their constructed example, I use the term 'storylines' to describe the abstraction of specific stories to generic, abstract ones. Storylines evidence the process of making sense of particular experiences with common sense and pre-existing models of belief and behaviour, and they show how people attempt to make sense of their day-to-day lived experience in terms of other experiences and patterns of actions they recognise as reoccurring in the world. In my own research (Pihlaja, 2014a), I have shown how the story of the Titanic can be told in different contexts, with metaphorical language being developed and extended to apply the storyline of disasters generically to other contexts. The abstraction can occur all across the cline of specificity, from a retelling of a historical account of the Titanic, to drawing analogies between the Titanic and one's own experience in extended metaphor, to simply invoking the storyline in a phrase (e.g. 'go down like the Titanic'). For those adhering to particular religious texts, the same use of storylines can be seen in accounting for actions, such as seeing one's own hardship in life as analogous to that of biblical characters (Pihlaja, 2017b).

Positionings might also evidence moral reasoning that is not produced as ad hoc explanations in exchanges between particular interlocutors, but they evidence larger cultural ways of talking about, for example, the actions of nation states. In the noughties, a storyline of terrorism and of good and evil was dominant in the accounting for actions of governments and terrorist organisations, with those represented in good positionings in one story being represented in evil positionings in other stories, as Harré and colleagues (Harré et al., 2009b) note in the discourse of George W. Bush about Osama bin Laden, and vice versa. Both leaders essentially followed the same storyline, with different people and entities serving as the goodies and baddies, in attempts to seize the moral high ground and position the 'enemy' in a negative way. Their research shows that the storyline of 'Good eventually triumphs over Evil' is a compelling one regardless of what side of an issue one is on (Harré et al., 2009a, p. 9). Storylines evidence ideology and cultural beliefs particularly when they are repeated at different levels of abstractions. The more abstract accounting for the actions of individuals with categorisation can then be used to understand groups of people – for example, when the story of Osama bin Laden organising and executing the 9/11 attacks becomes abstracted to a storyline of Muslims committing terrorist attacks.

The processes of abstraction and categorisation with different frames or schemas are a fundamental human process for understanding the world and for moving from particulars of experience to larger conceptual structures (Tsur, 2003). These are key concepts in Cognitive Linguistics, particularly in the study of metaphor from a conceptual perspective (Lakoff, 1987; Lakoff & Johnson, 1980, 1999) and categories (see, for example, Billig & Tajfel, 1973; Housley & Fitzgerald, 2002; Jayyusi, 1984; Rosch & Lloyd, 1978; Tajfel et al., 1971). Positioning itself might be described from a cognitive perspective – Cognitive Stylistics (Semino & Culpeper, 2002; Stockwell, 2005) provides accounts for how readers create mental models of characters, which include categorisation and prototypes. Rich descriptions of these processes can be seen in Text World Theory (Gavins, 2007; Werth, 1994, 1999), as an example, which shows how people construct conceptual models of the world based on discourse and how, importantly for the study of religious belief and practice, individual minds fill in absent information, dependent on their own embodied cognitive experience (Gibbs, 2006) – that is, the things they have thought and felt in the world in their particular body up to that point. These models differ from person to person but also show similarities for individuals who share sociocultural contexts and have similar embodied experiences of the world.

Approaching interaction from a discourse dynamics perspective requires viewing all elements of interaction as potentially in flux, including beliefs which can and do shift during dialogue, something Cameron's (2012) work on conciliatory discourse has shown, and look instead at the consequences of each positioning, each storyline on the trajectory of discourse over time. The point is not what discourse evidence shows about cognition (although it very likely does provide evidence for this), but what effect discourse has on what follows after it and how that develops over time. People may also feel a kind of 'emotional attunement' (Cameron, 2011a; see also Hoffman, 2000;) when speaking with others, showing concern not only for their perspective but also their 'moral principles and beliefs' (Richardson, 2017). When people speak together, they are not simply listening to claims and counterclaims about faith, but they may also feel and understand things they wouldn't if they weren't in dialogue with another. Considering this perspective can then offer explanations for apparent shifts in belief in the real-world interaction of individuals, good examples of which can be seen in, for example, Whiteley's (2011) and Whiteley and colleagues' (Peplow et al., 2015) work looking at the discourse of reading groups. What people say and how they position themselves are dependent on how they believe others are viewing them in a particular discourse context. The construction of *meaning* is empirically a discursive process, subject to the material conditions of interaction.

How people position themselves and others, and actions within the social world, and how they account for their actions with their beliefs evidence how religious belief and faith are conceived of as a coherent system. The positioning of self and others is particularly revealing when those positionings can be understood on higher levels of abstraction, involving categories of belief and practice. To answer the research questions posed earlier, considering how right practice and belief are represented and constructed in interaction and how religious belief and practice adapt to changing contexts, looking at the interactions of people of different religious beliefs and practices, speaking in a variety of different contexts, can offer some insight into how they understand themselves and others in the social world, particularly when the same storylines can be observed occurring and reoccurring in different discourse contexts.

2.2 Collecting and Analysing Discourse

Attempting to do close empirical study of religious discourse inevitably confronts the difficulty of deciding what discourse should be studied, particularly when researchers are interested in writing more generally about discourse practices. Following my previous work (Pihlaja, 2014a, 2018), I base my analysis on exemplar case studies, rather than large, representative samples. There are several reasons for this decision: first, case study research quickly shows how problematic generalising about religious believers really is and begins from an assumption that the analysis will reveal discourse processes, but not necessarily reveal anything about the ways in which Christians or Muslims or any other category are different from one another. Second, case studies allow researchers to follow discourse as it develops, without any constraints on what might or might not be included. The nature and context of the cases will be different, with different kinds of discourses and different kinds of speakers. There must, of course, be principles governing what is collected and why; once those principles are agreed upon, the approach and methods can develop in creative ways. And third, case studies tend to capture more interesting discourse, the sort of interaction that is compelling in and of itself.

Religious discourse can be observed in a variety of different places, but given my focus on language-in-use and the development of religious belief and practice, public dialogues about religion, in both supportive and antagonistic settings, offer several key advantages. In public spaces where the orientation of talk is explicitly towards religious belief and practice, the focus of the talk is on the key topics the research questions hope to address: instances in which the speakers are addressing challenges to the beliefs posed by social changes, such as shifting views about sexuality. To find instances of these discussions, my own ongoing, now ten-year longitudinal observation of religious users online following principles of Discourse-Centred Online Ethnography (Androutsopoulos, 2008) provided many possibilities for the kinds of discourse I might collect.

Mediatisation and 'personal publics' (Schmidt, 2014) have become a key change to religious discourse in contemporary life, and both formal and informal talk between people of the same faith and debates between people of different faiths – namely, Christians and Muslims – taking place in public forums is abundant. Moreover, the nature of media distribution in the contemporary world means that talk of all kinds can be accessed through the Internet, with differing degrees to which their online distribution impacts the original discourse events. Representing these different kinds of public interactions from a mix of Christian and Muslim speakers, the following discourse was collected for analysis:

- Videos made by the Muslim social media user Ali Dawah, a young British Muslim man who describes his goal as 'Calling people to Islam' (Ali Dawah, n.d.). As an online *dawah* (the teaching and propagation of Islam often akin to evangelism) preacher, Ali Dawah's posts include videos of him discussing issues with Muslim friends, question and answer videos with Islamic authority figures, and debates between him and other users (including Christians and other Muslims). At the time of analysis in 2018, Ali Dawah's Instagram posts regularly received thousands of likes and his videos regularly garnered tens of thousands of views on YouTube. Although ministry is ostensibly the focus of Ali Dawah's site, he does occasionally engage in 'drama', or antagonistic debates (Burgess & Green, 2008) with other people on the site. Ten videos (total time 2 hours 58 minutes, 33,572 words) were selected, including examples of Ali Dawah's approach to religious teaching and featuring Ali Dawah speaking to other Muslims about contemporary issues. The majority of the videos were posted in 2016 and 2017.
- Episodes of the *Bad Christian* podcast, one of the most popular Christian podcasts in 2017, regularly garnering more than 100,000 downloads a month during that time. The podcast web page describes the podcast as 'Matt, Toby and Joey discuss funny, controversial, and personal stuff with guests from the music business, leaders in the Christian world, and interesting folks from well outside of the Christian world' (*Bad Christian* podcast, n.d.). The hosts of the podcast hold or have held different professional ministry roles but speak in personal capacities in the podcast. Ten podcasts (total 13 hours 16 minutes, 131,946 words) were included for analysis, which represent a range of topics that occurred in the 100 episodes prior to June 2017.
- Five debates (total 10 hours 16 minutes, 112,860 words) between the Muslim scholar Dr Shabir Ally and a variety of Christian opponents including James White, Richard Lucas, and Dave Hunt. Shabir Ally is the host of the Canadian TV show *Let the Quran Speak* and is both a leader in ministry and an academic scholar of Islam, holding a doctorate from the University of Toronto in Islamic studies and '[f]or over 30 years, he has been an active member of the Muslim community in Toronto, as well as an active participant in interfaith dialogues and initiatives' (Quranspeaks.com, n.d.). Although *Let*

the Quran Speak has its own YouTube channel, videos of Shabir Ally debating Christians in a variety of international settings are often uploaded by others and shared broadly. These will be the focus of my analysis.

The videos made by Ali Dawah, the debates, and the podcasts contain different kinds of scripted content. Although all of the videos and podcast have predetermined themes, often with the hosts doing work before the recording to invite guests and make plans for the production, the discussions that occur are not scripted, with evidence of this lack of planning in the regular overlap of speakers, interruptions, and self and other repair. The discussions also regularly shift into other topics and include conversations, particularly in the case of the podcast, which don't necessarily relate to theology and religion. The podcasts also include the reading of scripted advertisement copy, which is clearly introduced with a marked change in tone and focus and little or no overlapping talk during the reading of the advertisements.

The debates represent a different form of naturally occurring religious discourse, as they are more scripted and, in some cases, include the debaters reading from pre-prepared comments. Most of the discourse does have evidence of preparation, particularly when arguments are made in numbered outline. These can be constructed prior to the debate or during the debate, as preparation for rebuttals. In one instance, Shabir Ally makes a thirteen-point rebuttal, following his notes from the opposing statement immediately preceding his response. The debates therefore represent some of the best examples of prepared theological discourse, with the debaters also holding positions of authority within their religious communities.

In some ways, the talk analysed here represents a range of speakers of different ages and from different national, ethnic, religious, and class backgrounds. However, all the prominent speakers analysed in this text are men. This lack of gender balance has been a historical difficulty in my work on religious discourse, looking primarily at new and social media texts, where men have dominated debates between Christians and Muslims, dawah videos, and Evangelical Christian podcasting. For the ten years I have been observing these interactions, men have been the prominent figures in all three of these domains. Although my choices of whom to analyse reflect an interest in finding representative examples of podcast, dawah, and debate discourse, I recognise how the analysis of men's talk in religious discourse to the exclusion of women's talk contributes to the marginalisation of women in religious contexts, and I will address the issue again in the final chapter.

Within the videos and podcasts, different voices represent the categories of belief – the Christians in the *Bad Christian* podcast have little in common, at least stylistically, with a Christian apologist like David Hunt, who appears in one of the debate videos. The diversity of speakers then leads to a lack of consistency in and among people who nominally are members of the same faith. Among the *Bad Christian* podcast hosts, for example, there was often a lack of consistency in the positions taken by people ostensibly claiming the same confessional faith. The presence of this diversity and how these differences in positions were managed both explicitly and implicitly allowed for a rich analysis of how interaction among people within a particular faith builds consensus or accommodates disagreement. At the same time, the diversity of voices makes clear the difficulty of speaking authoritatively about any one speaker as representing their faith. Instead, the discourse makes obvious the messy reality that confessional faiths are not monolithic entities, and the processes by which people shift positions are observable in close analysis of discourse.

Some of these affordances might be seen as particularly unique in a world of social media consumption, but they should be viewed as larger issues with media consumption and production. The development of publishing and the changes in context that occur from the production of a text and its consumption over time are often the same issues that are confronted in social media contexts. Something is said or written down in one context, and the artefact then travels in time, with different people interacting with the text in different ways as it goes forward. Considering the context of production and consumption is then always essential to understanding how and why people might be speaking the way that they are.

All of this interaction took place in public or on publicly available platforms – the speakers are all in different ways oriented towards both the interactants who are physically present with them and an audience, which is either physically present (in the case of the debates) or imagined (in the case of the podcasts and YouTube videos). Although, of course, all social interaction can be understood as performance (Goffman, 1959), this public position undoubtedly creates a heightened sense of performance for all the speakers, who are aware that they are being watched. Although this likely affects how people talk about themselves and others, it also reflects the nature of the contemporary world wherein private spaces and private discourse, particularly in digital contexts, can never be guaranteed. At the same time, particularly in the podcasts, the speakers made repeated claims about their own authenticity and presentation of themselves on the podcast: they often made claims that they were not performing and who they were on the podcast and who they were off the podcast were essentially the same. Still, the public performance element of the discourse should and will be considered throughout the analysis when considering how speakers might be adapting their own positions.

Despite being public-facing interaction, the nature of each audience for each video or podcast was not necessarily straightforward. The videos in particular represent the ways mediatisation can change how different events are recontextualised over time. For example, several of the debates which are analysed were recorded in front of live, local audiences, and the recordings were originally made available as DVDs or VHS tapes through the organisations which sponsored the events. The debates were then posted on YouTube many years later, recontextualising them. The *Bad Christian* podcasts also exist on several media platforms simultaneously, first as traditional podcasts listeners can download through programs like iTunes, but they were also made available as live events on Facebook and YouTube, wherein people could watch and interact with other users while the recording was being made. After the live recording of the video, the video remained on YouTube and Facebook for people to watch.

After identifying the *Bad Christian* podcast and Ali Dawah as good examples of public in-group religious discourse, videos that were representative of the different topics and content that the podcast and video makers produced were chosen for analysis, keeping in mind the research questions and focus, which centred on right belief and practice in discourse and how the speakers talked about the challenges facing them. I then identified debates to compare how people spoke with those outside of their beliefs, particularly around issues that were considered contentious, with the apologist Shabir Ally appearing in all of them. These debates were all collected online, having been posted on YouTube, but the debates are, with the exception of that in which Richard Lucas appears, not posted by the individuals appearing in them. The debates also all appear to occur in front of live audiences, some of which are shown at times in the videos and which were occasionally asked for contributions in the form of questions. One debate appears to have occurred in a recording studio, with no interaction with a live audience. The selection of debates was also done with a focus on identifying exemplar cases with a range of topics covered. Although there is consistency in the issues that are discussed, the discourse represents a diverse set of topics from numerology to the reliability of the sacred texts.

In all, there was 23 hours, 39 minutes, and 14 seconds of talk, that totalled 278,378 words of transcribed text. Further information about the videos and podcasts can be found in the Appendix, including the URLs for the videos and dates of posting. In regards to the amount of discourse gathered, I balanced an attempt to gather a representative sample of the content from each source with an attempt to gather similar amounts of discourse. Although both the debates and podcast amounted to 10 hours, Ali Dawah's videos were only about a third of that time. However, the nature of Ali Dawah's videos was a more condensed approach to each topic with much of filler content that is present in, for example, the *Bad Christian* podcast, edited out. By looking at ten videos, I was able to represent the diverse kinds of discourse present in his videos, as a video on a single topic often covered a similar amount of ground as one podcast.

Much discussion has occurred in recent years about the ethics of using discourse taken from sources online. The increasing availability of and interest in differing forms of online discourse have led to applied linguists calling for a more carefully considered approach to the ethics of analysing online media texts (Spilioti & Tagg, 2017), something I have seen shift significantly in my ten years of looking at YouTube videos. The discourse analysed here, although collected from online spaces, represents a diversity of media and discourse types. These include debates recorded for distribution on DVD and VHS tapes and for television broadcast, which were posted on YouTube well after their initial recording. The podcasts are distributed through a variety of different digital platforms, including social media. The dawah videos made my Ali Dawah are the only videos produced on YouTube for YouTube audiences, but those too can be recontextualised, edited, and posted in different ways on different social media sites, like Instagram.

Potential harm is inevitable when reproducing and recontextualising texts, since the researcher exerts control on how individuals and what they have said are presented to new audiences. I have argued elsewhere and in my previous work (Pihlaja, 2017a) that the key ethical concern in dealing with creative content posted in online spaces is copyright, and representing texts in a way that respects fair dealing and fair use laws (US Copyright Office, 2006; Limitations on exclusive rights: Fair use, 1976). These laws stipulate that creative content be attributed to the copyright holder and without compelling reason not to reproduce them (i.e. clear harm could be posed to the copyright holder if they were identified); there is no ethical or legal reason to not cite them. This may be the case in terms of legal obligations, but further consideration is also needed in the consequences of recontextualising someone's copyrighted words for academic analysis.

The application of fair use laws in online spaces has been problematic (Freund, 2014); however, as an ethical principle, for public figures, the full and accurate representation of their position with full attribution of the source of the text should be the primary concern. For users who are not necessarily public figures, but producing discourse in response to the videos or other online content of public figures (someone commenting, for example, on a YouTube video page), the position is more complicated, and it seems less likely that a user's expectation would be that their comment might end up in a book about religious discourse, even if their use of the site includes an explicit acceptance that what they have written or said can be publicly accessed.

Because the main texts (the videos and podcasts) are produced not only in public spaces but also with an explicit awareness of the text producers about their public nature, the speakers do seem to assume that their words will be subject to criticism – indeed, this is often an explicit point of the videos and podcasts. I have therefore chosen to acknowledge and cite their words with reference to the source from which the excerpt is taken. However, in cases where comments from videos have been reproduced, the usernames have been anonymised. Although good arguments can be made for referencing usernames, particularly when users commenting are themselves well established in the community and their use of a site evidences a full awareness of the potential consequences of publishing their comments online, this cannot necessarily be confirmed. Moreover, when reproducing comments that might be viewed as antagonistic, there appears to be little added value and more potential for harm by including usernames in the text.

The videos and podcast were transcribed using whole word transcription, arranged in intonation units (Chafe, 1988). The discourse analysis procedure follows the principle that analysis must always be done, where possible, of the recording of the interaction itself, and transcription serves the purpose of making the discourse searchable and allowing for the talk to be represented in writing when needed. Transcription must also take into account the competing interests of the quantity of discourse to be analysed and the accuracy and detail that can be achieved. Because the analysis included some need to accurately measure the extent to which certain words or topics arise in the talk, utterances and words were not marked for stress, accent, and rising or falling intonation. This allowed for searches of the texts using tools like AntConc (Anthony, 2014) to identify and quantify uses of particular words and terms when needed. In the extracts that follow, transcription is presented as intonation units with minimal added capitalisation and (when absolutely necessary) punctuation to assist with ease of reading. Occasionally parts of the transcription have been cut for comprehensibility and marked with [. . .].

My process for discourse analysis then followed these steps:

1. Transcribe discourse event
2. Segment discourse event (following Cameron, 2011b)
3. Identify all explicit positionings in each segment
4. Consider potential implicit positionings, including of the speaker and audience, searching for further evidence of these positionings elsewhere in the event
5. Identify the explicit narrative or storyline, or implicit narrative or storyline the positionings constitute
6. For each positioning, describe its trajectory in the discourse event
7. Compare positionings of speakers within discourse event and across discourse events

Analysis focuses on the interaction between people in the videos and podcasts, with the comments on videos, where they are present, included as supplementary information, particularly when discussing listener and viewer responses to positionings. Because my research focuses primarily on how people talk about their own position and the position of others in the moment-by-moment interaction, I began my analysis identifying discourse segments where right belief and practice were specifically discussed, identifying where possible explicit positionings were occurring and contested often in the form of categorisations. Explicit 'small stories' told by individuals about their own experience (Labov & Waletzky, 1997) were also identified, including stories taken from sacred texts and stories-in-interaction between participants (De Fina & Georgakopoulou, 2011), particularly when these stories were used to establish or challenge generic or abstract positionings of individuals within particular categorisations. With attention to the trajectory of the talk, account was also taken for what had occurred before and after each positioning, from the intonation unit level to the discourse segment level, considering how the positioning followed from previous interaction.

The process of analysis can be illustrated in looking at one section of a debate between the Muslim Shabir Ally and the Christian Joseph Smith (D4, see Appendix). Ally says:

Extract 2-1
Second point I'd like to respond to
is the idea that
Smith said Muslims
impose their understanding
of revelation
upon the Bible
so we demand that since the Bible
the Qur'an was revealed
as a dictation from God
The Bible should also be revealed as a dictation
I don't think that I would impose
that understanding on the Bible

This extract comes from a debate between Ally and Smith. The particular segment is Ally's response to Smith, and further the 'Second Point' of that rebuttal. Ally is explicitly positioning himself ('I'), Smith, Muslims, the Bible, the Qur'an, and God. Given the context of the debate, and the use of the category of 'Muslims', Ally may also be making an implicit positioning of 'Christians', of whom Smith is a representative. From the action of 'Muslims imposing their understanding on the Bible', a potential storyline of 'Muslims imposing themselves on others' might be emerging. In positioning himself as opposing Smith and potentially Christians like him and saying 'I don't think I would impose that understanding of the Bible', he offers the opposite story-line, 'Muslims don't impose themselves on others.'

The durability of any of the potential storylines and the extent to which they feature in discourse around the same topics requires considering the point to which Ally is responding and following the trajectory of the conversation back to Smith's original positioning of himself, the Bible, and the Qur'an and the context of the discourse segment in which he made the claims. The development of the storyline going forward, particularly in the context of debates where there is an incentive to respond to previous positionings, is also important to understanding its role in the discourse event. Positionings and storylines show the properties of *heteroglossia,* in that they are both produced at particular moments to meet the requirements of particular discourse events and at the same time embedded in larger sociopolitical, sociocultural contexts with well-established ways of talking about oneself and others, particularly when the discourse is oriented towards issues of religious belief.

Textual evidence about the relative fixed nature of positionings and storylines need then go beyond looking only at evidence in a particular discourse event, but the extent to which similar positionings and storylines might be observed in other discourse events and indeed in any of the background research which may be relevant. Established ways of speaking can be seen particularly in debate settings when specific questions from debaters to one another lead to topics that don't have a clear relationship to the initial question and the debaters revert to established positionings. An example of this might be a debater in a discussion about the reliability of the Qur'an, negatively positioning Mohammad based on his marriage to Aaisha, an established storyline about Mohammad in Christian apologetics that is not necessarily relevant to the topic of debate.

The analytic aim is to uncover the implications of positionings and storylines for right belief and practice and the consequences talk about oneself and others has for how actions and beliefs are evaluated. This includes moral judgements on the personal, individual level and on the categorical level, when judgements about individuals are abstracted to groups which are positioned to share particular characteristics with the individual. These moral judgements can become fossilised and serve as heuristics for how people understand themselves and others. They both help and hinder mutual understanding where people talk about their own faith and that of others. Discourse analysis provides the tools to uncover how those same patterns can provide deeper insights into how people talk and think about those around them, about their social world, and how the world does and should work.

3 Naming, Changing, and Contemporary Contexts

Depending on your position, religion is either in dire straits, stumbling into oblivion or it's never been stronger, standing as an existential threat to secular, modern life. In a speech to the fundamentalist Christian Liberty University, American Vice President Mike Pence warned of an impending 'shunning' of Christianity (Puckett, 2019), brought about by a secularised culture that rejects faith. The speech was newsworthy for its apocalyptic prediction of the future for Christians, but there was also an obvious lack of continuity – the vice president, speaking in his capacity as one of the leaders of the government, was arguing that his faith was being marginalised.

The persecution polemic has played a crucial role in Christian identity in the recent past (Castelli, 2005) and can serve to bind people together in a shared identity. The sense of persecution of religious believers is not limited to Christians and, perhaps more realistically, a sense of persecution among Muslims also exists, with high religious group identification correlating with a higher feeling of being under threat (Obaidi, Kunst, Kteily, Thomsen et al., 2018). For some, simply living as a religious person in the contemporary world includes the perception that your religious identity is constantly being challenged.

Regardless of whether Pence's prediction for the future is accurate – one can't help but see the speech as a way of stoking resentment and suspicion rather than a genuine concern for religious believers – the truth about how religion exists in a contemporary context is not necessarily straightforward. What does seem to have changed for people like Mike Pence in the recent past is that people of other religious beliefs and people of no religious belief are now increasingly visible and recognised in contemporary Western life where Christianity has been seen at least publicly as the dominant religious force in culture. A key feature of modern, contemporary contexts is now the presence of the 'Other' in our day-to-day lives – in our Twitter feeds, the foods we eat, or the people we see on the street in many urban centres across the world. How we talk about this diversity and position ourselves in relation to those around us is a necessary skill in contemporary life. This prospect can potentially be quite daunting, particularly when religious believers hold exclusive positions about their own right belief and practice, and challenges to those beliefs have important existential consequences. Where it may have been possible to ignore minority positions in the past, the contemporary world makes it far more difficult to overlook the different beliefs, and religious believers now must increasingly work to differentiate and distinguish between themselves and others and hold firm against a perceived sense of an increasing secularism.

3.1   Representation and Categorisation

A basic element of religious identity is the labelling of one's faith in a way that is recognisable to others. Religious categorical labels, much like religion itself, are porous and contextual, dependent on who is speaking with whom and what possible categories are available – one couldn't claim an identity as an agnostic, for example, until 'agnosticism' emerged a category of non-belief. Confessional statements might help people differentiate among Christians and Muslims, but in authentic, real-time interaction, categories of belief and what beliefs and actions should be attributed to each category can become contested. The plasticity of categorisation and the situational nature of categorisation processes are key considerations in the development of Sacks' (1992) concept of 'membership categorisation' discussed by Housley and Fitzgerald (2002). The categorisation of Christian or Muslim, and what those particular categorical labels mean, is a fundamental and frequent form of religious discourse. What should or should not be seen as Christian and Muslim and who gets to make those decisions play an important role in the management of individual and group identity.

Discussion about how categories should be defined occurs frequently in debates, particularly when speakers are attempting to position negative actions or beliefs, either of people who might be seen to be affiliated with themselves or in attempting to associate their opponent with the negative actions of others who share their categorical affiliation. That process of making sense of actions and beliefs in terms of categorical labels is not, however, linear. When two people from different points of view are attempting to position each other in different storylines, conflict can occur and results in speakers adjusting their own positionings to adapt to the emerging conditions of the interaction. In exchanges between the Christian Dave Hunt and the Muslim Shabir Ally, in their debate (D1, see Appendix), who gets labelled as a 'real' Christian or a 'real' Muslim is a recurring theme.

Hunt is introduced as the author of a variety of books on Christianity and Islam, and he speaks with a laidback authority. He very much looks the part of the Christian theologian, in a knit jumper and neatly trimmed white beard. He is relaxed and confident and introduces his position at the beginning of the debate as a straightforward and simple reading of the Bible:

Extract 3-1
> Now I want to make it very clear
> I'm not here
> to represent
> or preach
> or defend any religion
> Protestantism
> Catholicism
> method
> Methodists
> Methodism
> or
> [...]
> Calvinism
> or Presbyterianism
> or anything
> I'm here to defend
> and explain
> and defend
> Biblical Christianity
> [...]
> people call themselves Christians
> you wanna
> you wanna make up a religion
> go ahead
> make up any religion you want
> you're free to do that
> but you can't call it Christianity
> unless you follow the teachings
> and example of Jesus Christ
> that you get
> Christianity
> that you claim
> to be following
> you get it from
> the Bible
> God's word
> so that's why I define it
> as Biblical
> Christianity

In this extract, Hunt positions himself as 'not defending any religion' and goes on to list denominations of Christianity as examples of 'religions' he is not defending. In contrast, Hunt claims to 'defend and explain and defend Biblical Christianity', a category that others have used to describe belief that foregrounds the supremacy of the scriptures as inerrant (Piper, Taylor, & Helseth, 2003) and which Hunt elaborates saying that Christianity must be derived from the Bible, rather than the history of beliefs or practices associated with certain kinds of Christians. Instead, for Hunt, something or someone cannot be Christian if 'you do not follow the teachings and example of Jesus Christ' which comes from the Bible. Hunt subsequently rejects any possibility that his criteria for categorisation, essentially following the Bible, might be complicated because he views the text as self-explanatory and claims the Bible 'interprets itself'. By taking this conceptual position on what Biblical Christianity is, he attempts to establish the category as something fundamental and his use and understanding of Christianity as the 'true' representation.

Hunt's positioning of himself and his beliefs highlights the complexity of representing one's own beliefs. Hunt's marked Biblical Christianity shows both his own conceptualisation of his belief as the original representation of Christian faith and the reality that the term is used in a variety of different ways and that use requires further distinction. Although his own Christianity may be the dominant conceptualisation of Christianity, Hunt recognises in his statement a need to further clarify what he means by 'Christian' because of the myriad ways the category is used. However, the distinction that Hunt makes does not, in fact, distinguish between any of the categories of Christian 'religions' that he lists. Adherents of Protestantism and Catholicism, for example, would both presumably also claim to be following the teachings of Christ. The category of Biblical Christianity is not something he has defined as he suggests, but a recognised category of fundamentalism.

Hunt's use of categories positions himself as standing outside of the histories of any denomination, but not because of a particular concern over their doctrinal positions – Hunt himself presumably has been a member or regular attender of particular churches with particular doctrinal positions. The categorisation of the beliefs he is defending as Biblical Christianity allows him to avoid having to defend actions of any particular Christian which his Muslim opponent in the debate, Shabir Ally, may bring up. The beliefs and practices of Christianity are simply those practiced by Jesus Christ, and anyone who does anything contrary to those beliefs and practices, which Hunt claims are self-evident, is not truly a Christian. The position inoculates him from any criticism by Ally because he can subsequently claim that any action taken by a professing Christian that he sees as positive is an example of Biblical Christianity, and any negative action is evidence that the person follows some other kind of Christianity.

Hunt does not elaborate on the 'teachings and example of Jesus Christ' that he views as essential to Biblical Christianity. Despite also claiming to hold Islam to the same standard as Christianity (judging Islam only by what is written in the Qur'an and Christianity only by what is written in the Bible), Hunt says instead, 'I think it's equally important to scrutinise the fruit of Christianity – I'm talking about Biblical Christianity – and scrutinise the fruit of Islam. What is the fruit of each?' He subsequently describes actions of

Mohammad and mixes both historical claims about Mohammad with quotations from the Qur'an to create the sense that what he is claiming is written in the Qur'an, including the following anecdote:

Extract 3-2
Mohammad solidified his power
with about twenty five murders
a number of his first victims
were poets
who wrote disrespectful verses
so he justified himself by a passage
added to the Qur'an
and I'm not going to have time
to get to many of these
but Mohammad often got
uh
uh
a revelation
recorded in the Qur'an
cause he was the one that was dictating this
that justified his actions
how about that
his first victims
some of them
were poets
uh
who wrote disrespectful verses
so
what do you know
along comes a passage in the Qur'an
sura twenty six
two twenty one through two twenty four
declaring that all poets
were inspired
of Satan

Hunt presents evidence in his positioning of Mohammad as a violent figure, but this evidence is not drawn from a specific source. Instead, Hunt describes Mohammad as 'solidifying' his power through murder and particularly through the killing of poets who Hunt describes as having written 'disrespectful verses'. After this claim, Hunt then cites the Qur'an directly, saying that Sura 26:221–224 declares that 'all poets were inspired of Satan.' Hunt's use of evidence in this way makes it appear that the whole of the story comes from the Qur'an, including the details he has included in the beginning of the story, with Hunt's own explanation for why Mohammad took the action that he did. The citation of the specific sura, with the verses, adds authority to Hunt's claim as a second-order discourse, one in which his own words are presented in the authoritative voice of the Qur'an. However, there is no clear connection between the two points, and Hunt's use of the Qur'an in this way appears to be an attempt to position himself as an authority on the Qur'anic text, a strategy also used by Evangelical Christian preachers in incorporating biblical references in their preaching (Pihlaja, 2013).

The particular example establishes a storyline about Mohammad as a self-serving political leader who used his claims to have received a revelation from Allah as a means to justify his own actions often including what Hunt describes as immoral killing or sexual activity. The storyline also draws on an implicit view in the West of Islam as a violent religion (Ghadbian, 2000), an underlining theme throughout Hunt's statement. The positioning of Mohammad in a specific story of violence reinforces and is reinforced by this cultural misunderstanding, one that conflates political and religious violence to challenge the integrity of Islam and positions Muslims as a threat. Hunt's talk is a single, specific instantiation of a storyline that is likely already familiar to the audience.

Hunt goes on to tell another story which negatively positions Mohammad, wherein Mohammad sees 'a scantily clad Zaynab', the wife of his adopted son, and then receives a revelation about divorce that allowed Mohammad to marry Zaynab. This positioning also draws on a well-established, negative storyline of Mohammad as sexually deviant (Spencer, 2006) meant to delegitimise Islam. In the same way as he did in recounting the story of the poets, Hunt uses his own words, without specifying the source of the information, but ends with an explicit reference to a specific sura: 'Another timely revelation came along that was added to the Qur'an sura thirty three.' The same pattern implies the connection between Hunt's own words and the words of the Qur'an, without a clear demarcation of where the information is coming from in both instances. Hunt goes on to say, 'I could cite a few other revelations that were uh equally self-serving', suggesting that the instances of Mohammad acting in his own interest are common and that Hunt is taking his information in all cases explicitly from the Qur'an.

The extent to which Hunt is successful in convincing the audience with his argument is difficult to judge. Using selective and inconsistent citations from the Qur'an seems unlikely to convince a Muslim audience, as Hunt is not a scholar of the Qur'an. Instead, Hunt's positioning of himself as knowledge-able about the Qur'an is important in his role as a Christian apologist, arguing for the supremacy of Christianity before a mixed audience. As Hunt has been introduced as an expert on Christianity, and a learned scholar having written numerous books, he already has a position of authority. By presenting his arguments against Mohammad citing 'chapter and verse' of the Qur'an in the same manner as he argues for Jesus, citing the Bible, Hunt uses the same strategies to position himself with relation to both sacred texts. Although the Muslim audience may recognise that he is not an authority on Islam, the strategy allows him to be heard as one to non-Muslim audiences who are less familiar with the Qur'an and Islamic theology.

Hunt's positioning of Jesus and Mohammad is part of two opposing story-lines, wherein Jesus Christ and Mohammad are similar characters in Christianity and Islam, respectively, but the actions and examples of both represent very different moral actions. Hunt says, following the stories about Mohammad acting in his own interest:

Extract 3-3

Now
there's no comparison between Jesus
and Mohammad
and the followers
Peter said
Christ left us an example
that we should follow his steps
who didn't know sin
neither was guile found in his mouth
but the Qur'an frankly admits
that Mohammad was a sinner
urges him to confess
his sins
and I don't
uh
think that we would
uh
want to follow
uh
some of the things
that Mohammad did
the history of Islam
has been
shameful
his followers
killing one another
by the
hundreds of thousands

Hunt's argument is fundamentally built on a contradiction. He first says that 'there is no comparison between Jesus and Mohammad and the followers', reflecting his view of each figure and their followers as moral examples. However, contrary to this hyperbolic statement that there is 'no comparison', Hunt's positioning of the two actively encourages the listener to compare them as central figures and examples in both religions. Jesus is positioned as a leader 'who didn't know sin', while 'the Qur'an frankly admits that Mohammad was a sinner.' Hunt states that Christians follow the example of the 'teachings of Jesus' and that Christians 'should follow his steps who didn't know sin'. However, because Mohammad is positioned in a negative way as a sinner, the implication, although Hunt never explicitly says it, is that Mohammad's followers also took on his negative, 'sinful' attributes. The 'followers' of Jesus and Mohammad can then be broadened to include Christians and Muslims in the contemporary world; if Christians follow Jesus, then Muslims must then follow Mohammad, creating a 'shameful history' and 'killing one another by the hundreds of thousands'.

For Hunt, a connection should be made between the representation of the figures and their followers in both traditions. Whatever actions can be attributed to Jesus can then be attributed to Christians and whatever actions can be attributed to Mohammad can subsequently be attributed to Muslims. In both cases, the figurehead serves as the central example of the category of faith they come to represent. This line of argument is particularly expedient for Hunt, given the generally positive view of Jesus Christ, something Ally himself recognises, saying Jesus is known as the 'Prince of Peace'. Furthermore, few stories from the gospels about Jesus could be characterised in a negative way, allowing Hunt to make the argument that Jesus was, as he highlights, 'without guile', particularly compared to Mohammad, whose actions as both a spiritual and a political leader are more extensively recorded.

Hunt's argument provides an opportunity for Ally to respond by further arguing against what he sees as 'common' issues in the Bible and the Qur'an. Ally, like Hunt, looks the part of a theologian, although his long beard and traditional Muslim attire contrast with those of Hunt. He also speaks in a more organised manner, with notes that he reads from and point-by-point rebuttals to Hunt's arguments. Ally says, near the end of the debate:

Extract 3-4
> What I've tried to show
> even though
> many people think that the Qur'an is a violent book
> and by contrast
> the Bible must be a peaceful one
> especially it is
> since it is represented
> by a faith today
> which is characterised by Jesus who uh
> who is known to be the Prince of Peace
> I showed on the contrary
> that one
> when one looks carefully at the issues
> that are

common to both the Bible and the Qur'an
one can see that the Qur'an is in fact
a peaceful book

Ally doesn't address Hunt's positioning of Mohammad; instead, he continues to make the argument that Christianity and Islam both struggle with similar issues, suggesting that Hunt's point that a distinction can be made between the Bible and the Qur'an is not accurate. Ally disputes the claim that the Bible is 'peaceful', arguing that it is based on a representation of Jesus as the 'Prince of Peace' and argues instead that the contrary is true: that the Qur'an is 'a peaceful book' once one looks 'carefully at the issues'. The argument suggests that the 'representation' of the Bible and the Qur'an has been inaccurate, but that these inaccuracies can be eliminated through study. Ally doesn't take issue with Hunt's representation of Jesus or the Bible, but rather Hunt's incomplete description of both books. Ally's response to Hunt's argument about terrorism and Hunt's positioning of Mohammad is not to argue against the claim that Islam is a violent religion but instead challenges the claim that the Bible is a peaceful book.

While Hunt made a comparison between Jesus and Mohammad, Ally takes a different approach, arguing for the necessity of returning to the source texts and studying them. Rather than position Jesus in a negative storyline, Ally focuses on parts of the Bible that include violent imagery that is also problematic in a contemporary context. This strategy essentially cedes the centrality of the Bible. Rather than appeal to parts of the Qur'an that could be seen as exemplifying its peaceful characteristics, Ally chooses to highlight problematic parts of the biblical text – if the Bible and by extension Jesus himself are seen as peaceful, any story of violence in the Bible is relevant to the debate and to how both books should be perceived. As an example of violence in the Bible, Ally appeals to the story of Samson, arguing that it represents an example of a 'suicide killer':

Extract 3-5
In the nine eleven
uh
terrorist bombing
which we should all
reject and denounce
but we should
uh
at least be clear
that
uh
there is nothing in the Qur'an
that justifies the events of

uh
September eleventh two thousand and one
but we have something in the Bible
which actually celebrates
and glorifies
a suicide
killer
Samson
whom we learnt to love
in Sunday School

In responding to Hunt's claims about violence in Islamic teaching, Ally first rejects the idea that the Qur'an supports the 9/11 terrorist attacks, although he leaves out the specifics of that rejection and doesn't offer a detailed rebuttal of Hunt. Instead, he makes the point that the Bible's teachings could also be interpreted as supporting 'terrorist' violence, as in the case of Samson, which Ally says the Bible 'actually celebrates and glorifies'. Ally further makes the point that Samson was a person 'we learnt to love in Sunday School', and the use of 'we' reinforces an earlier statement that Ally made, highlighting that he too attended Sunday School as a child in Canada, and the stories that the audience would be familiar with were also the stories that he was familiar with. The reference to Sunday School then suggests that violence in Christian doctrine is a basic and common part of biblical teaching.

Ally's decision to not negatively position Jesus or his followers doesn't necessarily reflect Ally's hospitality towards the opposing position, but rather how Ally's arguments need to accommodate a Christian audience. Hunt's negative positioning of Mohammad in a storyline where Mohammad is a sinner committing violence appears to show little concern for creating common ground with Ally or the Muslims in the audience. Ally, on the other hand, positions obscure characters from the Bible in negative storylines and uses this not to attempt to delegitimise Christian belief but to argue instead that Hunt's storyline about Islam and Mohammad as engaged in *uniquely* violent actions is unfair. Whereas Hunt's argument calls for a complete rejection of Islam (something acceptable to the Christian audience), Ally does not call for a rejection of Christianity but rather a more critical approach to the content of the Bible.

The weakness of this positioning of the Bible is embedded in Ally's own introduction: the Bible has not been represented as a book of violence. This representation is, of course, inaccurate, and the Bible has been used to explicitly and implicitly justify violence (Ariarajah, 2017), including in contemporary discourse about the Iraq War (van Noppen, 2012) and in Evangelical apologetics for violence depicted in the Bible (Richardson & Pihlaja, 2018). However, Ally is working against a negative representation of Islam in contrast to Christianity, in a context where terrorism is primarily associated with Islam (Ghadbian, 2000). Although it may be logical to describe Samson as a 'suicide killer', Ally himself admits that Samson is a figure 'whom we learnt to love in Sunday School'. These positive representations of Christianity, particularly when contrasted with ongoing negative media coverage of Islam, create a difficult context in which to make this argument.

The exchange shows how debate, however fair or equal the structure may appear, is constrained by the cultural and situational context. Hunt is afforded a substantial advantage from the beginning, arguing in front of a Canadian audience where Islam is the minority position. The cultural understanding of the Bible favours a Christian storyline, one that even if the audience doesn't accept as a part of their personal confessional faith, they likely have some familiarity with. By contrast, Ally is making a positive argument for the Qur'an, a text that has not played an important role in the cultural history of the country, and one with which the non-Muslim Canadian audience members are unlikely to have read. To the extent that these non-Muslims may be aware of Islamic teaching and Muslim practice, Hunt's positioning of Mohammad, the Qur'an, and Islam suggests that a negative representation does not require justification in the same way that a negative representation of a Bible does.

Ally's attempt to undercut Hunt's negative positioning of Muslims and Islam ultimately revolves around the argument that Hunt is inconsistent in the way that he addresses the Bible and the Qur'an. Ally says,

Extract 3-6
Just as Dave was saying
there are good Christians and bad Christians
well
there are good Muslims and bad Muslims
there are people who follow the true teachings
and people who do not
and
uh
it is interesting
that Dave
uh
in
speaking about Muslim activities
would blame all of the activities of Muslims
on the Qur'an
but then in speaking of the
the facts that he has documented in his own book
that Christians slaughtered so many Jews
and fellow Christians
and so on
he says

okay
those are not real Christians
okay
so
[…]
then let's be fair
and do it with both books

Ally argues that 'there are people who follow the true teachings and people who do not', accepting Hunt's claim that there are some who don't follow the 'true teachings' in a religion. Ally also accepts Hunt's differentiation between 'good' and 'bad' members of particular religions – there can be both 'good' Muslims and 'bad' Muslims (Mamdani, 2002). When Hunt comments on the negative situation for free speech in Saudi Arabia, for example, Ally accepts the point and makes an effort to distinguish between culture and religious practice and belief. However, instead of condemning Hunt's use of the actions of terrorists to represent typical Muslim belief, Ally says that to be consistent, Hunt must also then accept the same argument when it is shown to be true of Christians. For Ally, the fact that 'Christians slaughtered so many Jews' is essential to take into account if one is going to be 'fair', implying that Hunt's selective use of evidence is not. Ally does not position himself as an authority in the same way that Hunt does. Instead, he is both a critic of the Bible and the Qur'an, someone who is 'fair'.

However, Hunt doesn't make the same sort of concessions. Instead, he uses the introduction of violence to speak directly about Islamic terrorism. In the five debates, violence and terrorism are very rarely mentioned by the Christian debaters in relation to Islam, but Hunt explicitly refers to suicide bombing in one of his final statements, around 90 minutes into the 2 hour 40 minute video. Hunt makes the argument that violence is implicit in the praise for suicide bombers in an editorial in the newspaper *Al-Hayat* which Hunt says praised the suicide bombers of 9/11 as 'the salt of the earth, the engines of history, the most honourable people among us', suggesting that terrorism could come to 'shopping centres in America' and that the goal of this terrorism is 'you either submit to Allah or, or else'. Hunt positions all Muslims with the actions of the terrorists saying, 'These were not fanatics, these were Muslims by the thousands shouting *Allah alakabar* . . . . Allah is the greatest.'

The argument includes a malignant positioning of Muslims, wherein the actions of terrorists are represented as following the teaching of Islam and foregrounds a religious motivation (to make others 'submit to Allah') for the 9/11 attacks. The positioning of 'Muslims by the thousands shouting' in support of the terrorist attack gives a specific instance in a storyline of terrorism, where individual Muslims act in violent ways and are supported by other Muslims. By foregrounding the shouting of '*Allah alakabar*', Hunt highlights a religious motivation for the terrorist act and conflates the goals of terrorists with Muslims – this is not about 'good' and 'bad' Muslims, but Muslims more generally.

The positioning of Muslims in a storyline of terrorism, based on the actions of a small number of people, shows how abstraction of an individual action can be both exclusive and inclusive, depending on the speaker's goals, and moral reasoning need not be logical – for Hunt. Although Muslims can be grouped together based on the particular actions of the 9/11 terrorists, one must also differentiate 'good' or 'real' Christians and 'bad' Christians. The two abstract categories allow Hunt to position Christians within different storylines. By making these careful distinctions, he can represent all 'good' actions as exemplars of his belief and of those who share that same belief. He doesn't, however, have to apply the same logic to Muslims.

Hunt's reasoning about Muslims and his representations of Christianity and Islam are not impromptu rebuttals of Ally. The use of evidence and the quoting of the article suggest that it is a planned argument; although Ally challenges Hunt in this instance, the same argument could be used in discussions among Christians where someone like Ally isn't present to offer a counterargument. Similarly, the storyline about 'Biblical Christians' shows how Hunt can both reject the undesirable actions of some Christians and reinforce solidarity among people who already agree with him. Even when these claims are shown to be logically inconsistent, Hunt does not abandon the line of reasoning. The context of the debate allows for the voicing of the counterargument, but it doesn't remedy inconsistent logic.

Hunt's argument that the violent actions of some Muslims represent Islam more generally and Ally's reticence to make the same argument about Christianity further reveals the privileged position of Christianity, wherein Hunt is able to define his and others beliefs in contrast to a particular narrative about Christianity, and Ally's position must, in some way, address the false or illogical statements that Hunt has made. Within the debate context, Hunt as a white, male Christian authority is able to claim without qualification that his beliefs and practices represent Christianity. At the same time, Hunt does not afford to Ally the same authority, to define the fundamental beliefs and practices of Islam in an accepted storyline about the violent nature of Islam (Baker et al., 2013; Bruce, 2017). Ally's discussion of biblical violence by contrast does not attempt to silence Hunt's own claims about Christianity but to argue that both Christians and Muslims must take into account the less desirable portions of their sacred texts. In this way, Hunt's and Ally's approaches to debating and the positioning of each other are fundamentally different. Hunt negates and erases Ally's own positioning of himself and Islam and propagating his own storyline, while Ally positions Islam as comparable to Christianity, arguing for its legitimacy through analogy to Christian belief.

The interaction between Hunt and Ally reveals two important characteristics of representing one's belief and positioning oneself and others. First, the audience and the dominant belief in a particular context determine the positions available to an individual. If Christian belief is dominant, then Islam is understood in analogy to it. Second, debate can become a means for disparaging another's belief and platforming one's own belief. The debate between Hunt and Ally is described as 'the Bible against the Qur'an' and 'the Bible versus the Qur'an'. However, the debate becomes about larger issues of how each faith is represented and shows little evidence that either debater is attempting to resolve theological issues between the two faiths.

3.2 Religion in a Diverse World

The debate between Shabir Ally and Dave Hunt ostensibly centred on the vague idea of 'the Bible versus the Qur'an', but the arguments and subsequent positionings suggested that the key issue was the extent to which violence can or should be justified using religious belief and how violence done in the name of Christianity and Islam should be treated in contemporary society. The focus on and rejection of religious violence highlights the broader context of the contemporary world in which the debate took place wherein terrorism is viewed as abhorrent and potentially an existential threat, particularly after the 9/11 attacks. The focus on violence is not incidental – it reveals the particular concerns about religious belief and practice at a particular point in time.

Within this context, debate is positioned as a remedy to religious violence, because it requires listening to and speaking with people of different beliefs, a practice that supposedly promotes peace and understanding in a multicultural, diverse world. Michael Coren, a Canadian broadcaster and clergyman, serves as the moderator of the debate and offers an introduction, describing the benefit of dialogue between different religions:

Extract 3-7
It is so important
in contemporary Canada in particular
I believe
that ideas are expressed openly
I know some are offended by some ideas
that's the nature of being a grown up
in a
pluralistic world
some ideas offend
get used to it
we coexist
we live together
so respect for people willing to stand here

sit here
participate
and give their opinions
I think it's a wonderful thing
and
uh
it's one of the
the great triumphs of democracy

Positioning the debate as a 'wonderful thing' and one of the 'great triumphs of democracy', Coren makes clear that what is most important is being able to hear differing opinions and respect others. The goal of the debate is not to win the argument and prove the other side invalid, but rather 'getting used to' the existence of those with differing opinions, so that people can be 'grown up' and 'coexist' and 'live together' in a 'pluralistic world'. Importantly, however, Coren does not suggest that it is necessary to accept the views of the other, and his introduction to the debate only includes an implicit negative evaluation of those who can't live together with others, not those who believe strongly that they are right and others are wrong. The introduction also condemns feeling 'offended by some ideas' as childish. The material conditions of the debate represent mutual respect and tolerance, as well as participation and engagement with the opinions and views of others, with 'democracy' as the key organising principle.

    Although Coren focuses on these principles, the extent to which both Ally and Hunt accept them as the goal of the debate is not clear. Neither Hunt nor Ally suggests that they are offended by the views or existence of the other, nor do they explicitly suggest that the other's view should not exist. Instead, the statement seems to address underlying concerns about multiculturalism and religious diversity. Coren doesn't talk about terrorism in his introduction, but the mention of 'contemporary Canada' and 'democracy' suggests that the debate plays a role not only in resolving disagreements or seeking truth but also in performing tolerance as resistance to radical belief. Debate then becomes a public rejection of extremism simply through non-violent engagement of the other.

    How people talk about their own faith and that of others depends heavily on who is listening and whether their positioning is likely to be challenged. Of the two debaters, Ally makes the clearer attempt at finding common ground between Christianity and Islam. When he does speak negatively about the Bible, he is careful to hedge, for example, saying at one point that the Bible's description of a command to the Israelites to 'kill everyone' in a land they occupy is 'unfortunate', positioning himself as not being happy to point out contradictions in the Bible. By contrast, Hunt's approach to the Qur'an, as I have shown, is much more indignant and aggressive. Because the debate is hosted by a Christian organisation and oriented towards a largely Christian audience, the general principle of living in a 'pluralistic world' and showing respect for one another doesn't appear to apply equally to both Ally and Hunt.

The other debates include different physical conditions, topics, audiences, and debaters. However, debate is always positioned both explicitly and implicitly as a positive way for people of different faiths to interact. In a debate at a University in South Africa, hosted jointly by the Christian group Campus Crusade for Christ and the Islamic Propagation Centre for Islam, Shabir Ally and the Christian apologist James White argue over whether the earliest followers of Jesus Christ believed Jesus was God (D2, see Appendix). Like the debate between Hunt and Ally, the moderator who identifies himself as a Christian emphasises the importance of mutual respect. The moderator says the following:

Extract 3-8
In a place like South Africa
where
uh
tolerance
is the big word
and we don't want to offend everybody
and we must just hold hands
and sing kumbaya
and not disagree
about
uh
about big things
I can tell you
that these guys
are two examples
of people
who can disagree with one another
but in a civil manner
and
uh
the basis for that disagreement
uh
or the basis for it happening in a civil manner
is not relativism
it's not the lack of truth
but it's
it's mutual respect
and love
and I think we can learn something uh
from that sort of
uh
uh
discussion

'In a place like South Africa' foregrounds a difficult contemporary context and positions dialogue between Christians and Muslims as an alternative to other forms of conflict, but the moderator, apparently speaking ironically in the voice of a common sense South African cultural perspective, says, 'We don't want to offend anyone' and we must 'hold hands and sing kumbaya'. Tolerance in this sense is a 'big word', something that is implicitly linked to 'relativism' and 'lack of truth' and rejected as the basis for the debate. Instead, Ally and White are put forward as examples of disagreeing in a 'civil manner' based on 'mutual respect', 'love', and learning from each other. What the two are meant to be avoiding in their disagreement, and what kind of disagreement might be considered 'uncivil' is left unsaid. Although 'relativism' and 'lack of truth' are rejected, the goal of the debate is not to decide which position is right. Moreover, the moderator doesn't suggest that the debaters are attempting to change either their or the audience members' minds; despite implicitly positioning a tolerant society in a negative way, the representation of the debate is the perceived need for people of different faiths to respect one another despite their disagreements.

The positioning of the specific debate between Ally and White suggests a storyline about how Christians and Muslims should interact. Ally and White are positioned as representatives of their respective faiths and their interaction as an exemplar case of dialogue between people who disagree. After two incidents occur during the debate, one where a mobile phone notification with the call to prayer is heard and one in which a Christian loudly reacts to a claim by Ally, audience members are also explicitly positioned as representative of their belief categories. The moderator, in his concluding remarks, refers to both of these incidents as representative of both groups acting negatively. He says, 'Let's call it square and say both sides have misbehaved. We had Muslim prayers and Christian chanting.' The disruptive actions are attributed to categories of people rather than individuals, and they are treated as equally negative intrusions, even though they are materially quite different: a Muslim spectator had not silenced his mobile phone ('Muslim prayers'), while a Christian in the audience had disrupted Ally at one point shouting out their disagreement ('Christian chanting'). Instead, the incidents are abstracted as 'misbehaviour' attributed to 'both sides' and reveal an emerging storyline that 'both sides' act inappropriately in debates.

Within the debates, the moderators, and at times the participants, position both extremism and relativism as threats to society and religious belief. People who do not listen to what the others have to say are also positioned in a negative storyline. However, everyone who speaks also explicitly rejects the idea that both sides can be 'right' and asserts that the goal of the debate should be to decide what is and is not 'true'. A tension then arises, as the debates are intended as both examples of positive inter-religious interaction and means for the audience to make judgements about the opposing truth claims of both sides. These two intentions are not always in conflict – Ally in particular makes an effort to show common ground between the Bible and the Qur'an, between Christianity and Islam – but none of the five debates ends with both sides making concessions and coming to a common conclusion.

The debates position religions as systems which inform how and what people believe, but only in contrast and comparison to an opposing side – how a Christian sees the world rather than how a Muslim does. These constructions can be limiting and political with a focus on refuting individual points which are ultimately inconsequential for lived religious belief; the debates remain focused on arguments about abstract meaning rather than questions of ethics. The contemporary world provides an impetus for these debates because of an apparent perception that dialogue and interaction between religious believers are necessary to avoid unwanted conflict and, more importantly, violence. However, the contemporary world is not foregrounded in the disagreements.

By contrast, stories and positioning about the contemporary world between people of the same faith can focus on practical elements of religious belief and practice. For Ali Dawah, the challenges of the contemporary world include substantial amounts of grey area, where young Muslims must decide whether or not they should engage in activities that might be seen as *haram*, or forbidden within Islam, if those activities are essential to their day-to-day lives. Two of the collected Ali Dawah videos address these issues specifically: *IS CAR INSURANCE HARAM? AskTheSheikh* (A2, see Appendix) and *CAN I SELL ALCOHOL & PORK AT WORK? (SPECIFIC FATWA) || AskTheSheikh* (A7, see Appendix). In both of the videos, Ali and a guest, Sheikh Haitham, discuss how Muslims should deal with elements of contemporary life that appear to be both wrong from an Islamic perspective and unavoidable. The process of 'asking the Sheikh' for advice is well established in Islam (Agrama, 2010) and provides the basis for making decisions about what actions should or should not be considered permissible in a changing world. The videos tend to also present a visual contrast between Ali, who is in his twenties and dressed in street clothes, and the older Sheikh Haitham, who is in a robe and *kufi*, the traditional cap worn by Muslim men, and has a long beard. In the discussion of selling and touching pork and alcohol while working at a supermarket, Ali introduces the topic saying,

Extract 3-9
> For today's question
> is we had an email from a sister
> who works in Tesco [British Supermarket]
> and she's asking
> that
> obviously

she's supporting her family
she has no other choice
um
is she allowed to serve
alcohol
or
touch pork
um
et cetera
is she allowed to do that

Ali presents the topic as a genuine question from a sister who has emailed him, although her actual words are not quoted. The sister works at a large UK supermarket, Tesco, and Ali states that she is 'obviously' supporting her family, without explaining why this would be 'obvious'. This caveat positions the question which follows as resulting from necessity rather than a choice. Ali's positioning of the young woman suggests that she wants to avoid potentially doing anything wrong. Ali then asks if she is 'allowed' to do two activities that are positioned as exemplar cases of potentially haram actions: serving alcohol and touching pork. Ali's use of 'allowed' suggests that the questioner is seeking permission from a religious authority, although Ali's revoicing of the question and the lack of specifics make it difficult to deduce what Ali's concerns are and what the woman's concerns are or if indeed she is an actual viewer or rather a constructed example of an issue that is reoccurring in the community. Ali specifically asks if she is allowed to 'serve alcohol' or 'touch pork' with the tag 'et cetra', and the question makes subtle distinctions to clarify what is or is not permissible, and if there is a difference between 'serving', 'selling', and 'touching' different products.

What exactly the woman is doing when she is working and how her actions in that role are described are important for moral reasoning and deciding whether or not the actions she takes are appropriate. Ali's positioning of the questions reveals a storyline in the actions of a specific viewer, a Muslim who is working in a shop and required to do certain actions. The specific story is useful insomuch as it can provide an exemplar case for how Muslims should act in similar situations. Although the title of the video reads *(SPECIFIC FATWA)*, the wording of the question and Ali's exposition of all actions to broader categories – ultimately, is some action halal or haram – shows how moral judgements as they unfold in discourse events can reveal higher order, abstract reasoning, and consequentially how that higher-order, abstract reasoning can be applied to other issues.

Sheikh Haitham's response makes the context of the contemporary world in the West relevant, saying,

Extract 3-10
First of all
uh
you know
in this
country and in the West in general
it is
very rare for anyone
a brother or a sister
to find
a job that is purely halal [permissible]
that is free from any haram [prohibition]

Sheikh Haitham begins by highlighting the context of 'this country' and the 'West in general' as places where purely halal jobs are 'very rare'. Sheikh Haitham doesn't further elaborate on how this might contrast with non-Western, presumably Muslim countries, but the answer suggests, from the outset, that a part of living in Britain will likely include taking a job that requires doing some things that are considered haram. The sheikh, however, follows up on the point further in the conversation, saying that 'these days' even in Muslim countries, 'It is very difficult to find a job that is purely halal.' The answer reveals two abstract categories for physical locations: the 'West' in contrast to 'Muslim' countries. Further, by positioning the story in 'these days', the sheikh again makes the contemporary context relevant. The question is not whether or not haram actions can be completely avoided in contemporary life but rather which haram actions can be 'overlooked'. This is not just an issue for those living in Britain, but it applies around the world, positioning Muslims living in both Muslim-majority countries and the Western context of Britain as confronting the same problems.

Implicit in the discussion of right action for Muslims working in supermarkets is the public nature of the work. Making decisions about right and wrong action involves not only a simple question of what is and is not allowed in Islam, but complex choices about how one's religious identity, and particularly a Muslim identity, can and should be present in contemporary, public life. The difficulty holding minority religious commitments in a secular context is a pressing issue, particularly for young Muslims who have been the object of suspicion and derision in public discourse and the media (see Ahmed, 2015; Gholami, 2017; Pihlaja & Thompson, 2017 for the myriad pressures that young Muslims face in day-to-day life in the West) and are the subject of negative perceptions in Britain, particularly for individuals who are seen as performing religious identities publicly, for example, women wearing hijabs (Hopkins & Greenwood, 2013). For young Muslims, the question that Ali asks Sheikh Haitham has repercussions beyond simply what is permissible, but what the position of young Muslims in contemporary British society should be.

Despite the reality of discrimination and suspicion, Sheikh Haitham's response does not engage with any of the larger societal issues about the perception or treatment of Muslims in working contexts or on what the effects of making one choice or another might be for how the particular young woman is perceived, by her colleagues or managers or customers. The only other factor that is suggested as relevant is that she is relying on the job to support her family, but the sheikh doesn't engage with this point either. As the specific positions are abstracted, the storyline becomes almost exclusively focused on what is or is not right action. The moral judgement that follows then explicitly downplays the importance of intent and circumstance, instead embedding intent in the way the actions are described. Sheikh Haitham does this by focusing on the issue of 'serving alcohol' as a physical action that can be judged as haram or halal regardless of individual intention:

Extract 3-11
It is true that khamr [alcohol]
leads to a fasad [depravity]
drinking alcohol leads to fasad
that's why
the Prophet as-salam [peace be on him] said
about khamr
it is khamr
but
the amount of dealing with khamr
in working for a Tesco
or
Sainsbury
or the likes of that
is minimum
is minimum
and you are not
really facilitating that
and you are not selling it
you are just
passing [scanning it]
or
yeah
you are not even serving it

The verbs describing 'scanning' the items become relevant in thinking about the position of the Muslim worker in relation to the item they are touching – the sheikh makes clear there is a distinction between 'selling' and 'serving' the item and simply 'passing' it (Ali corrects him to say 'scanning' in the next turn of the conversation). This positioning of the action changes the storyline from one of selling alcohol and 'facilitating' another person's depravity to the less intentional moving an item from one location to another. The nuance of the processes changes the storyline and with it the way in which the person can be positioned in relation to the action. The storyline becomes one in which young Muslims in contemporary society take part in haram acts that should be overlooked, because the actions themselves are done without intent. The moral position of the young woman is not then entirely dependent on the actions she does in her place of work, but the story that can be told about them. The way those actions are talked about, Sheikh Haitham shows, is essential to understanding what is or is not permissible.

Sheikh Haitham's response also includes the Arabic words for alcohol and depravity, or sin, with a reference back to the teaching of the Prophet. Arabic words describing religious principles are used without translations in this extract and suggest that both the sheikh and Ali expect the audience to understand the terms, as Ali doesn't clarify them or add any annotations or text to the video in post-production (which he does in other videos). Of course, one is able to understand the majority of the message of the video without understanding the specific terms, but their use shows that the audience is positioned as having some background in Arabic and some knowledge of these key terms – they are Muslim viewers with a basic understanding of the religion and the Qur'an.

Although there is no explicit discussion of the woman's colleagues or her supervisors, the implicit message is that she should go about her work without causing any undue attention to her religious belief:

Extract 3-12
Sheikh: We ask brothers and sisters
to try their best
to find the minimum haram
[. . .]
to find the jobs with the minimum haram
and also
we try to speak to the
any management
with the Tesco
in any other of this
uh
superstores
yeah
so that they should work
only in halal
uh
facilities
Ali: If they can
yeah
Sheikh: If they can
Ali: Inshallah

The sheikh does insist that, where possible, workers should attempt to 'try their best' and 'to find the jobs with the minimum haram', but this is the extent of the responsibility expected of the worker. The sheikh then uses the collective 'we' to talk about this request of 'brothers and sisters' and then to discuss the possibility of discussing the issue with management, saying that 'we' 'speak with' the managers of the Tesco that 'they' are working in, so that they 'should work only in halal facilities'. Ali follows this statement with the qualifier 'If they can', which the sheikh repeats and Ali uses the Arabic, phrase 'inshallah', meaning 'if Allah wills it'. Who 'we' are in Sheikh Haitham's statement is not entirely clear. The first use, with 'we' asking brothers and sisters to follow a route with less haram, implies people in leadership roles, possibly limited to sheikhs like himself giving advice to Muslims, but it could also apply to any Muslim.

The suggestion to speak to management is carefully hedged with the caveat 'if they can' and both Ali and Sheikh Haitham work to make clear that attempting to avoid particular tasks at work isn't a requirement. Moreover, Sheikh Haitham says that 'we' 'speak with' managers, rather than saying they 'ask' or 'demand'. Requests are therefore positioned as being done in amenable ways, and without demanding changes from management to account for issues of minor haram. When major haram is involved, the impetus is on the Muslim worker to simply not take the job in the first place. The sheikh, however, doesn't suggest that the supervisor or shop owner must accommodate the worker; rather, the worker must do their best to balance their own needs with religious teaching. The answer seems to implicitly consider an awareness that the demands may be viewed negatively and that there is a need to reduce the possibility of discrimination when making a claim based on one's minority faith position.

Ali Dawah and Sheikh Haitham's response, particularly in a public discussion of Islam on social media, counters storylines which position young Muslims, particularly Muslim women, as failing to integrate in society (Baker et al., 2013). Although there has been concern about the role of the Internet and social media in online extremism, particularly in reporting on extremist groups like Al Qaeda (Seib & Janbek, 2010) and ISIS (Lieber & Reiley, 2016), research has also looked at the numerous ways in which extremism is combated in online spaces (Abdulla, 2007; Ashour, 2010; Etling, Kelly, Faris, & Palfrey, 2010). In discussions on Ali Dawah's channel, and in this video in particular, the focus is on how young Muslims can adapt practices in contemporary contexts, and when potential issues arise, the onus is placed on Muslims to be accommodating and not make demands on the basis of their religious beliefs. Accepting 'minimum haram' in the workplace and a magnanimous attitude towards those who find themselves in situations wherein they must make similar decisions is a stark contrast to storylines wherein Muslims are positioned as attempting to stand outside of Western society. On the contrary, the discussion is entirely on how to behave in ways that respect both Western norms and one's religious commitments.

Of course, the video is a public representation of Islamic belief for a public audience and might not necessarily be understood as an authoritative *fatwa* or Islamic legal judgement, nor does it imply that Ali Dawah or Sheikh Haitham might argue for different standards in private contexts. Still, previous research has shown that the Internet has become an important resource for young Muslims for finding information about their faith (El-Nawawy, 2009; El Naggar, 2018). For those searching for advice about the choices they need to make in their day-to-day lives, the content available to them online can be crucial guidance. In this video, there are no caveats that the viewer, or indeed the specific woman asking the specific question, should speak to their own imam about or to search out advice offline. It would then be very difficult to present a moderate view of Islam to a public audience while teaching a different position privately, without the public position affecting individuals' choices and actions about what activities are appropriate.

However, little evidence on the video page, and particularly in the comments, indicates that the opinion is used as a resource for making decisions about right behaviour. In terms of positive responses, there are comments praising Ali and the sheikh and one clear comment where a user claims to have experienced peace from watching the video:

Extract 3-13
I used to work in a city hall kitchen, preparing food for staff and cleaning dishes. My duties were mainly cleaning dishes, but one day the chef who was a really nice guy asked me to grab the bacon from the fridge and place them on a tray to put them in the oven, as he was very busy. I did it, but I did not touch the bacon physically, I used a tool to place the bacon on the tray and the chef did the rest. Ever since I have the feeling of having committed this big sin, thank you brother Ali for giving me peace with this video.

At least in one instance, some empirical evidence shows that the video can lead to a change in how a user feels about themselves and has some effect on their moral reasoning. The struggle the commenter describes is primarily one of their conscience, 'the feeling of having committed this big sin' rather than being judged negatively for their actions by others or having been confronted about their actions. The comment suggests that the concern raised in the video is not limited to one individual and taken with the number of views that Ali and the sheikh have hit on a topic that is of concern. However, whether or not the comment is genuine is difficult to judge and what is much more apparent are the disagreements about whether or not the fatwa that the sheikh has given should be accepted. A clear majority of the comments that receive higher ratings respond to whether the fatwa is accurate. The opinion of the sheikh is roundly rejected in these comments, but the extent to which this is indicative of the average viewer's response to the video is also difficult to judge as arguing in comments sections about the content of a particular video is not necessarily representative of how an average viewer interacts with it.

The video which follows, entitled *IS CAR INSURANCE HARAM? AskTheSheikh* (A2, see Appendix), addresses a similar discussion. The conversation focuses on whether or not the buying of insurance involves *riba*, or money made in an unjust way – 'money for money' as the sheikh presents it – because the person buying the insurance is not necessarily clear whether they may receive more money in payment from the insurance company than they have paid into the insurance. The conversation includes a discussion of 'necessity' in the contemporary world, much in the way of the discussion of the job at Tesco, with Ali and the sheikh attempting to work out what is or is not needed to live in the contemporary Western world. Ali draws this issue back to the different challenges that Muslims face in their lives.

Extract 3-14
So have understanding brothers and sisters
you might look at something
and it might be like
wrong
but understand the situation behind that
because
when it's your necessity
with a car for example
you say
ah
I need my car
in reality
do you really need it
but we don't question that
we just say
look the scholars said it
let's go
but let's
not have double standards
let's understand the other person

Ali and Sheikh Haitham's discussion of insurance first focuses on how different people see necessity in different ways and argues that 'brothers and sisters' must have an understanding of other people's situations. As with the discussion of selling alcohol and deciding what is and is not haram, the action of buying insurance is abstracted to a 'necessity'. The positioning of an individual then dictates the way their actions should be viewed, again showing how positioning of people and actions contributes to moral reasoning. In the example of car insurance, a person's actions may be viewed as 'wrong' until you 'understand the situation behind' the person's car ownership. 'Need', both here and in the earlier example, is fundamentally an abstract and, therefore, ambiguous concept. Ali makes the point that 'in reality', need might be something that one feels but isn't actually real. The focus is on taking specific situations into account to 'understand the other person'.

The presentation of the issue, and the nuanced discussion that follows on how to decide whether actions include riba, focuses on a balancing of scholarly input and personal responsibility. Ali and Sheikh Haitham, however, do not comment specifically on the actions of any individual and stress instead the importance of fellow Muslims not judging the actions of others. Having clarified the overall principles of riba, Sheikh Haitham and Ali encourage viewers to both consider their own actions ('Do you really need [a car]?') and their view of others ('Let's not have double standards'). Where the particular action in question is open for interpretation and there is not a clear answer to whether something should be avoided as haram, both Ali and the sheikh encourage viewers to do their best with the advice they've been given and avoid looking down on the choices of others in similar, difficult predicaments.

The focus on the reasoning and how words like 'need' are used in accounting for actions again shows that positioning and storylines have consequences for how moral judgements are made, and the same action – like having car insurance – can be deemed either right or wrong depending on the storyline. Ali's talk about the actions of others and how he positions them shows how abstraction facilitates moral judgements, as he moves between several scales of specificity. Stories of individual Muslims with cars can be abstracted to generic Muslims with cars, to generic Muslims taking part in generic actions that might be seen as being haram. Once the principle is agreed upon and a particular incident can be abstracted to a storyline, that storyline can be applied at different levels with consequences not only for a specific question but also more broadly to right belief and practice for everyone.

The issue of car insurance also has fewer consequences for how Muslims are viewed publicly, in a way that perhaps making special requests of a manager at a supermarket might not. Perceptions of actions then become primarily issues of in-group membership and how the community relates to itself. However, actions that are clearly haram and committed publicly by Muslims (and therefore reflect negatively on Muslims more generally) are treated much more negatively.

These same issues emerge in a video entitled *'EMOTIONAL INTERVIEW WITH SISTER IN TWERKING VIDEO ... '* (A4, see Appendix) Ali Dawah interviews a young Muslim woman who has had a video of herself go viral online. In the viral video (which Ali doesn't show), the woman is said to be seen twerking, or dancing in a sexually provocative way, while wearing a hijab. The video caused a significant controversy, and Ali Dawah initially publicly admonished the woman and condemned the video. Subsequently, Ali was contacted by the family of the woman and told that she struggled with depression and 'mental issues'. Ali then posted another video in which he interviews the woman, who is not shown and whose voice is disguised, telling her that Allah forgives her and she need not worry about Allah's judgement because she has repented.

After posting and taking down the video where he clearly vents his anger about the situation, Ali posts a second, more measured response where he plays a clip of the interview with the woman and takes a more conciliatory tone. However, Ali begins the second video by explaining the anger he showed in his first response video. Ali suggests that he responded too strongly, saying,

Extract 3-15
We
when we see such videos
we
take it too far
we start insulting individuals
swearing
insulting
calling them all kinds of names

Unlike the discussion of selling alcohol at Tesco or buying car insurance, there is no ambiguity in the rightness or wrongness of twerking. Instead, the focus is shifted to the online response to these actions and what people should do when they see a Muslim behaving in an inappropriate way. Even though Ali's description of the event began with a discussion of the particular response to the particular video, the whole incident is abstracted to a storyline that is regularly followed where 'we take it too far' in response to the actions of 'individuals'. Ali positions himself as a part of a collective 'we', and by using the present tense of the verb 'see', he suggests the actions are the kind of thing that people in his position do, including 'swearing', 'insulting', and 'calling . . . all kinds of names'. They are not, however, in this construction the thing that he himself has done at a particular time towards a particular person. The positioning of 'we' in an abstract storyline obscures his own responsibility. His actions become the sort of thing that everyone does.

Despite not directly taking responsibility for his response initially, Ali's self-positioning emphasises his own humility in addressing controversial issues and dealing with others. Ali plays part of his video that he posted and took down, but only after the caveats about his own 'confusion' and 'frustration' with the situation. In the first video, Ali says to the camera,

addressing the woman, 'What the hell is going through your head?' Ali
doesn't explicitly apologise for his initial angry response, but says instead:

Extract 3-16
Okay guys
so you saw for yourself
like how frustrated me and Musa was
I was
I couldn't
I was just banging the table
like
I was just frustrated
cause I was like
why would somebody do that
and it was just
it
it taught me a lesson
like in a way
where I was like
okay
I should be angry
for the sake of the religion
but I should always
think
okay
there must be reason
you know what I'm saying
so I learned a big lesson myself

In this accounting, Ali stresses that his anger was 'for the sake of religion',
positioning the violent response, exemplified in his 'banging on the table', as
being motivated by positive intent, making the actions understandable.
Although the accounting for his actions and self-positioning includes 'learning
a big lesson', that lesson is simply to focus on the point that his anger should
always be motivated by religion. By positioning himself as acting in defence of
religion, he differentiates himself from the other negative responses to the
incident. The same logic applies to the woman in the video, whose intent,
when it is revealed, changes how Ali positions her and her actions. For both,
their actions must be understood in their accounting, and in reconsidering the
women's intention, Ali can position himself in a new, positive storyline.

Intention and knowledge are crucial in moral reasoning (Jayyusi, 1984), with
both playing a role in how people and their actions should be viewed (Edwards,
2008). Intention affects how storylines develop, offering explanations for
actions and events. Things which appear negative may actually be positive,
and vice versa. Whether Ali's initial response is acceptable will depend on why
he acts the way he does. If his anger is motivated by personal spite, it is not

acceptable; if it is 'for the sake of religion', then it is acceptable. Intention emerges in the positioning of himself and his actions. By providing a post hoc accounting, he maintains his positioning as an authority, someone who can make judgements about others and defend Islam in public spaces. He is a passionate arbitrator for Islam online and an authority on how Muslims should be seen in contemporary society rather than an angry troll, attacking a woman for making a mistake.

Ali eventually plays his interview with the woman from the video wherein she describes struggling with depression and then breaks down, crying. Ali says,

Extract 3-17
Okay so
basically
don't worry sister
don't worry
don't
don't be upset
this is
wa'Allahi [I swear]
this is the work of Shaitaan [Satan]
believe us
the only reason I'm doing this
is because
unfortunately
people are going to watch the video
and judge you
based on that
so don't cry
Allah Subhanahu Wa Ta'ala [Allah most glorified most high]
is the most merciful
and don't ever
and you said
you [...] started to practice
so sister
wa'Allahi
I make dua [prayer] for you
inshallah
that you get well
don't be upset
that is good that
one part
the fact that you're crying
wa'Allahi
this is a sign of repentance
and remorse

and it shows that you have iman [faith]
yeah
so don't be upset

Ali's response positions the woman as primarily concerned with her own spiritual condition. Although he positions himself as intervening because 'people are going to watch the video and judge you', he focuses on her needing not to worry about Allah's judgement because she has 'started to practice' and that she has 'iman' because her crying shows repentance and she has remorse for her actions. Ali's injunction for her to not worry and not be upset focuses exclusively on the judgement of Allah, positioning her in a storyline of repentance and religion. Ali suggests that by returning to religious practice, she has proven herself to be remorseful and doesn't need to worry. His use of Arabic also increases at this moment in the video, suggesting a heightened spiritual importance to what he says and adding weight to his language.

This storyline does not take into account the disapproval and hate the woman received from others in the online context and the positioning of her and her actions as reflecting negatively on Muslims. The woman's actions, given that she is 'practising-looking' (i.e. wearing a hijab), are more greatly scrutinised (Hopkins & Greenwood, 2013). Ali says, 'Unfortunately people are going to watch the video and judge you,' with the suggestion, given what follows, that the 'judgement' is coming from other Muslims who view the action as inappropriate. However, considering Ali's storyline about 'practicing-looking individuals' doing 'certain things' and evoking anger from people like him, the concern can also be heard of how the woman comes to represent Muslims more generally, particularly in a context where Muslims are already disliked and discriminated against (Bleich & Maxwell, 2013). Ali's message to the woman doesn't include any real advice about this issue; he simply acknowledges it as something that will happen and focuses on the woman's own repentance.

Ali's positioning of the sister's actions again shows how storylines about right action are important for moral reasoning, particularly in judging the intentions of others. Although his initial response to the video was completely negative, the retelling of the actions of the woman, taking into account descriptions of her own depression, requires a retelling of the story. Whether these accounts are plausible does not play into the reasoning about the actions of the woman – Ali does not appear sceptical that the woman's accounting is entirely true. Instead, the storyline of repentance and Ali's own role in the controversy allow him to further position himself as an authority in the Muslim community, particularly in the online context, and in representing right Muslim practice to a broader, non-Muslim audience.

Throughout the examples in this section, Ali places importance on 'understanding' the other person and considering the conditions of a particular question or controversy. 'Understanding' is performed through telling a story about people and their actions that gives them the benefit of the doubt. The owning of a car, for example, which requires purchasing insurance may or may not be haram depending on the needs of an individual and how those needs are positioned. The three examples in this chapter also show how the telling of stories can position Ali as a neutral, moderate figure in controversies around right and wrong belief and practice. Ali and those who appear with him make clear that although the contemporary world does create challenges, they can be navigated by seeking guidance from scholars and attempting to live with piety, depending on one's own circumstances and abilities.

At the same time, the Western contemporary context, where Muslims can be viewed with suspicion and derision, is an implicit, underlying theme in the dawah videos. Ali's approach highlights the pressures placed on Muslims to appear *moderate* and amenable to the contemporary context without placing unnecessary requirements on Muslims but does not lead to actions which clearly contravene acceptable religious belief and practice. To do this, Muslims must practice their faith in a way that carefully balances piety and adherence to a halal path, and acceptance of diversity within that practice, with different people having different needs. This positioning results in negativity both from non-Muslims who view the religious with suspicion and from hard-line religious adherents who attack Ali for taking moderate positions, creating frustrating 'damned if you do, damned if you don't' conditions for Muslims online.

This positioning of the Muslim, and the religious believer more generally, between the contemporary secular context and fundamentalist elements within one's faith can be played out in deciding which actions are acceptable and which are not but also in how religion is talked about in public contexts, where there is pressure, as we have seen in the debates, to be tolerant of others' beliefs and practices while seeking truth and holding firmly to one's own convictions. The challenge of the contemporary world for the religious believer is to manage these contradictory forces, taking care to find a balance between piety and tolerance. The struggle to find this balance is exasperated for members of minority religions whose religious practice is not normalised in the dominant culture. However, with members of dominant religions also suggesting that they too are subject to discrimination for their views, positioning becomes particularly important in how religious believers see themselves and others in the social world.

3.3   Adapting to Change

Religious belief in the contemporary world is often understood in comparison and contrast to other beliefs and a larger secular context, and the precise effect of living with and among others who don't share the same beliefs has been a long-standing question in the Sociology of Religion (Chaves & Gorski, 2001). Plurality has the potential to pressure members of religions to adapt and adjust their beliefs and practices, but these pressures can manifest themselves in different ways (Wuthnow, 2011). Although the reasons for change are often explicitly blamed on modernity and secularism, reformation of orthodox ways of believing and practising faith can and does often emerge internally (Wuthnow, 1985). These changes, like those that come from interaction with the secular world, are worked out in the interaction among believers, often in informal settings.

The discussion about what should or should not be considered essential in religious belief is a recurring theme in the *Bad Christian* (BC) podcast. In their persona as 'Bad Christians', challenging orthodoxy is crucial to the podcast's brand. One of the key underlying issues is how the American Evangelical Christian church treats the Bible and understands its role in Christian faith. The view of scripture most commonly associated with Evangelical Christianity is 'Biblical literalism' (Bartkowski, 1996) – that is, the belief that the Bible in its entirety is literally true. This position, along with a view that the Bible is completely without error, sees the Bible as central to Evangelical belief and treats scripture as having 'supremacy' (Bebbington, 1989), positions that the influential Evangelical theologian J. I. Packer (1978) describes as a fundamental of Christian belief.

This belief, however, is not shared among all Christians. Indeed, inerrancy is not included in the Nicene Creed, one of the earliest statements of Christian belief. Moreover, even within Evangelical and other fundamentalist movements, views of the Bible can differ depending on the experiences of individuals in particular communities (Moon, 2004; Ammerman, 2013), with a particular shift seen in younger people who may be more likely to reject both traditional views of the Bible and institutional Christianity more generally (Smith et al., 2015; Hinch, 2016). Arguments about the inerrancy of scripture have been a perennial issue in fundamentalist interpretations of Christian doctrine, historically related to evolution and creationism. However, cultural shifts particularly around changing views of homosexuality make the issue particularly relevant, with popular arguments made both for a changing view of the Bible (Hamilton, 2014) and against it (DeYoung, 2014). Belief in literalism can have larger effects on how individuals view the world (Oberlin & Scheitle, 2019) and can be worked out in a variety of ways in lived religious experience, as Besecke (2007) shows in her analysis of teaching within an American Evangelical church.

Arguments made for and against different views of scripture are often presented as theological in nature, but they can also be addressed and debated in interaction among religious believers in day-to-day life, drawing on individual knowledge, experiences, and the authority of theological figures. The BC podcast hosts discuss the issue most explicitly in an episode titled *Andy Stanley makes the Wolf List* (BC3, see Appendix). The episode focuses on a statement made by the megachurch (large Evangelical churches with thousands of members [Saunders, 2015]) pastor Andy Stanley on whether or not a belief in the infallibility of the Bible is essential for Christian faith. Before the discussion starts, Stanley is introduced as 'a really awesome teacher' and 'a pretty solid dude', but a controversy about Stanley's position on the 'inerrancy of the Bible', which one of the podcast hosts, Toby, describes as 'a belief that everything in the Bible, every single word, every single scripture, every single book, everything that's in there, is supposed to be in there and it's perfect ... it does not make any mistakes.' Andy Stanley's view on the issue as the pastor of a large Evangelical megachurch and a national leader in the Evangelical movement is seen as particularly important and his shifting position on the topic could have important repercussions for how Evangelical Christian orthodoxy develops. Joey, who works full time as a pastor, says of Stanley, '[He] represents mainline Christian culture.'

At the beginning of the podcast segment covering the controversy, Toby reads from a news article that highlights Stanley's influence within the Evangelical Christian church and the potential controversy of taking a position against the essential principle of Biblical inerrancy, with Toby reading: 'Stanley has definitely caused some ... waves in the church world. Some people are already calling him a heretic.' Toby further introduces the controversy about Stanley as follows:

Extract 3-18

> What Andy Stanley is saying
> is
> he believes in inerrancy still
> but he doesn't think it should be an essential
> if that's gonna cause people
> to not come to the faith
> [...]
> this is what Andy said
> he said
> [...]
> if the Bible is the foundation of our faith
> as the Bible goes
> so goes our faith
> it is next to impossible
> to defend the entire Bible
> and while you
> may be able to hang on to it
> your kids
> and grandkids
> and the next generation will not

Stanley's position, as the hosts represent it, is that although Stanley still views the Bible as inerrant, he recognises that the position may be untenable in the future. The reasons for why future generations will not be able to 'hang onto the belief' are not clearly stated, and the conversation between the hosts doesn't clearly identify the actual issue with inerrancy. No examples are given as to why the position is problematic or why a changing view is necessary, highlighting the assumptions the hosts have about shared knowledge. The audience is presumed to know and understand why inerrancy is an important principle of Evangelical Christianity and why Stanley's position is problematic. Joey says, 'We're supposed to believe that everything in the Bible is perfect. It just doesn't make sense,' but what specifically is the issue, what imperfect thing about the Bible 'just doesn't make sense' is left for the listener to fill in.

The other leaders and figures that are mentioned suggest that inerrancy is actually a way of discussing evolution and specific biblical teaching around gender and sexuality, which are highlighted in other episodes and ongoing themes in the BC podcast. Toby, in discussing Stanley's positions, mentions a website where Stanley is listed as 'one of the five most dangerous wolves preying on Christians'. The use of 'wolf' refers to Jesus' teaching in Matthew 7:15, warning his followers to 'Beware of false prophets, which come to you in sheep's clothing, but inwardly they are ravening wolves.' The verse is commonly used to warn Christians about the dangers of following beliefs that might be seen as deviant (Pihlaja, 2016), and a way of policing right belief. The 'wolf' list includes other progressives like Matthew Vines, who has advocated for not viewing homosexuality as a sin, and Rachel Held Evans, a prominent Feminist theologian. In this storyline, Stanley and other leaders who take unorthodox positions in Evangelical theology are false teachers who are leading Christians astray and must be confronted as dangerous threats to the community.

The hosts treat the positioning of Stanley and the other 'wolves' as laughable, but they also recognise the rejection of inerrancy as an important change, with the repetition of the term 'heretic' throughout the discussion. Regardless of whether they themselves view Stanley this way, they all recognise his statement as consequential: a 'big deal'. At the same time, the three hosts disagree about how important Stanley's theology actually is in terms of lived belief and practice. Joey takes the strongest view about the importance of Stanley but is challenged by Matt, who asks 'What's the big deal?' and argues that most people don't care about theological arguments. Joey responds: 'I'm saying it is a big deal because churches make that an essential and it shouldn't be that's all I'm saying.' Matt, however, argues, 'The people in leadership make it an essential. The congregation, they don't give two shits about it. They just don't.' A point Matt again reiterates in a joking way:

Extract 3-19
> That's one of those things
> that theologians
> and Christians
> talk about like it's some big ordeal
> you think Steve the plumber's going
> holy shit
> this motherfucker just went off

Matt's use of profanity in both cases when speaking about or in the voice of members of the congregation highlights how he views disagreements about theology. The theological term 'inerrancy' is contrasted with 'Steve the Plumber' – for Matt, it's laughable to think that average, lay members of the congregation would consider Stanley's position on inerrancy to be a 'big ordeal'. From Matt's perspective, the congregants of a church are simply less concerned with the specifics of theology and the theological positions taken by the leadership, particularly in the case of inerrancy of the Bible, which potentially has little influence on the actual practice of an individual's faith.

For Joey, however, Stanley's position has far-reaching consequences for how faith is practiced. He says, 'It's a big deal in the sense that it has profound implications which way you come down on it,' but what those specific implications are is not made explicitly clear at any point. Instead, inerrancy is presented as a specific example of a larger category of fundamentalist beliefs, including a belief in a literal hell. The rejection of inerrancy is not necessarily about specific changes in practice or faith, but about what they come to stand for. This move, however, is seen as a positive development, particularly for Joey, who says,

Extract 3-20
> I've thought now
> for at least two years
> that inerrancy
> shouldn't be an essential
> I'm fine with people believing in it
> and I'm fine with not believing it
> it should not be an essential
> like someone's faith in Jesus
> for their salvation
> you don't need to believe in inerrant
> inerrant Bible
> it should not be an essential

The development in Stanley's theology is also understood in comparison to the experiences of the podcast hosts, particularly Joey, whose evolving position on several key issues, including inerrancy and a rejection of belief in a literal hell, comes up several times in the collected episodes. Joey positions his rejection of inerrancy as a part of a storyline about his own development as a Christian and his movement away from a fundamentalist belief. At the same time, he hedges his position on inerrancy, saying, 'I'm fine with people believing in it and I'm fine with not believing it.' The point is not whether any individual believer is right or wrong, but that biblical inerrancy should not be fundamental to Christian belief and those holding more progressive views should be seen as 'normal Christians'.

How his own rejection of the belief, specifically as it relates to controversial topics like belief in a literal hell or the acceptance of LGBTQ+ Christians, shows the importance of inerrancy in Evangelical circles. A deviation is more than a difference of opinion – Christians who reject inerrancy can be seen as not real Christians, heretics, and wolves. Joey further voices concern that a rejection of inerrancy is likely to have an effect on how they as individuals are viewed. Speaking about how several other Christians are seen, he says, speaking in the voice of their critics, 'They're really out there. I don't even know if they believe. I don't even know if they're Christians. That's – that's messed up. I can't believe they just said that.' These people are seen by some as 'heretical, radical, full of bullshit people'.

The potential danger of being called a 'wolf' or 'false prophet' is clear throughout the podcast, with all three of the hosts frequently hedging declarations that might fall outside of the orthodox Evangelical belief about inerrancy. This contrasts starkly with other potential problematic beliefs and actions the hosts engage in and discuss: for example, the hosts often use coarse or vulgar language with impunity and discussions of other common sins like drunkenness, lust, and anger or violence, these topics are often the object of joking and represented without any hedging. The hosts do little to mark profanity, for example, as being problematic. Rather these features of their talk and behaviour are what might be expected of themselves as self-identified 'bad Christians', sinners who are in need of salvation. A rejection of inerrancy, however, is fundamentally different, a core belief that potentially changes the very nature of the faith.

The importance placed on belief over behaviour in Evangelical faith is highlighted in this discussion about inerrancy. The problem with Andy Stanley, both in being placed on a 'wolf list' and in the discussion about him in the podcast, is not that he has *done* something wrong, but that he has *thought* something wrong, and has become dangerous because he has suggested that a core belief might not be essential and allowed for a dilution of a key theological principle by accepting a diversity belief that does not conform to an orthodox biblical understanding. In a malignant positioning of Stanley and others, their own accounting for their belief is rejected; using the biblical words of Jesus, they are warned to be wolves attempting to destroy Christian faith from the inside. This positioning closes down dialogue and protects orthodox belief.

Similar discussions about what belief or actions are essential in Islam are less common in either the Ali Dawah videos or Shabir Ally's presentation of Islam in the debates. Instead, discussions of what is cultural and what is essential for right living in Islam are recurring themes. In discussions of marriage, for example, who should be considered an acceptable Muslim is discussed in a round about way through addressing Ali's complaint that many young Muslims are put under undue pressure to marry people of the same ethnic background or discouraged from marrying divorced women. In a conversation with Mufti Menk on the subject of *zinnah*, or sexual immorality (A9, see Appendix), the question of what makes someone a good or acceptable Muslim becomes the explicit topic of discussion. The video titled *Mufti Menk & Ali Dawah Parents rejecting proposal & Forced marriages* is the fourth part of a live event wherein Sheikh Menk and Ali are in front of a crowd and Ali is interviewing Sheikh Menk about haram (unacceptable) relationships. Sheikh Menk is positioned in the video as an authoritative figure, dressed in a white *ghutra* (head covering) and a black *bisht* (robe) over his *thobe* (long, male tunic). Ali, in the course of the discussion raises the issue of parents who 'make it hard' for their children, by insisting that the children marry fellow Muslims from their own 'tribe'. Raising the issue with Sheikh Menk, Ali says,

Extract 3-21
Couple of weeks ago
a brother messaged me
and said
Aki [brother]
okay okay mashallah [thanks be to Allah]
you talk about how you need to protect yourself from Zinnah [sexual sin]
et cetra
but I want to do it the halal way
the halal way is not possible for me
because my father
or my mother is rejecting a sister
or a brother
because he's black
or he's white
[…]
this is the main question
and one of the
biggest reasons which I believe
from what I've seen out there
the
the reason why
the youth

take the road to Zinnah
so how could one
pretend
protect themselves and how
what kind of advice would you give to the parents
who are
making it hard
for the children
to do it in a halal way
the marriage

In this extract, Ali voices his concern in a story of a brother messaging him 'a couple of weeks ago'. The question follows a similar pattern to the one seen earlier with the young woman questioning the sheikh about whether or not selling alcohol as part of her job was haram – very few specific features in the story clearly link it back to a specific individual. Indeed, in this question as well, the story shifts from a specific message to a storyline when the person who is supposedly 'rejecting a sister' is 'my father or my mother' and the reason for the rejection is 'because he's black or he's white'. In the telling of the story, all the positions become abstract: a young Muslim individual, either male or female, is unable to marry whom they want to marry because of their parents; Ali presents this as resulting in young people 'taking the road to Zinnah' as opposed to the halal way. Ali doesn't condemn the parents but takes a neutral position, asking Sheikh Menk, 'What kind of advice would you give to the parents?' rather than asking Sheikh Menk to advise the children.

The abstraction of people within the question again shows the importance of storylines in moral reasoning. Whether or not the actions that any individual takes are appropriate depends on how they and their actions are positioned within the story. Ali's telling of the story positions the young man, the brother, as wanting to protect himself from zinnah. This initial positioning introduces him in a positive way, as committed to do right and trying to follow 'the halal way'. The positioning of others within the story then occurs in relation to this initial positioning – others are either helping or hindering the individual in their efforts to live in a halal way. This hindrance can come from inside the community and from people like one's parents.

In another 'Ask the Sheikh' video (A5, see Appendix), Ali's co-host Musa poses the same question to Sheikh Haitham, positioning young Muslims wanting to marry people of other races or 'tribes' as acting with good intentions. Musa says,

Extract 3-22
A lot of sisters specifically
they want to get married
they find the brother

they like each other
they want to take it the halal route
the sister
she takes it to her parents
and
her parents
say no
but for no
Islamic reason
so
they say no
maybe because of the brother's race
or maybe because of something very petty
because they don't want her to marry for example
a
brother from a different race
you know
so
um
what is
the ruling and what is the like
uh
advice in regards to this

In this extract as well, Musa presents the issue of parents 'saying no' to requests by their children to marry people of another race, but for no 'Islamic reason'. Musa calls this 'a huge problem', one that he links again to sexual immorality. This issue is presented not as the result of pressures of the secular world, but rather a changing world wherein 'tribal' positions are not only dated but also wrong. They might not only be the racial but also 'maybe because of something very petty'. In this storyline, Musa appears to respect the authority of the parents but asks for a 'ruling' or 'advice' in regards to this. Musa and Ali position themselves as respectful of authority structures, with Ali mentioning elsewhere the importance of *shariah*, or Islamic judiciary, councils. At the same time, they are also comfortable challenging authority, suggesting that injustices occur when not all members of the community act in good faith.

Instead, the problem and the need for rethinking come from a cultural bias, a recurring issue in Ali's videos. How cultural issues are presented as being core parts of Islamic religion is a key problem that Ali can be seen arguing about both within the community and with antagonists attacking Muslims, particularly around issues like forced marriage. In a conversation in another video entitled *THE REALITY 12 || Why marry a divorcee??* (A6, see Appendix), Ali talks with a man named Ayman who married a woman with a young child. Ali praises Ayman as an 'amazing brother' and bemoans the negative beliefs within the community around marriage, saying,

Extract 3-23
> This cultural thing
> wa'Allahi [I swear to God]
> I
> I
> I personally
> like
> for the sake of Allah
> I hate it
> this cultural thing
> this
> oh
> she's this colour
> she's not from my caste
> she's not my
> from my tribe
> wa'Allahi
> disgusts me aki [brother]

Although in his discussion with Sheikh Menk, Ali positions himself as neutrally seeking advice, in this conversation with a peer, he is much more determined in his rejection of the practice of parents forbidding their children from marrying Muslims of other races. Ali is passionate in his rejection of what he positions as the 'cultural' elements of belief, something he 'hates' 'for the sake of Allah'. Ali uses the word 'tribal' in describing the positions of the parents, and his positioning of himself and others suggests a generational split, one where the children hold a more enlightened view than their parents with regard to race, because they are willing to marrying anyone that Islamic faith allows. Ali positions the children in these contexts as the victims of an archaic way of thinking which, though accepted, goes against the teaching of Islam by mixing cultural belief about colour, caste, and tribe with Islamic teaching.

In Ali's storyline, parents are positioned as a potential hindrance to the practice of religion because they hold onto cultural views. The children are positioned as the pious, eager to continue their journey on the 'halal route' and avoid the 'road to Zinnah', but roadblocks to this path come up within their own communities, and that other Muslims, in this case, the parents, cause difficulties for the practice of right religion. For Ali, this is the result of changes in the contemporary world wherein Muslims from different ethnic and national backgrounds live in the same communities, in this case in the United Kingdom, and the resistance from parents is the result of 'cultural things' that Ali implies are presented as religious objections to particular relationships among people of different 'tribes' or 'castes'. The children are positioned as enlightened in their contemporary, urban outlook, while parents hold unenlightened views on race and class; in Ali's storyline, the parents must be told to adapt to the changing cultural context.

In responding to Ali's question asking for advice for parents, Sheikh Menk agrees with Ali, while taking a more dispassionate and conciliatory tone, noting that the practice of marrying within one's 'cultural line' has roots in a misreading of *hadith*, or stories about and saying of the Prophet Mohammad. Sheikh Menk says,

Extract 3-24

If someone comes to you
the deen [religion] is okay
and the character is okay
they speak to you with respect
they're ready to respect your child
they have a sense of responsibility
let the marriage happen
let it happen
so someone might say
oh but the hadith speaks about khufu
you know what khufu is
it means
they need to be on a similar cultural line
that's a misinterpretation of the word
you have not interpreted the hadith correctly
you're talking of similarities in terms of the upbringing
so if you brought up in London
you've been to the similar schools
you've gone up
you've had similar upbringing
you know what's
happening
that's khufu
the colour
is never an issue
the tribe
is not an issue

Sheikh Menk's response answers Ali's question directly, noting that if 'the Deen is okay and the character is okay', and the person is respectful, parents should allow for a marriage to go forwards. 'Deen' refers to the extent to which a person follows their religious commitments, their good works, something that Ali's question doesn't address. Sheikh Menk, however, doesn't wholly retell the same storyline that Ali does, and there is little indication that Menk has the same experience or opinion as Ali that the problem is widespread. Instead, Sheikh Menk considers the potential that belief about marrying within one's own 'tribe' might be taken from hadith that appear to teach something similar: one should marry someone from the same cultural line: instead of thinking of culture in terms of colour or tribe, which he says is 'never the issue', but rather having a 'similar upbringing'.

Sheikh Menk, however, raises 'interpretation' as the key problem – a mistake, albeit an understandable one, in the interpretation of sacred texts. This positioning of the parents is more neutral than Ali's, positioning parents as not making it difficult for children to follow the religion but instead doing what they believe to be right. His response includes hermeneutic activity to understand the meaning of the word 'khufu', but his claim about the misunderstanding of the word is simply asserted: his basis for making the claim is not clearly articulated. However, this interpretation is essential to his positioning of the actions of the children seeking to marry someone who is not of their tribe. The storyline that emerges of Muslim parents allowing their children to marry those whom they choose, provided their Deen is 'okay', takes into account and preemptively rejects counter storylines that might position these marriages as haram based on the reading of the hadith.

Sheikh Menk provides a clear accounting for right belief and action, based within Islamic tradition with the caveat about the necessity of an 'okay' Deen. A storyline then emerges wherein both the parents and the children are acting in appropriate ways with regards to their religion and the parents' and children's actions are, unlike Ali's storyline, motivated by good intentions. Sheikh Menk's answer doesn't include any suggestion that parents need to reject cultural practices that are holding them back, just to correct a misreading of the hadith. Ultimately, both Ali and Sheikh Menk arrive at the same conclusion, that marriages between Muslims of different races is acceptable, but the different storylines leading to that conclusion emerge from significantly different positionings and moral reasoning.

Coming to the same conclusion does not, the exchange shows, mean that there is agreement on the particular elements of any given storyline. In a similar way to Sheikh Menk, Sheikh Haitham's response to Musa is less accepting of the positioning of the parents as often acting unjustly or with racist motives when rejecting potential marriage partners. He starts by suggesting that the first questions that must be asked in any relationship are how two people met and whether or not they were 'loose in terms of their relationship'. Sheikh Haitham suggests that this first step, of 'looseness', is what leads to the problem, one that can develop into much larger issues. Sheikh Haitham says,

Extract 3-25
I always say
if
a brother
uh
meets a sister
or a sister meets a brother
before they take it further
and before the Shaitan [Satan]

[...]
deceives them
and they start
communicating with each other
and developing love
yeah
they should check
whether they
their parents
would allow them
to get married or not

In Sheikh Haitham's abstraction of the same story, the positions of the children and parents are reversed. Key to the sheikh's story of children asking for the parents' permission to marry is the threat of 'Shaitan's' (Satan's) deception of them. Although Musa positions children as acting in good faith, Sheikh Haitham's storyline implies that the children have developed a relationship without their parents' permission and that these relationships are prone to Shaitan's deception if the children 'start communicating' and 'developing love'. The storyline includes the same actions as Musa's but attributes different intentions to the parents and the children. The parents are positioned as acting to protect their children, with Sheikh Haitham further supporting this storyline with anecdotes about people he has known falling into trouble when not properly seeking permission from their parents, or going against what their parents have explicitly warned them not to do. The symmetry in the storylines highlights how the same actions can be positioned in opposite ways to support moral reasoning. For Sheikh Haitham, the parents' actions are positioned in a storyline of protection of their children. The storyline implicitly challenges the assumption that the contemporary world and parents' inability to adapt to change have created situations that cause children to suffer.

Storylines about marrying outside one's cultural background also represent the different levels of abstraction that can be used in moral reasoning. Ali never discusses specific cases of parents telling a child whom they may or may not marry. Instead, the positionings represent categories of people in similar situations – parents and their children. The storyline of marriage and the halal course for young Muslims can be abstracted to a higher level, perhaps described as 'Children disobey their parents' or, conversely, 'Parents unjustly limit children's freedom', storylines that have values and ideologies which represent different ways of understanding religious belief and practice. The telling of the stories, whether they are real or constructed, or some mixture of the two, evidences both the trajectory of the particular discourse event (in this case, question-and-answer sessions) and the goals and intentions of the participants.

These two videos also show how response to contemporary pressures and what should be thought of as right belief and practice can be contested within individual faith communities. Key to making a case for the rightness or wrongness of particular actions requires storylines that account for them. Positionings within these storylines might use resources like sacred texts to justify actions, but as Sheikh Haitham's response shows, tacit understanding of shared principles within a religious tradition, in this case, beliefs about the role of parents and practices around marriage, is enough to justify positionings. Where particular claims against the positioning might be anticipated (as in admonishments around marrying someone not in one's khufu), the storylines can take into account potential alternative positionings and account for them.

Positioning in moral judgements can face different levels of resistance and acceptance depending on the shared beliefs within particular discourse contexts. The practical issues of Christian belief and practice centred on discussion of gender and sexuality in the BC podcast provide clear examples of how change can be rejected when storylines emerge that go beyond accepted practice within a particular tradition. In the episode *#282 Is Pastor Judah Smith Gay affirming?* (BC7, see Appendix), the hosts discuss a particular pastor, Judah Smith, who appeared to take an inclusive position towards LBGTQ+ people, suggesting that they should be included and treated as accepted without judgement and allowed to participate fully in the church. The comments were included in both a sermon and a tweet, both of which were publicly posted and then removed after they created controversy in the Christian community.

The topic itself, however, is never clearly introduced in the podcast, with vague language, Matt saying in faltering way,

Extract 3-26
This is going to be a very interesting
uh
podcast
and we're going to be talking about
uh
affirming
uh
our
our
all
<general laughter>
people
Toby's getting super uncomfortable already

The hosts' discomfort is palpable from the beginning of the episode, evidenced in the absence of the words 'gay' and 'homosexual' in the introduction. The point where Matt might be expected to say something explicitly about homo-sexuals or homosexuality devolves into general laughter and the acknowledge-ment that 'Toby's getting super nervous already'. The word 'affirming', presumably an ellipses of 'affirming [of gays and lesbians]', is repeated twenty-eight times in the episode and comes to represent churches and Christians accepting gay and lesbians as full members of their communities in contrast to churches where homosexuality is viewed as a sin, which they imply to be the more common view. However, what 'affirming' means precisely is also never explicitly discussed, with only one instance of the phrase 'affirming for LGBT' said when Matt is speaking in the voice of Judah Smith.

Although the BC podcast by definition champions transgression within the Christian faith, the analysis here has already shown the limits of challenging orthodox belief, particularly when those progressive positions are seen to be driven by broader changes in culture. To discuss Judah Smith's comments and 'gay-affirming' churches more generally, the hosts welcome a gay-affirming pastor, George Mekhail, whom they refer to as George, to discuss the issues. George's introduction includes few specifics about his work, except that he had written an article that the BC host Matt found interesting, and 'We wanna have a conversation here about it and we don't know what we're gonna say about it.' What the 'it' refers to is not necessarily clear and instead of further describing the controversy, the hosts of the podcast play the following clip of Smith preaching,

Extract 3-27
Jesus
systematically opposes
all
forms
of exclusion
he
he opposes it
he is
against it
any form
any system
any policy
or any programme
that excludes
anyone
Jesus
diabolically
and
very obviously
opposes it
so when it comes to our own country

and when it comes to exclusions of all kinds
and any policies
or systems
or world views
or perspectives
that you and I might have
and maybe has never been challenged or questioned
Jesus
if you follow him long enough
he will take you to Matthew's house
and all of us together
as followers of Jesus
will have to deal with any
exclusions
we have allowed
in our mentality
our perspective
or in our heart

Like much of the discussion up to this point, the comments themselves do not explicitly address the issue of homosexuality. However, the statement that Jesus opposes 'all forms of exclusion' was taken to mean by many (including George, the guest) opposing exclusion of homosexuals in the church. Smith makes the point that Jesus 'will take you to Matthew's house', a reference to Matthew the tax collector and Jesus' reputation with religious leaders for affiliating with 'sinners'. Smith's claim that 'followers of Jesus will have to deal with any exclusions' was specifically heard to imply that Smith believed Christians must become 'inclusive' or 'affirming' communities.

Throughout the episode, the hosts focus on the lack of clarity that churches in the United States have on the issue of homosexuality and, in particular, what exactly is the controversy with Judah Smith's comments. Instead, the position of churches towards homosexuals highlights the difficulty Evangelical communities face with holding conservative social positions, while attempting to 'reach out' to their communities. The extract from Judah Smith shows how pastors and authorities can make statements that co-opt the language of acceptance and affirmation but in ways that allow for ambiguity about the meaning and consequences of particular statements. At the same time, Smith speaks in an authoritative second-order discourse that draws an analogy between the Jesus' followers in the gospels and Christians living in contemporary contexts.

Smith's lack of specifics in describing the 'exclusion' to which he believe Jesus 'diabolically and very obviously opposes' positions himself and Christians in a storyline of acceptance, but one that can be heard differently depending on the beliefs of the listener. 'Acceptance' need not necessarily include acceptance of a so-called homosexual lifestyle. Smith's positioning of himself and his belief in this way then shows how the lack of specificity in positioning and the storylines that emerge can allow for multiple meanings and within contexts where contentious social issues are difficult to address. The comment shows how potential new storylines might emerge that don't necessarily follow a binary response to any particular challenge or contentious issue, in this case supporting or rejecting homosexuality as a corporate body.

The hosts' reticence to discuss the issue is acknowledged throughout the podcast, along with the problematic nature of homosexuality within Evangelical Christianity, particularly in the United States where Evangelical Christians have historically been mobilised to oppose gay rights in political contexts, including opposition to gay marriage (Sherkat, Powell-Williams, Maddox, & de Vries, 2011). At the same time, despite clear institutional positions about homosexuality, the hosts represent shifting attitudes within the Evangelical movement, and the discussion shows how, as Walls (2010) has argued, complex, in-group differences can be masked by overly simplified doctrinal statements. Walls uses Moon's (2004) concept of 'everyday theologies' to account for these in-group differences, arguing that individual theology is not a static assent to a particular doctrinal statement but 'formed in communities' and 'shaped by [religious believers'] life experiences' (p. 62). As the episode progresses, all three of the hosts evidence moral reasoning based in everyday theology, using their own experiences with gay and lesbian Christians to account for changes in their beliefs.

The pressure to assent to traditional doctrinal positions, however, is obvious in the discussion of homosexuality. The hosts hedge their positioning of themselves and others in storylines that reject orthodox positions on sexuality, acknowledging the problems with being seen as accommodating and 'evolving' with the changing culture. In describing his position several years earlier, Matt says that a cultural shift was inevitable, and 'we're gonna start to look real bad because of our views here'. He recalls telling his wife, 'It looks like our culture is headed to a crossroads' where Christians would feel pressure to change their views on homosexuality. At the time, he says that he felt strongly that he should 'hold firm' in his belief, suggesting two possible storylines, one in which Christians change their beliefs to fit cultural norms, which is seen as negative, and one in which Christians continue to hold the same beliefs and practices, which is seen as positive.

However, within this episode of the podcast, the abstraction of homosexuality as a theological issue is challenged in the recounting of authentic experiences, like George's description of a multisite megachurch in Seattle which became inclusive and subsequently was forced to close seven locations. George says,

Extract 3-28
> I think a lot of critics of people would say
> oh
> they're just going this way
> to get more
> audience
> and to go with the flow of culture
> but clearly
> it doesn't work out that way
> it sounds a lot more
> the opposite of that
> that's the what
> the weird thing about it is
> pick up your cross
> tell the truth
> do what you think is right
> is hard
> and might be costly

George voices the storyline of 'critics' who position affirming Christians as changing their beliefs and practices in response to culture because they want to 'get more audience' and 'go with the flow of the culture', ostensibly to increase their own popularity and be more broadly accepted. George's story, however, shows that 'it doesn't work out that way' and that an opposite outcome is actually more truthful, that Christians who affirm homosexuals in their churches are actually more likely to lose attendees. This changes the positioning of the Christians who affirm homosexuality as believing and acting in the right way, with the imperative 'pick up your cross'. This implicit reference to Matthew 16:24 in which Jesus implores a man who wants to follow him to 'Take up your cross and follow me' positions affirming Christians as true followers of Jesus, willing to suffer with him because it is 'hard' and 'costly'.

George's positioning of affirming Christians shows how changes in belief and practice might be accounted for with different storylines that reposition people and their actions. By implicitly referencing the Bible and speaking in an Evangelical Christian register, another storyline emerges, one in which Christ's followers rebel against religious leaders in a spirit of following Christ rather than following religion. The storyline of reformation includes affirming Christians being positioned in a positive way, and those who oppose them in a negative way. The affirming Christians are positioned as facing persecution for their belief and practice and should be seen as 'picking up [their] cross' to join in Christ's suffering.

In terms of their own particular beliefs, all three of the hosts eventually position themselves as supporting inclusive or affirming churches and theologies, although they hedge their responses. Toby says, in describing his own change of view to inclusion: 'and I understand I'm going along with the culture at large', positioning himself as being aware of the claims that could be made against him. Matt also hedges his response to the question of whether or not he supports an affirming theology, saying, 'I don't wanna earn brownie points and virtue signal here that now I'm affirming,' suggesting that he is also aware of cultural capital that can be gained by appearing progressive and highlighting the negative valence associated with being seen to acquiesce to pressure to change one's beliefs and practices because of cultural shifts.

The connection between the BC podcast's treatment of sexuality and Ali Dawah's and Sheikh Haitham's discussion of working at the supermarket and car insurance shows that the presence of the contemporary world in the day-to-day life of religious believers inevitably requires adaptation to how they act. What each individual should or should do is not always straightforward, and the processes of moral reasoning, as Jayyusi (1984) has argued, are discursive. They are rooted in categorisation processes that move between different levels of abstraction and don't necessarily have clear boundaries between right and wrong. This can apply in any case where there is moral ambiguity, where rationalisations might be made for individual actions. Of course, this ability doesn't guarantee the acceptance of others (something I will return to in Chapter 5). However, how particular people and actions are positioned in particular communities and the new storylines are a crucial component of *everyday theologies* (Moon, 2004) and can provide evidence for how cultural change occurs in the moment-by-moment interaction of religious believers.

The ability to truly innovate and establish new ways of believing and acting in the world does seem limited, as evidenced in both Sheikh Menk's response to Ali, where he argued that the belief that Muslims should not marry outside of their tribe is based on a misunderstanding of an Arabic word, and George's story about affirming Christians being persecuted, which referenced the Christian concept that religious believers will suffer for doing right. Both storylines are accepted ways of making sense of the world, but who is positioned and how they are positioned within them is not fixed. They exhibit the unifying and disunifying process of *heteroglossia*, where new ways of viewing the world are constructed out of the old. The changes that come about in right belief and practice don't necessarily require establishing new ways of talking about the world, but rather finding ways to position people and their actions following recognisable storylines. If new positionings within these storylines are accepted, new outcomes are also possible.

4   Inspiration, Authority, and Interpretation

One of the features of religious discourse in the contemporary world is the presence of a diversity of opinions and authorities in decentralised contexts. Although religious institutions continue to retain power, the ability of any person to access information and distribute its content has increased substantially since the turn of the century. The effect of technology on faith is, of course, nothing new: the printing press brought drastic change to religion through dissemination of information and the repercussions of this technology can be traced through history. But describing the development of the printing press as simply democratising information and providing access is an oversimplification of how people read and write. The books and pamphlets and literature that were produced with the printing press initially represented the possibility of access to information. The traditional institutions of power did continue to spread their own message and ideologies through the new technology, but the ability for new voices to make themselves heard also increased drastically. Importantly, how a person came to be heard, what processes selected and deselected for whose book or pamphlet got read, also changed.

The Internet and the variety of platforms that have developed with it have had a similar effect on not only access to information but also how a person can become an authoritative voice on a topic. The position of 'influencer' (Bakshy, Hofman, Mason, & Watts, 2011), or a person who can exert influence on a large number of social media followers, is based on the scale of popularity rather than expertise or knowledge. The consequences of this for social life, politics, and business have changed how campaigning and marketing are done. The consequences for the development of religion are also significant. Whereas historically the authority for right belief and practice, particularly as they relate to named confessional religions with clear doctrinal positions, have sat with institutional authorities, in the contemporary world, it's more difficult to identify who has this power. A Facebook preacher may have two million 'friends' and speak directly to them on a day-to-day basis, with no oversight from a traditional religious institution.

We've seen, however, that discourse doesn't appear in a vacuum. Even when shifts in technology might occur, historical ways of discerning right belief and practice persist. Believers, particularly Christians and Muslims, still base their religious faith on authoritative, sacred texts, which function as the starting point for their religion. How they understand the Bible and Qur'an is situated in long histories of reading and commenting on these texts. The influencers and evangelists who appear on places like Instagram and Facebook and YouTube have the freedom to interpret the texts as they want, but the constraints around what is considered acceptable still exist. At the same time, institutions and individuals who have held power in the past also adapt to changes in technology and society. All of this has consequences beyond what happens 'online', with contemporary models for reading and applying texts appearing in both the imam's weekly *khutbah* and the YouTube evangelist's vlog.

4.1   The Word of God

When the Christian apologist David Hunt repeatedly makes reference to his belief in 'Biblical Christianity', he is making a claim at the foundational, primary authority of the Bible. Hunt's claim is not uncommon in Evangelical and Fundamentalist Christianity where the Bible is seen as an inerrant authority (Packer, 1973; Bebbington, 1989) – his statement represents a common positioning of the Bible in a storyline with a clear authority structure. The Bible dictates what people should and shouldn't believe, and true religious believers follow it. The belief itself, however, is problematic because so many people do read and interpret the Bible in different ways, leading to a diversity of positions across a range of denominations of Christian belief. The Bible is still, after all, a book and people have different interpretations of what books mean.

Hunt's approach before the Evangelical Christian audience suggests that his representation of the Bible as the inspired, inerrant word of God can be unproblematic for certain audiences. Indeed, a look at denominational statements of, for example, the Southern Baptist Convention claim that the Bible was inspired by God and is 'totally true and trustworthy' (Southern Baptist Convention, n.d.). At the same time, Malley's (2004) work shows the complex interaction of both finding and creating meaning in biblical interpretation by Evangelical Christians because they also believe God speaks to the believer and guides their reading (Nuttall, 1992). What the Bible should include, in terms of the particular documents and their translations, can also be the object of disagreement among Christians, creating divisions and new denominations.

In Christian contexts, the Qur'an is often understood in analogy to the Bible, and the proliferation of debates both on and offline with themes like 'The Bible vs. the Qur'an' evidences how they can be seen as equivalent texts. This understanding, however, masks the fact that the two are fundamentally different, produced in very different times and contexts. The Bible is compiled from documents spanning thousands of years, but the Qur'an is believed to have been dictated directly from Allah to Mohammad, over his lifetime, although Mohammad did not write down the text himself; the compilation of the written Qur'an occurred after his death sometime around 650 CE (Cook, 2000). That said, Islamic belief holds that the Qur'an, in the original Arabic, is the revelation of God to humankind delivered through the angel Gabriel, verbatim. The belief then is that the Qur'an as it is preserved includes the actual words of Allah and is therefore completely authoritative and without error. Although arguments may be made about later writings (importantly the hadith, or reports on the sayings or actions of the Prophet Mohammad) the Qur'an is held in a particular place of authority. The Qur'an is memorised by Muslims, recited as part of daily prayer, and is the foundation to any discourse about the faith.

Sacred texts are essential in religious discourse both as providing the foundational principles of faith and as ongoing authorities. Religious believers are willing to accept whatever is included in their texts, if those texts can be trusted as the word of God. The process of 'trusting' or 'believing' the text is a complicated matter and includes discourse around problematic topics and using different apologetic arguments to support the specifics of one's own belief and practice. How these processes work become clear as the texts are discussed with both fellow believers and those who don't necessarily share the same belief.

Putting aside the theological arguments about the Bible and Qur'an and whether they can reasonably be considered the result of God communicating with humankind, the discourse about them constructs Christian and Muslim belief and practice and storylines about meaning with empirical effects on how religious believers subsequently behave in the world. Moreover, there are empirical relationships between what people believe about sacred texts and their sociopolitical and socio-historical contexts, something we observed in discussing how believers adapt to developments in the material conditions of the contemporary world – it is simply impossible to adhere entirely to a text written in a different time and place. The consequence of these changes creates constraints on how texts can be interpreted and applied, shaped by a complex interaction of cultural and hermeneutic practices.

Interaction about the meaning of the Bible or the Qur'an is itself the process of establishing and confirming a text as 'scripture' (Smith, 1994) and of 'everyday theologies' (Moon, 2004), as well as storylines that affect moral reasoning about how humans should interact. Arguments about how religious beliefs should be adapted in different contexts, and, indeed, if any adaptation should occur at all, are often rooted in readings of sacred texts, with different understandings and readings leading to different practical applications. Although some theological understanding is required in discussing religious texts, arguments always occur as interaction between people, with all the features, patterns, and complexities that interaction entails. And arguments

made about correct belief and practice built on sacred texts are further prob-
lematised in interaction with people of different faiths with religious texts of
their own, where common storylines are not necessarily shared.

How the Bible compares to the Qur'an is particularly important in the
debates between Ally and his Christian opponents, but often not in terms of
what either of the texts actually says or teaches. The debates over whether
a sacred text is the 'word of God' are fundamentally different from debates
about theology. They begin with shared assumptions – first, that there is a (one)
God; second, that the one God communicates with humanity; and third, that
texts written down by humans can include the word of God. These shared
assumptions may not be explicitly stated, but they play an important role in how
the texts are positioned and the debate participants engage with them.

The argument of what the Bible is, how it compares with the Qur'an, and to
what extent it can be believed as an authoritative text is a central question for
religious interaction, because it establishes a *primary discourse* from which
secondary discourses (in the Foucauldian sense) can arise. Getting this sacred
text right, and establishing the parameters for how it should be read, is essential
for faiths 'of the book' which look to written text to guide decisions about right
belief and practice. In debates between Christians and Muslims, arguments
often centre on which book is 'true', something discourse analysts of religion
will be less interested in. However, in the study of religious discourse more
generally, the process of establishing an authoritative text, how a person comes
to believe one book to be the word of God rather than another, has consequences for how interaction about faith and practice subsequently develop.

The debate between Shabir Ally and Jay Smith (D4, see Appendix) explicitly
addresses the question: 'Which is the word of God, the Bible or the Qur'an?'
This debate took place in 1998, at the University of Leicester in the United
Kingdom and then was subsequently uploaded to YouTube in 2016, titled
a 'Classic Debate' between the two. The debate revolves around the phrase
'the word of God' as it relates to the Bible and the Qur'an, establishing
a dichotomy where both texts cannot be equally the word of God, and both
debaters seem to accept this premise without qualification. Shabir speaks first
in this debate, describing the issue as follows:

Extract 4-1
How does one tell
if a book is from God or not
and more precisely
how does a Christian tell
if the Qur'an is not from God
now in a debate like this one
obviously the
Muslim would be interested

in showing that the Qur'an
is the word of God
The Christian would be interested in showing
that the Bible is the word of God
and each would be interested in refuting each other

Shabir's description of the core question of the debate includes very few specifics about what they are attempting to establish, beyond 'telling if' something is or is not the word of God. The phrase 'the word of God' occurs sixty-one times in the whole of the transcript, but problematically, what is meant precisely by 'the word of God' is never clarified by either of the speakers. In the extract, Ally uses the phrase 'from God' as synonymous with being the 'word of God': if something is from God then it is God's word. Ally seems to believe it is possible to 'show' that a text is the word of God (and, conversely, to 'refute' others, presumably proving that texts are not the word of God), but these processes are never explicitly stated.

The introduction reinforces the idea that there are fundamental differences in Islam and Christianity and that both the Bible and the Qur'an cannot be, at least equally, the word of God. Moreover, whether a sacred text is the word of God is positioned as of fundamental importance. Christians and Muslims are interested in proving the position of the text as a proxy for the truthfulness of their belief. This introduction implies that if a text could be proven not to be the word of God, then a faith could be refuted as well. The move is important in establishing a *primary discourse* (Foucault, 1971) – this primary discourse must be nothing less than the word of God to provide the foundation for a faith system.

The Bible and Qur'an are therefore positioned as equivalent, not in terms of their constituency, but in the position they hold in both faiths. Doing so obscures the significant differences between them and creates a subsequent argument that reveals more about how Ally and Smith view their own sacred texts than how one might actually differentiate between them for oneself. The question of the debate is presented as deciding between two options but in practice becomes a defence of their own beliefs; the debate isn't about deciding the truth between several different options, but exercising arguments about one's own religious belief in relation to what others might claim.

Ally further complicates the concept of the 'word of God' by presenting some criteria that might be applied in differentiating between the two texts:

Extract 4-2
So to prove that a book is the word of God
is extremely difficult
if you show me
a million
proven Bible

prophecies
I might ask you
what about the million and oneth
how do we know that this will definitely happen
and we will have to rest that on faith
same thing can go for the Qur'an
so it is easier to disprove
how do you disprove
then
a book to be from God
I think we can all agree
that if we find a book
contradicting itself
then
this obviously would not
be a book
from God

Ally points out the problematic nature of the debate given the extreme difficulty of 'proving' a book to be the word of God – the question of whether a book is the word of God is not an empirical question. Ally doesn't explicitly state the criteria needed for evaluating whether something is the word of God but implies that the extent to which what a book prophesises about comes true might be a criterion, although a flawed one because a religious believer can never be sure that what a text says will happen in the future will indeed happen. Ally then makes the point that contradictions in a sacred text might also disqualify it as being legitimately from God – presumably because if a text makes two contradictory statements, the reader would be unable to decide which to follow in terms of right practice and belief. This also establishes another criterion for books to be the word of God, although it is again a problematic one in that what counts as a contradiction is also a question of interpretation.

Ally's statement offers some insight into what the relationship between the word of God and the written word might be. First, the word of God can be contained in a book, and an individual book can be considered the word of God, but proving that a book is the word of God is extremely difficult. Second, positioning a book as the word of God will always require some faith because the reader and believer must project from experience onto the future. And third, that contradictions cannot exist within a book that one deems to be the word of God. Taken together, these three criteria show the way in which authority can be constructed around a book, by asserting its uniqueness and requiring some amount of faith based on that claim to uniqueness. The third criterion presumably does include aspects of a book that might be empirically observed, but what should qualify as a contradiction is not a simple empirical question, particularly given the contextual nature of reading and interpreting books.

Ally's argument for the reliability of the Qur'an and the lack of reliability of the Bible then follows these criteria, stressing the care with which the Qur'an was passed down through the generations, particularly highlighting the point that the Qur'an is not translated into different languages, preserving the original meaning. Ally illustrates this point by saying that the same Qur'an is recited 'in a cosmopolitan city such as our own here and where I come from', referring to his home in Canada. The unity and continuity of the Qur'an are particularly important for Ally, because he can contrast these features with the Bible which Ally points out is constructed from a variety of different manuscripts. Ally illustrates the point with this example:

Extract 4-3
    I'd like you to look in your own Bibles
    at John chapter eight
    you notice that the page that I've taken here
    from the revised standard
    version
    of the Bible
    has a curious arrangement
    you notice here
    that chapter eight seems to begin
    right at verse number twelve
    and the reason for that is explained in the footnotes
    what the translators have done here
    and for good reason which I will explain
    is that they have taken the entire portion
    starting with John chapter seven verse fifty three
    going into John chapter eight verse one
    going all the way to john chapter eight verse eleven
    they have put that at the bottom of the page
    as a footnote
    so you can refer to it if you choose
    but to indicate
    that this is no longer the word of God
    why
    because
    the ancient manuscripts
    do not have
    this passage

Ally uses the example of John 8:1–11 to illustrate how the Bible has been constructed through a process of 'transmission, corruption, and restoration', terms that he claims to borrow from Bruce Metzger, an American biblical scholar. Ally shows how this certain passage has been removed from contemporary Bibles because it was believed to have been added at some point after the original manuscript was completed. The implicit point is that because the

Bible has changed, it could potentially continue to change. The specifics of what was written in the John 8 passage that was subsequently removed are not discussed at this point in the debate, and Ally doesn't seem to take issue with the contents of the insertion, simply the fact that it had been inserted and that something was at one point considered the word of God and was later not. He goes on to list several other examples wherein potential contradictions might be observed in the Bible, showing places the writer of the gospel of Mark has misidentified a quote coming from Jeremiah as actually from Isaiah, and discrepancies about what hour Jesus was crucified.

For Ally's criteria about what might be considered the word of God, this is disqualifying. The point, however, isn't only that the Bible is not reliable, but rather that the Qur'an by contrast *is*. Ally's argument is made in opposition to the Bible – it's not what the Qur'an says that matters at this point, just that it differs from the Bible. Ally doesn't, initially, make the point that what is written in the Qur'an is unique or contains a kind of special truth; indeed, the contents of the book are not mentioned in his initial defence. Instead, what is important for Ally's argument is how the Qur'an came to be transmitted. Ally's argument leaves out what could be seen as comparable issues with the compiling of the Qur'an, implicitly rejecting them. He simply claims that the Qur'an was produced and passed down in a supernaturally reliable way, a characteristic that satisfies his first criterion for determining if a book is the word of God: he positions it as unique among other texts.

Smith, in his response to Ally, starts off with stating several assumptions that highlight the monotheist context. The first assumption is that 'everybody here believes in God', a statement that he uses to forgo having to make an argument about the existence of God, he claims. The assumption, however, does give insight into the audience's composition, or at least Smith's perception of them: he sees them as Muslims and Christians come together to debate rather than a forum which might include people of other faiths or no faith, and those assumptions have consequences for how he positions himself and his belief. This is reflected in the framing of the debate as well, between the Bible and the Qur'an, without a third option that neither of the books is the word of God. Smith goes on to list several other assumptions he holds at the beginning of the debate:

Extract 4-4
> I'm assuming also
> that
> uh
> this God
> does speak
> does communicate
> does reveal himself

that's one reason why Shabir and I are here today
thirdly
I'm assuming
that everybody here
agrees at least
that when he does speak or reveal himself
we can know
when he does so
that we can
recognise
when God speaks
or we can recognise
that this is the word of God
or this is not
the other is not the word of God

Smith's explanation of the word of God is built on theological assumptions, but ones he sees as being shared between Muslims and Christians. The assumption that 'God does speak, does communicate, does reveal himself' shows a shared belief in the interaction between God and humankind. In that interaction, Smith positions God as wanting to be understood and that God's interaction with humans happens in good faith, that is, that God is interested in speaking in a way that 'we can recognise', and that humans should be able to discern between things that are the word of God and things that are not. Importantly, in Smith's initial description, the Bible and the Qur'an are not named in the assumptions, but rather only the concept of the 'word of God', which he again doesn't offer a clear description of, just that he expects God would want his followers to be able to recognise something as either the word of God or not.

Smith's description of the interaction of humans and God includes the words 'speak' and 'reveal', which are potentially metaphorical but are also often used in biblical texts when describing the interaction of God with humankind and can suggest physical interaction in some cases. 'Speaking' may or may not refer to an actual physical voice being heard, and 'reveal' can ambiguously suggest a physical presence particularly when referring to Jesus (see in the King James Version Luke 17:30, 2 Thessalonians 1:7, 1 Peter 4:13). Ally, by contrast, only uses the word 'reveal' to talk about the Qur'an and the Bible, speaking in the voice of a Christian: 'Smith said Muslims impose their understanding. "The Qur'an was revealed as a dictation from God: the Bible should also be revealed as a dictation." I don't think that I would impose that understanding on the Bible.' Ally's point is that he doesn't view the Qur'an and the Bible in the same way, but he does continue to use the word 'reveal' to describe the Bible, only emphasising that it wasn't 'dictated', in contrast to his understanding of the Qur'an.

For Smith, 'revelation' of the word of God necessarily implies the revelation of Jesus (per John 1:1, 'In the beginning was the Word, and the Word was with God, and the Word was God'). Although Smith argues that the Bible is the word of God, his description of it differs from the description of the Qur'an by Ally. Smith never says, for example, that the Bible was 'revealed' to humankind, in contrast to the introduction by Ally which focused on the question of how 'to prove that a book is the word of God'. Smith does, of course, go on to defend the Bible as containing the word of God and being superior to the Qur'an, but his initial introduction is focused not on the Bible as a book, but the speaking and revelation of the word of God as a concept, far more nebulous than the discussion of the Bible as a physical artefact. The word of God and the physical Bible are, at least in principle, not necessarily the same thing.

The use of 'reveal' in the debate shows how the way words are used in sacred texts influences how they come to be understood in interaction among people of different faiths. Dorst and Klop (2017) have shown in their research with Dutch Muslims, how commonplace Christian understandings of theological concepts might be acceptable to Muslims, but understood in different ways, for example, around the idea of 'God as father'. Ally uses the word 'reveal' to describe how the Qur'an was compiled, whereas Smith uses it more generally to discuss the interaction of God with humankind, an interaction which includes the revelation of Jesus as a physical person in the world. Although both Smith and Ally do agree that the 'word of God' is revealed to humankind, materially they are speaking about something very different, even if the Bible and Qur'an can function in similar ways within Christianity and Islam.

Smith's stated assumptions position God and the word of God in a way that reflects an Evangelical storyline about God's interaction with humankind, part of what Bielo (2019) refers to as 'Creationist Poetics', or a way of framing debates about evolution in Evangelical Christian terms. Smith calls the 'relationship' that God desires to have with his creation a 'unifying theme' of the Bible, starting with the story of Adam and Eve, and following through to the story of Jesus Christ. He then argues that the same unifying theme is not seen in Islam; although Smith is correct in his assumption that both Christians and Muslims agree that God can and does communicate with God's creation, a 'relationship' is absent in Ally's positioning of humankind's interaction with God. The 'speaking' and 'revealing' of the word of God are compared with the relationship of Adam and Eve with God, one which is described as a physical relationship (Genesis 3:8), something that is not present in Islamic belief.

Despite this fundamental difference in how the debaters understand the interaction between God and humankind, and the acceptance that there are fundamental differences between the Bible and the Qur'an, they use contrastive arguments which position the two books in opposition in similar ways. Smith focuses on how the Bible has been accepted in a variety of contexts and attempts to establish it as the word of God through a series of claims that highlight its popularity, its longevity, and its applicability across a variety of contexts. Smith further challenges Ally's arguments about the differences across biblical manuscripts by arguing that the Bible was produced in a fundamentally different way from the Qur'an. Importantly, the arguments focus almost exclusively on the way in which the Bible was compiled, with almost no discussion of the content of the books. Instead, both debaters seemingly accept that in relationship with each other, the development of the texts is more important in establishing their trustworthiness than their content.

The trustworthiness of manuscript evidence appears to be less important in Smith's argument. Smith's response to Ally's initial claims that the Bible contains discrepancies is to focus on its impact throughout history and its impact on modern society and laws, using examples of places where the Bible has been influential. For example, he claims that 'almost every one' of the articles of the United Nations Declaration of Human Rights is 'biblical in context'. He particularly focuses on the point that the Declaration ensures 'Freedom of Thought and Religion' and contrasts this with a 'Muslim context' where he says, 'a Muslim may not move out or change or become – move to another religion'. Fundamentally, this argument has little to do with either the genealogy or theology of either book and applies an oversimplification of biblical principles to make his own assertion about the Bible's uniqueness. Smith essentially focuses on what he sees are the positive strengths of the Bible in comparison to his understanding of the Qur'an. How this specifically supports a claim about the nature of the Bible as the word of God is not necessarily clear. Instead, Smith uses comparisons between the two books where the Bible can be presented as being more positive as a way of bolstering support for the Bible and subsequently discounting the Qur'an.

Smith continues to follow these lines of argument that essentially make the case for the Bible as a positive force in the world, in comparison to his negative portrayal of the Qur'an. Smith argues,

Extract 4-5
Ninety-three percent of the world's population
now has
the Bible
in its own language
in its own mother tongue
there is no other book in the world that can claim that
the Qur'an
cannot come near that
there's no other book that can make that type of claim
why is it

because we know
that the Bible has to be put into the people's language
so that they can read for themselves
what God is saying to them
why
because it is very important that God
wants to relate to them personally

Smith's comparison of the Qur'an and the Bible positions the Qur'an as having a deficiency where Ally positions it as having a strength: the fact that the Qur'an is not meant to be translated. For Ally's description of the Qur'an, this increases the fidelity of the text over time, assuring that no changes are introduced. For Smith, the translation of the Bible reflects a relational character of God, focused again on the 'speaking' of God to humankind and the 'personal' nature of the relationship between God and humankind. Ultimately, Smith's point is not about whether or not the Bible is more reliable than the Qur'an, but that people are able to read it and feel some connection to God. The theological position of the Evangelical Christian puts a focus on 'what God is saying' to go beyond humankind in general, to the individual. God, in this story, is positioned as wanting to 'relate to [people] personally'.

Smith's argument shows the way in which belief about the category of the word of God is shaped by the theological positions he holds before the debate begins. This goes beyond the assumptions that he stated, to include the Evangelical belief about the personal nature of God's relationship with each individual human being. This belief informs the position he takes about the Bible, using the Qur'an as a contrasting foil. The criteria that both are applying to their own sacred texts are not likely to provide any increased clarity about what the word of God is or is not, just how their own sacred text is unique. The debate does little to resolve the underlying question about which text is the word of God, a question that seems fundamentally unanswerable in the context of the debate. Instead, the debate is useful because it provides both Ally and Smith a platform to position their own sacred texts as unique in relation to another sacred text and tell a story about the positive effect the texts have had on the world

Ally's response to Smith follows a similar pattern, taking the arguments that Smith has made to position the Bible in a positive way and using them to contrast negatively with the Qur'an. Ally does this in a thirteen-point rebuttal, but it is Ally's description of the 'word of God', used eleven times in this extract, that shows the fundamental differences in their views of the term. To make his point, he reads out from the biblical Old Testament passages which include particularly violent commands to kill innocent people and raze cities:

Extract 4-6
Some of the Bible is
the word of God
and if you apply that
great
but just because some people apply the law
doesn't prove it's the word of God
because some people might not apply some other laws
like this one I just read out to you
and that doesn't
prove
that it is not the word of God
it just proves that people
do not want to apply it
there may be other reasons that you think
that's not the word of God
but whether people apply it or not
doesn't make any difference
for the word of God
you're using there
an ad populum
appeal
which is a logical fallacy
number ten
that the Sharia is not applied in certain lands
again
that doesn't prove or disprove
that it's the word of God
it just proves that some people don't want to
follow the word of God
if you have the word of God
Jesus came and he preached to the people
and the people don't accept it
does that mean that what he's preaching is not the word of God
or it proves that the people are wrong

In his response, Ally addresses Smith's claim that because countries like Japan and India, which are largely not Christian, have laws which follow the Bible, this provides evidence of it's unique applicability across cultures (an argument quite remarkably ignorant of the historical context of colonialism and the US involvement in the writing of Japanese laws following World War II). Ally's response includes the word 'prove', stating that Smith's argument failed to prove anything. Ally goes on to say, 'What do you mean by the word of God? What exactly is the criteria that will prove a thing to be the word of God?' For Ally, the claim that the Bible is the word of God must be supported with evidence that rules out other natural or simpler causes, something Ally argues is not true of the Qur'an, for example, in the numerical miracles which he debates with Richard Lucas (D3, see Appendix). Still though, Ally doesn't offer any specific way of evaluating the texts. The implication seems to be that because Smith has failed to make a positive, logical argument for the Bible as the word of God, it can be rejected out of hand because there is no overwhelming evidence in its favour.

Ally positions himself as a neutral arbitrator by conceding that parts of the Bible are the word of God, but then rejects Smith's use of 'logical fallacies', positioning Ally as oriented to a particular way of knowing, and further establishing himself as a more legitimate source of information because, unlike Smith, his position is rationale. That positioning, however, doesn't include judging the Qur'an in the same way as he has judged the Bible. Instead, he focuses almost exclusively on biblical problems, and how Smith's argument is inconsistent, for example, in praising laws based on the Bible, while ignoring parts of the Bible which encourage actions that might be universally seen as immoral, such as the killing of innocent people and the razing of cities.

How Ally and Smith position sacred texts potentially reflects the expectations of the audience of Christians and Muslims to see their own positions defended and opposing religious viewpoints challenged. Similar to the debate between Shabir Ally and David Hunt, the video occasionally shows images of the audience, but there is little sense of their overall demographic makeup, although the introduction to the speakers by two people (who appear to be students) suggests that the debate may have followed a typical format whereby a Christian organisation and a Muslim organisation jointly sponsored it. The fact that these specificities are left out of the introduction does show that the context, for the initial editor of the video and the user who posted it on YouTube without further information, is not seen to be essential for understanding the debate.

At the end of Ally and Smith's time, the audience is given the opportunity to write questions, all of which follow from themes touched on in the debate, with a focus on positioning one's own religious belief and practice in relation to those of others and which often signalled the author's own position in the wording of the question. A presumably Christian man asks Shabir Ally the following question, which is read out by one of the moderators:

Extract 4-7
God's word to his people
is more
is more than just the words of a book
God has a power to reveal himself to us
in many ways
we
we can discuss

we should discuss how the historical
evidence
for and against the Qur'an and the Bible
but is this the most important issue
I ask Shabir
do you and other Muslims
know God's word for your life
do you know God's love and power
manifest
God's amazing grace and mercy
do you and other Muslims know the joy
and the peace that comes from experiencing
a relationship with God

This question returns back to how God 'reveals himself to us in many ways'. The questioner agrees that the argument of the debate about what is or is not the word of God is important, particularly the historical evidence, but then reframes the issue in an important way, focusing on the topic of 'God's word for your life', which disregards the content of the debate around the ultimate reliability of the Bible and the Qur'an. The change in the syntax from 'word of God' and to 'God's word' and the addition of 'for your life' positions the issues of the debate as primarily about religious belief and practices. The questioner's description of a 'relationship' with God and the collocations of 'love and power', 'grace and mercy', and 'the joy and the peace' position knowing the 'word of God' as primarily experiential, something that one 'knows' not from the arguments presented, but in the way that they feel about themselves. 'The joy and the peace that comes from experiencing a relationship with God' has nothing to do with whether or not the texts are contradictory or can be proven to be close to their original source materials.

The disagreements between Smith and Ally highlight their views of how the 'word of God' should be revealed and interact with religious believers. Smith sees the word of God as necessarily situated in times and places and therefore, in some way, the product of those times and places, that they are 'inspired' by God, rather than dictated to be written word-for-word. The debates show differences in how the texts are categorised as sacred and the different social processes that lead to the establishment of 'scripture' within communities, empirical processes which are unique to each religious community (Smith, 1994). Given these differences in communities, contexts, writers, and historical circumstances among a myriad of other factors, their positioning of sacred texts within their religious faith and the purposes they serve are revealed to be fundamentally different, even as the two attempt to understand and argue about them in relationship with each other.

The fact that the debate happened and is indeed a 'classic', ongoing one suggests several important points about scripture in the contemporary world.

First, Shabir Ally and the Christians he debates view the uniqueness of their sacred texts as central to their beliefs, even if the content of those texts is not explicitly the focus of discussion about them. In one sense, what the books say exactly is irrelevant to the discussion. Second, while holding ecumenical positions with regards to other religions is good, believing that one's scripture is the word of God is exclusionary and can include the belief that one's own scripture is superior to others. And third, both believe the superiority of their own faith is empirical and can be proven.

The extent to which formal debates represent Christian and Muslim views of scripture is questionable. The formal debates in the physical locations where they occur and in their online second lives, where debates are now uploaded and viewed by thousands of users, are popular for their direct conflict of ideas. They are not, however, intended to represent a diversity of opinions – formal debates are fundamentally about binary opposition. The interaction has shown the problematic nature of similar words being used to mean different things, including key terms like the 'word of God', but also 'reveal', which can mean different things to different people. We've also seen the useful plasticity of these terms including the 'word of God' and how it can be positioned in different ways, depending on how a person is using it and to what effect. Sacred texts then may be viewed as fixed, foundational authorities in religions, but they can serve a range of different actual functions in talk about the religion, even without reference to their actual content.

4.2   Representing Authority

The word of God as it is revealed in sacred texts is central, at least conceptually, to the religious discourse of Christians and Muslims. The authority of sacred texts is often undisputed: Christians don't say outright that the Bible is wrong and neither do Muslims question the Qur'an. Even when arguing with people of other faiths in the debates, there were few instances where a sacred text was directly challenged. However, how authority is exercised by people and institutions speaking for and about God is a different matter and much more variance can be seen in who is accepted outright as an authority figure. Conceptually, the sacred texts are seen as foundational authorities which can't be questioned, but *who* gets to claim authority to use those texts and to advise religious believers on what they should and shouldn't do in terms of their faith and practice is less clear.

How different members of faith communities can and should exercise authority in either influencing the development of doctrine or making ethical decisions has been a recurring theme so far. In many cases, the positions that individuals take are rooted in the authority of a sacred text, as we have seen in the extracts of the debates. At the same time, institutional authorities, scholars, and teachers also appear in religious discourse to add authority, both when speakers position themselves and when others position them. All the main characters are in some way an authority since they are public figures speaking about their faith and have, to differing degrees, significant influence on the audiences to whom they are speaking. Who is or isn't an authoritative figure is a dynamic element of all the talk I've investigated so far, and this section will further explore the dynamic processes of becoming, representing, and disputing authoritative figures.

Within Evangelical Christianity, the Bible is the central authority (Packer, 1978; Bebbington, 1989), one that can be read and understood by any individual, with the help of the Holy Spirit. However, when the Bible is used in institutional and social settings, distinctions between the authoritative position of the Bible, the institution of the church, and pastors and leaders can become difficult to parse. The emphasis placed on a personal relationship with God further complicates how the Bible's authority can be exercised, when conflicting interpretations emerge from individuals who ostensibly hold the same beliefs. The Evangelical axiom 'The Bible says it; I believe it; That settles it' (Dictionary of Christianese, 2013) can only function effectively in contexts where there is a shared belief about what exactly the Bible says.

The Evangelical Christian understanding of the Bible and how it should be interpreted based on one's own personal experiences and other contextual factors, like the doctrinal statements of churches and their leaders, are a recurring theme in Christian discourse, where authority structures differ depending on denominations and their beliefs and practices, and different interpretations of the Bible abound. The importance placed on a believer's personal relationship with God and how that relationship should affect one's understanding of the Bible can be seen in a *Bad Christian* podcast episode discussing megachurch pastor Andy Stanley's questioning the importance of biblical inerrancy in Christian belief (BC3, see Appendix). The podcast host Toby says of Stanley:

Extract 4-8
> I think if he was completely honest
> he would say
> now I have my doubts too
> so it's not worth
> standing so firm on
> like come on
> we can believe in Jesus
> and all be on the same page
> we don't have to all believe
> that the Bible is
> absolutely perfect

Despite the importance placed on the Bible in Evangelical belief, Toby's interpretation of Stanley's statement positions 'belief in Jesus' as the primary marker of Christian religious belief. Toby suggests that Stanley may not hold the view that the Bible is inerrant; however, because of the position of the Bible within Evangelical Christianity, Stanley is unable to publicly take that position without hurting his own credibility. Instead, he needs to suggest that there is a possibility for others to believe something different, without taking the position himself. What the conceptualisation of the Bible as 'absolutely perfect' and a 'belief' in that concept actually entails, however, is never clearly stated. The same can be said of what it means to 'believe in Jesus', something that is also not clarified in the discussion. Instead, the belief is implied to be understood by the audience, without a need to further clarify what exactly belief in Jesus should entail.

Toby's and the other hosts' appreciation of the difficulties facing Stanley highlights the authoritative position of the Bible as the word of God within Evangelical Christianity, even when any specific theological point is not being discussed. What is more important than any particular point of theology is the role of the Bible as *the* authority within Evangelical Christian belief. It is part of a set of beliefs that indicates a commitment to an Evangelical world view. Throughout the discussion of this specific issue and the Bible more generally, the consequences for changes in belief about the inerrancy of the Bible are not clearly addressed, and there seems to be a shared understanding about what position the Bible should hold within Christian belief and practice. How the Bible is read, interpreted, and used follow common sense practices that don't need to be explicitly stated.

The absence of an explicit discussion about how the Bible should be read and interpreted highlights how people may perceive implicit, shared belief and practice within their community. The podcast has a large audience with several hundred thousand listeners a week, and the positions the hosts articulate reflect some of the common sense ideas about the Bible and what beliefs are acceptable, and its centrality in Evangelical Christian belief to instruction in 'practical, moral, and spiritual' matters (Bielo, 2008, p. 9). The evidence for this shared understanding is the ability of the hosts to talk vaguely about controversial issues without needing to explain in detail the position of the Bible. Its importance in Christian life is already assumed.

At the same time, throughout the *Bad Christian* podcast, there is little direct quotation of the Bible, although reference to it does occur in discussions of church authority, the teaching and preaching of pastors, and Evangelical Christians and Christian culture more generally. The hosts don't actually engage in any particular discussion of what the Bible says. This is of course, in part, the nature of the 'Bad Christian' show and a seeming attempt to focus on cultural issues within Evangelical Christianity, rather than being a source of religious authority. Still, the absence of the Bible reveals that 'Christian' discourse doesn't necessarily require the sacred text. Throughout the eight podcasts (131,946 words) included in this analysis, the word 'Bible' occurs ninety-two times with at least one mention in every episode and 'scripture(s)' occurs eleven times across six episodes. Examples of biblical language or commonplaces occur in the discourse, but the Bible is never explicitly quoted with chapter and verse or presented as evidence for particular positions.

The unique authority of the Bible within the podcast is, as I have said, implicit, but the hosts often appear sceptical of its practical role in Christian life. In discussing critiques made about a former megachurch pastor (BC5, see Appendix), the hosts talk about how he could be legitimately criticised. Toby says,

Extract 4-9
Should he accept responsibility
for the fact that
these
this criticism [of his bad behaviour]
is legitimate
like these people actually
whether it's right or wrong
they're making good points
it's worth a discussion
it's not worth saying
here's a scripture
you're wrong

The morality of the pastor's actions and the extent to which he should 'accept responsibility' for what the hosts' present as the pastor's 'bad behaviour' is positioned as a moral question that requires 'discussion' rather than confrontation with the Bible. Toby makes the point that 'It's not worth saying here's a scripture' showing that in the practice of challenging a person about correct belief or practice, the Bible can't necessarily be used to resolve disagreements, particularly when confronting practical problems of inappropriate behaviour. Toby also suggests that the behaviour is not a simple, single 'sin' that might be identified and condemned using scripture. Even if the Bible is an authoritative text, its authority cannot always and simply be exerted to resolve moral or spiritual issues.

The pastor's own positioning of himself within the institution makes any challenge of his authority, even with biblical evidence, difficult, because of the hierarchy of the church, a point made by Foucault (1971) in his discussions of the orders of discourse. The Bible as a sacred text functions within a social hierarchy and any attempt to upend that hierarchy is unlikely to be successful. The Bible must be used in conditions where those claiming its authority are in a position to do so and in contexts where people within the institution will accept those claims. The idea of a church member going to a church leader to confront them with the Bible is laughable for the hosts because the authority of the Bible can't just be taken up by anyone. The leader will have the power to dismiss its use and resources to delegitimise claims again them.

The use of the Bible to position oneself as an authority can also be unsuccessful when some incongruity exists among the use of the text, the audience, and the individual attempting to exercise its power. Throughout the podcasts, the hosts frequently deride pastors and their use of the Bible. In discussing how pastors are able to increase contributions to churches (BC6, see Appendix), the hosts play a clip of a megachurch pastor preaching about tithing, or regularly giving a part of one's income to the church. When the pastor, in support of his argument that talking about money and asking for donations is acceptable, says, 'I'm just preaching the Bible to you' to which the hosts respond with laughter, because the preaching offers a clear example of a pastor using the Bible to say something with which the hosts completely disagree, in this case asking the congregation of a church to give money when the pastor and church are both already extremely wealthy. In this case, the authority of the Bible is negated by its obvious use for immoral ends, something the hosts recognise as using Christian belief and practice to further one's own financial situation.

Despite these examples of using the Bible being positioned at times as practically ineffective, the foundational role of scripture in Evangelical Christian belief and practice is never explicitly questioned by the hosts and is often present in discussions particularly about diversity in views about Christian belief and practice. In the episode focused on the inappropriate actions of the megachurch pastor (B5), a discussion occurs about which ideas or beliefs are taken up as correct within Christian culture. Matt makes an argument that as collective human knowledge develops, 'silly and goofy ideas will just be pushed by the wayside' and that progress is inevitable. Toby, however, points out the power of fundamental belief in the Bible in response to development, and how particular passages can be quoted which suggest that people can be 'lead astray' by not following closely to biblical teaching. Toby says,

Extract 4-10
I
believe in Jesus
but everything else
is just a big question mark
but
the Bible
people can take a lot
and it's not just

cherry-picking scripture
people can take a lot of the Bible and say
yeah
everything you're saying
the Bible said would happen
I'm sticking with what the Bible says

Here, Toby positions himself as 'believing in Jesus' and his belief in the Bible as implicitly subordinate to that belief. Ideas that might challenge an inerrant view of the Bible, in this case evolution which is presented as 'truth', could be perceived as contradicting 'what the Bible says'. For Toby, however, the fundamental position for his faith is the statement 'I believe in Jesus', which implicitly places Jesus as an authority above the Bible. A belief in Jesus can be understood as more dynamic than a belief in the Bible, which is a fixed artefact and allows him to position himself and his beliefs in relation to principles rather than teachings in scripture.

This positioning of himself and his faith in a more dynamic way, again implicitly, juxtaposes with the positioning of other Christians as believing in an inerrant Bible. It also reflects the discussion of Stanley's statement which contrasted belief in Jesus with belief in the Bible. Toby said of Stanley: 'We all believe in Jesus' but 'don't have to all believe that the Bible is absolutely perfect'. At the same time, Toby says that people can use 'a lot of the Bible' to argue against positions that the hosts have taken, recognising that their statements could be a resource in moral reasoning about what they say and do. He recognises how his actions could be positioned negatively by others, as part of storylines where he is positioned as leading people astray.

The voicing of a fundamentalist position as 'I'm sticking with what the Bible says' highlights the belief that it is possible to deduce meanings and adhere to them. The position is intrinsically conservative: one 'sticks with' a belief rather than moving on to something new or different. The criticism of 'cherry-picking scripture', a term that occurs in another episode as well, also suggests the way in which views of scripture and particular positions are defended when they are convenient and without care to the context in which they appear. The criticism reflects a commitment to reading the Bible as a single artefact, one that can be used to interpret itself and views the Bible as a part of a larger coherent structure of beliefs. Individual verses must be read and understood in light of other passages of the Bible which can clarify issues that might appear to be problematic.

Although the hosts do not continue to explicitly discuss evolution after initially using it as an example, a belief in creationism as stated literally in the Bible is the exemplar case for the conflicts the hosts discuss. If the Bible appears to say one thing clearly and directly, and one explicitly rejects the factual nature of that account, the Bible can no longer be 'absolutely perfect' and can be further challenged as an authority on other factual, moral, and spiritual issues. The commitment to a hermeneutic which sees the Bible as the consistent word of God is important in these cases because problematic portions of the text can be reinterpreted using other parts of the Bible to assert certain beliefs and argue that divergent readings of the text are not taking into account the whole of the text. It reflects a persistent belief in Evangelical Christianity about the centrality, complete inerrancy, and clarity of the Bible (Marsden, 2006; Thompson, 2006). Indeed, one central tenant of the Protestant Reformation itself was the belief that Christians could read, study, and understand the text without an intermediary (Lazareth, 2001). By questioning specific points, the hosts understand that this positions them as questioning the entire authority of the text, and subsequently as threats to the whole of the belief system.

In the episode, the hosts avoid taking clear positions themselves, often hedging statements about their belief in the Bible or using imagined others to voice conflicting views. While they may accept they are 'bad Christians' in the eyes of others, they don't position those who disagree with them in the same way, as being in some way deficient. Moreover, the hosts, in this discussion, never appeal to actual comments or concerns they have received about their questioning the position of the Bible in their faith. Instead, the arguments against their own views are voiced by themselves, including representing past versions of themselves as shocked in their own questioning of their faith. These beliefs are represented as the norm for Evangelical Christians, beliefs that if rejected put their own faith in doubt. The hosts do not, however, position those who might disagree with them in a negative storyline, and fundamentalist Evangelical Christianity is not rejected as such.

The potential consequences of a shifting belief in the Bible appear to weigh heavily on all three of the hosts as the comment about 'a lot of the Bible' warning against their position shows, and this tension becomes a recurring theme as they discuss different cultural issues. The hosts position themselves and their views as changing over time in a positive storyline, one which also more abstractly positions being open to new ideas and interpretations in storylines of growth and development. These storylines, however, are often tempered by a fundamentalist critique. Matt describes his approach to belief and practice in a fundamentalist Christian voice, saying, 'The enemy's deceptive – he's trying to deceive you', where the 'enemy' is presumably Satan. Matt continues, recounting his specific beliefs:

Extract 4-11
    [I believe] that God is real
    and the truth is the truth
    and the truth will set you free
    and that

you don't have
anything to
be worried about
if you are seeking the truth
and Jesus and God are the actual truth
you don't have anything to be worried about

Adapting one's faith, particularly in terms of what the Bible says, can be positioned either as 'being deceived' or 'seeking truth', a conflict that the hosts of the podcast readily discuss. Matt's statement about searching for truth begins with saying 'God is real', an ontological statement with entailments that affect how he interacts with claims and counterclaims about what is right and wrong. The tautology 'the truth is the truth' positions 'truth' as essential and unchanging, something that is unaffected by the particular beliefs and interpretations of scripture by others, particularly those who say 'I'm sticking with the Bible' or adhering to a previous position. Within this positioning, the believer is active and engaged and 'seeking' truth rather than 'sticking with' what has been previously believed about the Bible.

The Bible, however, retains its foundational properties and its presence in Christian discourse, even in this discussion about its secondary relationship to Jesus. Matt recites a Biblical commonplace from John 8:32 (*New International Version*) ('Then you will know the truth, and the truth will set you free'), implicitly positioning those who 'seek truth' as doing what is commanded in the Bible. Positioning oneself as seeking truth and positioning God and Jesus as 'the actual truth' presumably provide an apologetic for the potential that the Bible could be read or understood in ways that are traditionally not accepted within their own communities. Like other anthropological work including Bielo's (2008, 2009) and Malley's (2004) investigations of Bible studies, the practices for reading and understanding the Bible are often left unsaid and the importance placed on 'seeking truth' and 'following the spirit' are fundamental to the practice of actually reading the Bible, where disagreements and competing interpretations can be present even within the same, local Bible study groups.

The role of the authority of scholars, academics, pastors, and sheikhs is a recurring theme, with the voices of different authorities appearing at different times to support the positions. Ally in his arguments uses Bruce Metzger, a prominent biblical scholar, to support his argument that the Bible has changed over time. Ally does this repeatedly in his arguments, particularly about the changes in the Bible, making appeals to Metzger, and other scholars such as F. F. Bruce, James Dunn, and Bruce Chilton among others, whom Ally is clear to position as Christian scholars and respected, in one case asking his Christian opponent in the debate, Jay Smith, to agree with him that Metzger is a 'reputable scholar' before continuing on with his argument. Ally also makes reference to 'conservative scholars' including Metzger particularly in his debate with Smith, at one time saying in an argument about whether all Peter's writing could be attributed to the Apostle Peter: 'Now, who said that? Not me. A scholar whom you trust, one of your conservative scholars.' By focusing attention on 'your conservative scholars', Ally highlights that Smith should accept the authorities he draws upon, because they both share the same beliefs and commitments to the Bible.

The positioning of scholars with these qualifiers, and in particular the positioning of some scholars as 'conservative', draws attention to conflict about whom should be considered an authority. Referring to 'your conservative scholars', Ally distinguishes between different kinds of authorities, and a storyline of conflict between conservatives and liberals can be observed in several interactions. In the debate with James White in South Africa (D2, see Appendix), 'liberals' and 'liberal scholarship' are positioned in a negative way, with the Christian apologist White saying, 'Liberals do not listen to conservatives and conservatives study liberals and respond to them, but it's a one-way street.' In making an argument about that Mark's was the first gospel that was written, Ally says that 'even conservative scholars accept that point', using the work of the biblical scholar F. F. Bruce to support his argument. Ally describes the Christian F. F. Bruce as 'a careful scholar': 'He's a conservative. He's trying to preserve the tradition.' By highlighting the ideological and political stances of the authorities he cites, Ally shows that who is or is not accepted as an authority is subject to a range of factors beyond an individual's theological knowledge. An authority who could be identified as a liberal, regardless of how robust their argument is, might be rejected out of hand because of their perceived ideological commitments.

With his reference to 'conservative scholars', Ally also attempts to position himself as aligned with authorities whom his opponents may accept, and who share similar theological convictions. This positioning of himself, and as a representative of Muslims, in line with the thinking of conservative scholars, is a part of the same emerging storyline wherein the beliefs, and practices of Christians are not necessarily contradictory to those of Islam but can be seen as aligned with Christianity. Ally in citing them is also showing his own commitment to conservative readings of the Bible which attempt to 'preserve the tradition', rather than search for novel or contemporary readings of sacred texts. Throughout the debates, Ally does not attempt to establish new authorities or suggest that White, Hunt, or Smith should accept criticism from outside their own traditions.

The Christian apologist David Hunt, in his rebuttal to Ally (D5, see Appendix), takes issue with the use of 'supposed biblical scholars':

Extract 4-12

The God of the Bible is
one would reasonably expect
he hasn't left mankind
at the mercy of certain experts
to interpret what he says
and I
don't believe in that
so I don't
quote the experts uh
Shabir
loves to quote
various supposed biblical scholars
at least in the
one or two debates of his
that I listened to
historians who
criticised the Bible
and Christianity
and they
don't offer any proof
endless speculation uh
tedious series of
suppose this
or
perhaps that
and
contradicting one another

Hunt stresses the importance of faith in 'the God of the Bible' and positions 'supposed Bible scholars' in a negative way, implying that accepting their opinions would put one 'at the mercy of certain experts to interpret what he [God] says'. Hunt's position is that the presence of 'speculation' among 'supposed Bible scholars' makes their conclusions unreliable, particularly when they contradict one another. In his argument against the use of scholars in the debate, however, Hunt does not refer to any specific examples of historians criticising the Bible and not 'offering any proof'. Instead, a storyline emerges in which academics and scholars are positioned as a threat to 'the God of the Bible' and 'what he says'. Hunt describes them as 'criticising the Bible' because their speculation can make things unclear. By avoiding any specifics, the argument is about Ally's approach as a whole, claiming that the reliability of the Bible hinges on facts about its historicity. If Hunt is unwilling to do that, then Ally is unable to convince him.

The belief in the ability of Christians to understand the meaning of the Bible without the need for an intermediary authority reinforces a 'hermeneutic circle' wherein one's biases and prejudices inform one's reading and interpretations of texts (Bartkowski, 1996). Winchester and Guhin (2018) have argued that 'normative frames', that is, the expectations about how a particular cultural practice should be performed and experienced, play a role in how authenticity and sincerity are gauged in Evangelical Christian discourse (prayer, in their specific study). These normative frames are the result of tacit knowledge about cultural religious practices rather than systematic processes for evaluating evidence, with an importance placed on the Bible not simply as a historical book with an empirical history but also as an artefact that is central to a cultural process of negotiating right Christian belief and practice (Bielo, 2008). The Bible then must be perceived to be reliable because of its centrality in religious faith, and evaluation of any evidence that challenges one's understanding of the Bible will therefore be treated as a threat to one's religious faith.

The 'normative frames' for talking about the Bible and its authority can be seen in Hunt's rejection of scholars whose conclusions might undermine its reliability. His argument is not that the research is problematic in its process, but that any challenge to the ability of Christians to read and understand the Bible for themselves challenges a foundational principle in the faith. The argument contravenes an important principle in Evangelical Christianity: that Christians interact directly with God and this interaction provides essential guidance (Winchester & Guhin, 2018). Scholars should not be needed to understand the Bible because God himself guides the Christian's reading of the Bible. This belief also clarifies why Hunt sees the work of historians as a 'criticism' of the Bible and, by extension, God's ability to communicate with humankind. If any argument is made that the Bible cannot speak directly to Christians or that additional context is needed, then the Bible ceases to be a reliable authority because a reader cannot understand the meaning of biblical passages themselves. To challenge the clarity of the Bible is to challenge God's ability to speak to his followers without a mediator.

This positioning of scholars as attacking the Bible plays an important role in Hunt's view of 'Biblical Christianity', because it allows him to position his own authority as sanctioned by the Bible. By rejecting shifting scholarship, he can position himself as following a fixed biblical standard rather than any tradition. Although Hunt is, of course, interpreting the Bible in a particular tradition with particular biases and prejudices, by ignoring them and claiming to read the Bible without any interpretative lens, he draws on the Evangelical and funda-mentalist Christian storyline that real or true Christians follow what God says, while others follow scholars. This position highlights the relational nature of Evangelical Christian belief, which focuses on the perception that one's belief and practice come directly from God, without any mediation.

By contrast, the use of Christian scholars and historians supports Shabir Ally's positioning of himself and his arguments about the Bible in a storyline of logic, because even other conservative Christians agree about them. The primary focus on logic contrasts with his Christian opponents who claim they are simply reading the Bible, most strikingly in Hunt's appeal to 'Biblical Christianity' and his emphasis 'on what God says'. At the same time, Hunt also positions himself in a storyline of logic, claiming that scholars 'don't offer any proof', suggesting that his approach to the Bible is also logical. The response, however, makes no specific reference to any of Ally's claims. Instead, Hunt simply dismisses any apparent evidence against his position as baseless 'criticism' of the Bible. It's not that he accepts that his reading of the Bible is illogical, rather that the crucial point is following Biblical Christianity, which, because it is God's truth, cannot by definition be wrong.

The response shows how positioning criticism of oneself and one's beliefs in terms of larger storylines about persecution can valorise Christians to stand strong against anything which appears to undermine the Bible. The same storyline was acknowledged in the *Bad Christian* podcast episode discussing the inerrancy of the Bible and claims that the Bible predicts criticism against it and warns Christians to be vigilant in opposing attempts to undermine it (see Extract 4-14). For those holding an inerrant view of scripture, the text itself can be presented to make an argument for its own authority. Although different readings of the Bible are certainly possible from fundamentalists holding the same view of the text, the readings must be supported by the belief in the inerrancy of the text to be accepted, as evidenced in Ally's attempt to make his arguments through appeals to conservative scholars.

The same tactic and the same positioning of scholars are taken by James White (D2, see Appendix) after Ally again appeals to the work of the scholar James Dunn, with whom White disagrees and says,

Extract 4-13
Shabir will say
over and over
listen to him
scholars have concluded
scholars have concluded
I dispute every single one of them
scholars can conclude anything
there's a scholar in Germany
that has concluded
he's a Muslim scholar
that Mohammad didn't exist
any Muslims ready to convert
oh
why not
Shabir says
scholars say

and you just accept it
well
I don't accept it
because scholars
say anything
scholars say that the original language of the Qur'an
was not Arabic
scholars say
all sorts of things
I don't believe
that it is meaningful argumentation
to stand before you and say
well my scholars say this
his scholars say that
now you decide

Like Hunt, White's argument here goes beyond simply disregarding the opinion of a scholar but challenges the whole strategy of appealing to scholarship to support one's argument. White focuses on the point that 'scholars' as a category is problematic because people hold differing points of view. Importantly, White focuses on 'scholars' rather than 'scholarship', highlighting the individual, human character of each scholar. White illustrates this point by listing claims apparently made by scholars about the Qur'an and Mohammad that Ally would see as potentially unacceptable. Although Ally's use of scholarship is carefully referenced with the names of scholars supporting their claims, Hunt refers to 'a scholar in Germany' who is a 'Muslim scholar', mimicking Ally's use of Christian scholars without the same level of detail. White then positions scholars as 'saying all sorts of things', implying that their authority cannot be trusted because, as with Hunt, there is the possibility that they may disagree with one another and their conclusions might be contradictory.

The context of the debate is likely to have played a role in these responses to scholars. Certainly, Hunt and White reveal at other points in the debate that they do allow for some role of scholarship in their own belief, and White's response suggests an exasperation with a certain argument to which he doesn't appear prepared to respond, rather than a fundamental disagreement with the premise of scholarship. Moreover, the authority figures in this context, for both Ally and the Christian opponents, are Christians, not Muslims or secular scholars. Although the debates between Ally and both White and Hunt ostensibly include comparisons between the Bible and the Qur'an, the focus remains on research and scholarship on the Bible, with only marginal discussions about the reliability of research about the Qur'an. The consequence of this focus is not a discussion of the value of scholarship more generally or how one might be able to use evidence in a productive way, but how evidence can be used to attack or defend particular points.

Ally's response to White makes clear that White's positioning of 'modern scholarship' in a negative way is a sign of weakness, and one that Ally rejects, at least rhetorically, because he doesn't believe it to be a threat to his own belief. He says,

Extract 4-14

James has not given any reason
for ignoring modern scholarship
except that
the modern scholarship threatens what he believes
and he's warning Muslims
that if you adopt the modern scholarship
then you will also be threatened in your faith
I don't believe that
[…]
be a
true threat

Ally's response to White reveals another storyline about scholarship, that it can be adopted in beliefs about sacred text and one which doesn't see it as 'a true threat' to one's faith. Ally positions White negatively by suggesting that he is 'ignoring' modern scholarship because he sees it as a threat and contrasts White's fears and warnings about scholarship to Muslims with his own positioning of himself as welcoming scholarship and saying it is not a 'true threat'. Ally positions himself as being more confident in his faith, reinforcing again the storyline that he, and Muslims generally, build their belief and practices on logic as well as faith. He positions Muslims as not needing to worry about modern scholarship because they are confident their position will be supported.

Although Ally positions himself as confident that modern scholarship will support his belief, the context of the debates means that he doesn't need to engage with specific criticisms of the Qur'an in 'modern scholarship'. Following this point, Ally continues to further position White's understanding of the role of Paul in early Christianity as misguided and argue that Paul's teachings opposed the original teachings of Jesus and his disciples. However, he doesn't engage with 'modern scholarship' about the Qur'an in any meaningful way; as White's examples about scholars criticising the Qur'an and Islam were only produced as examples of bad scholarship rather than genuine arguments, Ally's position and the potential complicating historical issues with the Qur'an are not addressed. For Ally then, the authority of modern scholarship can remain unproblematic in the context of the debate, regardless of whether or not the same issues of fidelity or authenticity may be at stake in research about the Qur'an.

The exchange highlights how power relationships and the dominant position of particular religious beliefs can continue to dictate how discussions among people of differing faiths proceed. The argument remains focused on the Bible rather than the Qur'an, and Ally is able to avoid having to deal with potential similar 'threats' against the Qur'an by modern scholarship that may undermine his positioning of the Qur'an as a unique document. Smith attempts, at one point, to describe the work of a scholar named Patricia Crone which casts doubt on whether Mecca existed, but the argument has little traction in the debate as Ally rejects the issue as having been dealt with in another debate. The debate continues on without the same level of criticism of the Qur'an.

The use of scholars to support his arguments about the Bible is not, however, replicated in his positive arguments for the Qur'an. Ally does not rely on any authorities to support his statements, and he seems willing to engage with modern scholarship about Islam and the Qur'an, except in reference to the arguments about the historicity of Mecca. Positive arguments for the uniqueness of the Qur'an are present in the argument about numerical miracles (D3, see Appendix). In this debate, Ally uses Muslim scholarship, but only in a limited manner, relying instead on what he claims are examples of numerical miracles in the Qur'an. The arguments made against Ally in this debate focus on the problematic nature of numerology more generally, rather than scholarship about the Qur'an. Ally's work positioning the Qur'an as a unique text is met with arguments against this claim and attempting to show that Ally's examples of numerical 'miracles' could be demonstrated in other texts.

Within the debates, authority is contested and subject to the specific conditions of the discourse in which it occurs, with a dynamic relationship to a series of different storylines. Authority is not a static entity and whether a particular text or person has authority depends on the conditions of any given argument. Ally's positioning of 'faith' and 'modern scholarship' highlights the dynamic relationships among evidence, logic, and faith in religious belief and practice. Which one has precedence at any one time depends on what the argument is about and how a speaker is positioning themselves. Although the debates position two faiths as opposed to each other, with the implicit assumption that there is a right position and a wrong position, in actuality, they do little to resolve disagreements among people of different faiths. Instead, they reveal how plastic arguments around sacred texts can be, with the speakers using them to serve particular purposes when they are expedient.

4.3   Establishing Authority in Changing Contexts

Ali Dawah Shabir Ally and his opponents, and the *Bad Christian* podcast hosts are implicitly seen as authorities, either because they have been chosen to represent a religious position in a debate or because they have large audiences. However, with few exceptions, they rarely appealed to their own knowledge or education to establish that authority. Instead, they relied on a variety of sources, including sacred texts and traditions. In this section, we will investigate how other authorities, particularly theologians and scholars, can be used to make a case for particular arguments about right belief and practice, and how authorities can be presented in diverse contexts and accepted by different audiences as authorities.

We've focused on how the authority of scholars is represented and contested in debates, but scholars are also regularly appealed to in Ali Dawah's videos. Beyond the physical presence of the sheikhs, often wearing traditional Muslim robes with long beards in contrast to Ali Dawah's Western clothing, there are also appeals to Islamic institutions and authorities. The role of these absent authorities in deciding on right belief and practice occurs in a disagreement around the appropriateness of *nasheeds*, a cappella vocal performances, in Ali Dawah's video *ARE NASHEEDS REALLY HARAM?? ALI DAWAH* (A8, see Appendix). The video is made by Ali and his co-host Musa as a response to criticism that Ali claims they have received for a video they made featuring a nasheed artist. The complaints argued that the video was not acceptable because nasheeds are or should be considered haram. In Chapter 5, I will return to further discussion of how the disagreement between Ali and those 'attacking' him is represented – for now, I would like to focus on how Ali positions himself in relationship to different authorities.

After acknowledging that they are not experts on the topic of nasheeds, Ali says, 'Basically what we did is, we said, you know what – let's look into this without being biased.' By responding to the criticism, Ali positions himself as willing to consider others' points of view, even if it also positions those who are attacking them as not acting in good faith and shows that he is willing to do further research on the topic. To 'look into' the issue of whether nasheeds are permissible, Ali's partner Musa claims that their video had been shown to several important sheikhs in Saudi Arabia by one of Musa's friends, studying in Riyadh, Saudi Arabia. These sheikhs are positioned as being special authorities, even though Musa and Ali are not able to clearly identify why exactly they have the authority that they do:

Extract 4-15
    Musa: I know a brother
    personally
    um
    so does Ali
    who's studying
    in
    Imam Saud University in Riyadh
    uh
    he's a very close brother of mine
    I speak to him nearly every single day

um
he's really really close
I'd consider him one of my best friends now
um
and
I spoke to him
and he has access to
some of the Kibar al-'Ulama
Ali: what does Kibar al-'Ulama mean
maybe
the people that don't know
Musa: yes
I'm about to clarify that
Ali: sorry
Musa: so the Kibar al-'Ulama are actually
a select
few
around
thirty
forty Ulama [scholars]
that are
very very big
so they are scholars that have been around
in Saudi Arabia for some time
they've studied
extensively
and they are actually picked
um
hand-picked
to actually serve in the council of judiciary scholars
um
currently I think
if I'm not mistaken
there's twenty-one of them
so he has access to people like that
so I said to him
bro
here's the video
please find out for us
is it halal
is it haram
what's wrong with it

In resolving the question about the appropriateness of nasheeds, Ali and Musa appeal to legal scholars and position themselves as willing to take the opinion of the scholars regardless of what they say. These authorities, however, are not necessarily known to and recognised by the audience, and Musa and Ali must not only name them but also explain why they have authority. Musa positions the Kibar al-'Ulama as 'very very big' scholars who have been chosen by others to serve, showing how authoritative positions are represented: they are people who are a part of the established religious hierarchy. Musa also positions himself and Ali in close proximity to the scholars, by claiming that a 'very close brother of mine' and 'one of my best friends' gives them access to those scholars who can help them validate their claim. Their positioning of the council also implicitly assumes the supremacy of Sunni Islam and the authority of Sunni clerics appointed by the king of Saudi Arabia, something that is not explicitly discussed, but is obvious in how they represent the authority of the Kibar al-'Ulama.

Ali, in discussing the location of the scholars misstates that they are from Medina, which Musa corrects, saying they are actually from Riyadh, and Ali responds, 'Riyadh, same thing', to which they both laugh. This moment in the interaction highlights that regardless of where they are precisely, the location of the scholars as being in Saudi Arabia, in close proximity to Medina, is an implicit marker of their authority – they are not sheikhs living in Western countries. Their particular qualifications are not extrapolated upon beyond Musa saying they have been 'around in Saudi Arabia for some time', 'they've studied extensively', and have 'been hand-picked to serve on the judiciary council'. These three features of the scholars reveal how Musa and Ali regard their authority. First, they are not based in a Western context, but close to the original source of Islam in Saudi Arabia. Second, they have a scholarly background and have studied Islam, presumably in a formal setting. Third, they have been recognised as authorities by others who also seemingly have the authority to place them on the council.

This example shows that it is not necessary to argue from the Qur'an or hadith to establish right belief and practice and that religious authorities can also be important in deciding what is and is not appropriate. In their discussion of the opinion, they recognise that not all Muslims will accept the authority of the council. Musa goes on to say,

Extract 4-16
We have gone to Kibar al-'Ulama
brothers and sisters
now this is the opinion we choose to follow
and it's a valid opinion
it is a valid opinion
now there are
there is another opinion out there
that because the Sufis do nasheeds
you should avoid them
and

certain scholars have even said that they are haram
in their opinion
scholars like Sheikh Saleh Al-Fawzan
so
he's also in the council of judiciary scholars
now his reasoning for it
is that the Sufis do it
and he believes that
it's wrong for that reason
he believed that
he believes that it's something people should avoid
and that's his opinion
brothers and sisters
I respect and love Sheikh Saleh Al-Fawzan for that

Musa further stresses the position of the Kibar al-'Ulama and that Ali and Musa are following that particular council's judgements, rather than choosing to follow different opinions as they see fit. Musa says, 'We are not like certain people that are taking one opinion from some random sheikh in Egypt.' The opinion, he stresses, is a 'valid opinion', but not one that is necessarily agreed upon by all scholars. The reference to Sheikh Saleh Al-Fawzan, another Saudi Arabian scholar, further positions Musa and Ali as not only having chosen to follow the opinion of respected scholars but also being clearly aware of opinions that disagree with them and showing their ability to engage with disagreements in a meaningful way. Moreover, Musa stresses that he 'loves and respects' the sheikh for his opinion, positioning himself as being respectful of authoritative figures, even when they do not necessarily agree with him. Musa positions himself as recognising that legitimate disagreements between scholars do occur and that he is respectful of everyone in authority.

Musa's positioning highlights how conflicting authorities can be present in a disagreement, even within one faith, and that this disagreement is not necessarily negative – positioning of oneself and others who disagree need not end in the language of 'attacks' or 'fights'. Indeed, the ability to engage meaningfully with contrasting opinions of others and represent them in a respectful way is positioned in a positive way in a storyline of striving for mutual understanding. The authorities in the religion are positioned as being able to hold legitimate opposing opinions when they are recognised as authorities and scholars. Musa makes the point to say, 'He's also in the council of judiciary scholars', referring to Sheikh Saleh Al-Fawzan who disagrees and sees nasheeds as haram because 'the Sufis do it', and does not argue with the point in any meaningful way, again positioning himself as respectful of the authorities with whom he disagrees.

Throughout the video, Musa and Ali position the traditional scholars in Islam as key for establishing their own authority. They show clear respect for authorities who disagree with them, provided those sheikhs and scholars are in respected positions. This is the same implicit claim to the authority of the sheikh seen in the 'Ask the Sheikh' videos, where Ali Dawah asks questions from viewers to Sheikh Haitham. In these videos, the sheikh's position and what sort of authority he has isn't even explicitly stated. Unlike the long explanation for the authority of the Kibar al-'Ulama, Ali doesn't offer any background into Sheikh Haitham's training or what particular branch of Islam he represents. Instead, he is simply positioned as the sheikh whose opinion is worthwhile. There are no videos on Ali Dawah's channel making arguments against Muslims leaders and once the authority of a figure has been established, they are spoken about with respect.

Positioning themselves and their opinion as validated by the Kibar al-'Ulama highlights an implicit potential weakness of Ali and Musa as young men making videos on YouTube. Because of their popularity, they may be seen as Islamic authorities themselves, but they appear to recognise that it is problematic that they are not scholars and that concerns about their background could arise, given their lack of education and training. Throughout Ali Dawah's videos, he never appears to explicitly position himself as an authority on the Qur'an, and his own credentials are never mentioned in the videos that are included. He does not regularly wear traditional Muslim clothing, and his discussions with friends on the channel always position him as a peer of those around him.

At the same time, because Ali is so popular on social media (including Instagram, Twitter, and Facebook in addition to his YouTube channel), he implicitly does have authority as an influencer. In the context of religious teaching and dawah more specifically, to maintain his own legitimacy, he must indicate that he understands his authority as a social media figure is not the same as religious authority. This position of authority does appear at times, most clearly in the controversy around the young woman in the hijab being recorded twerking (A4, see Appendix). In the video, Ali refers at times to his 'team', for example, when discussing how he might support the woman who has been recorded. By regularly hosting others on his channel and posting videos of himself interviewing prominent figures like Sheikh Menk in formal settings, he is implicitly positioned as a person with influence and access.

In terms of authority, the church as an institution is much more present in the Bad Christian Podcast than the Bible. Church is mentioned 397 times in the course of the eight episodes, and is a constant topic of discussion among the hosts, particularly so-called 'mega-churches', or churches with thousands of members which serve both religious functions in religious believers lives while also meeting a variety of 'spiritual, emotional, educational, and recreational needs' (Eagle, 2015, p. 589) and their 'mega-pastors'. Originating in the United States, megachurches may not be affiliated with larger denominations and can operate independently of institutional support and oversight, given their size and ability to financially sustain their own ministry. Megachurches are also often described as being 'seeker' oriented or 'seeker sensitive' (Sargeant, 2000), modelled after successful churches like Willow Creek Community Church in Illinois, which have reimaged collective worship to include contemporary music, drama, and comedy in their services (Gramby-Sobukwe & Hoiland, 2009). The churches focus on services and programming that appeal to a market of potential attendees who wouldn't normally attend church services. The result is programming and content that focus on the interests of seekers rather than traditional liturgy or biblical exposition and is therefore analogous in some ways to religious content posted on social media. The goal is to engage with audiences and become popular and, in so doing, spread a religious message.

The topic of megachurches and the status of their pastors are the focus of several episodes (see Appendix) including *Church Shopping vs. Car Shopping* (BC2), *The Perry Noble Mega church clown Show* (BC5), and *Is Pastor Judah Smith Gay affirming?* (BC7). In these episodes, the position, motivation, and authority of the pastor are often the focus, with discussions about the authority of the Bible as it relates to the institution of each individual church or pastor as a source of conflict. The marketisation of religion and the focus on the size and attendance of church services on Sunday mornings in particular is a site of conflict about the role of the church and how authority should be developed and recognised within it.

The problematic mixing of church authority with marketisation is organised as the focus of the episode *Church Shopping vs. Car Shopping* (BC2). In the episode, the *Bad Christian* podcast host Toby discusses his experience of looking for a new church to attend and compares the experience to shopping for a new car. Describing his frustration with the church he attended that particular Sunday, Toby says,

Extract 4-17
> I'm at a weird point in my life
> where I'm feeling more and more strange
> about
> God telling somebody
> that I need
> to hear this
> like that is getting harder and harder
> for me
> [...]
> there's a
> man
> almost always
> exclusively

that God talked to this week
at this church
and told them that
I'm there
and I need to hear this
and
one mile away in
God told
that man
to tell that church
this thing
and they're all
you know I mean
like it's
it's probably not that varied

Toby's description of preaching and the idea that God is speaking through preachers to congregations illustrate the limits of claims to authority. Toby positions his discomfort with the context by saying he's at a 'weird point in his life', a way of describing the changes and development of his faith from a fundamentalist position. The problem of being told that God is speaking to him, and there is something he 'needs to hear' from God, isn't necessarily a theological one – there seems to be little criticism in the podcast episode about the theological point of God speaking to humankind, even through other humans. In practice, however, the hosts are extremely critical of the misuse of this authority when other explanations for the motivations of a pastor might offer a better accounting for their words and actions. For the hosts of the *Bad Christian* podcast, the problem with the pastor's claim is that the message at this church is not unique.

The positioning of a message as from God and one that you can't receive without attending a particular church cannot be trusted in a context where the pastor is not only meant to be a spiritual authority but is also competing in a market economy for people to attend their service. The message of God, what one 'needs' to hear, being limited to a Sunday service where one's attendance has a direct financial incentive for the pastor has consequences for how the reliability and validity of the message are perceived. This observation illustrates the difficulty of authority in a marketised economy where the audience is the consumer and the perception that this might corrupt the message. Toby's criticism is not that the message preached at the church is wrong, but that the way it has been positioned is inaccurate – the pastor is simply following the same storyline that a majority of pastors are following on any given Sunday. He cannot therefore trust the authority of the preacher's claim that God has given them a message to deliver to the congregation.

The problematising of the claim reveals what Toby and the hosts who agree with him believe about the message of God: that it must be unique and it must not be motivated by spiritual reasons, not consumer ones. One must not be able to account for the message using simple, natural explanations that don't require faith. The extract shows that contextual factors can determine what pastors say at particular times and may be said for rhetorical purposes, rather than being genuinely 'from God'. The criticism, however, doesn't make a positive argument, suggesting what might be considered a valid claim that 'God is telling' someone a message that needs to be passed on to a particular congregation. How then legitimate spiritual authority might be exercised in this context is left unresolved, and the positioning is part of a storyline whereby Christians should always be suspicious of pastors in market-driven contexts.

The hosts go on to clarify that a message need not be 'unique', but that they bristle with the idea that a pastor is following a kind a 'formula' in their preaching, particularly when that formula reduces or diminishes suffering and sees the teaching of a church as 'ordained and comprehensive'. The hosts explicitly place the blame for this attitude about the centrality of the church on the need for churches to maintain their Sunday service attendance because it is central to their funding model. Without attendance to Sunday services, the church is unable to maintain its financial position, so other potential ways of 'growing' outside the context of the Sunday service are diminished. The criticism of the sermon is then not just what the pastor has said, but the larger sociopolitical context of the megachurch and the market economy where choosing a church is analogous to shopping for a car.

The questions that Toby and the other hosts raise in this extract resonate with the debates between Ally and Smith about what should be considered the word of God on what criteria should be applied to distinguishing whether or not an individual has actually 'talked to God'. The extent to which an individual recognises what is said to them as the word of God is, like the discussion of sacred texts, dependent on an individual's theology and whether what is being said to them comports with what they already believe. Toby's positioning of the questions he has about the preaching coming from a 'weird point' in his life suggests that he perceives himself as falling out of the norms and practices of Evangelical Christianity more generally, another recurring theme for the Bad Christians and that this has an effect on how he is able to hear the messages from authority figures within the church.

The problematisation of church authority because of market corruption has resonances with historical reformation in the Christian church and raises a central question about who should have authority in the production of second-order discourses and delivering the word of God to believers. The narrative of secularisation and individualisation of religious experience focuses on how those experiences can be varied, personalised, and unique. The *Bad Christian* podcast hosts describe a church that is monopolising and consolidating authority, with megachurches developing beyond the authority of Bible teaching and religious community, to larger comprehensive structures built on business models. Authority over belief and practice in this context is then best understood by the economic model of the church's context, rather than what may be the word of God.

One Evangelical preacher is treated with particular derision in the episode *The Perry Noble Mega Church Clown Show* (BC5). The topic of the episode is the resignation of the Evangelical preacher Perry Noble from NewSpring, a megachurch in South Carolina. They provided the reason for the resignation (identified by the hosts as Noble's use of alcohol) and talked about at what point Noble be should considered rehabilitated and allowed to preach again, either at his own church or other churches. In the discussion of this particular situation, pastors in megachurches are positioned negatively. Toby says,

Extract 4-18
That's what got me on this big kick is
how many pastors
mega pastors especially
tell you all this stuff
about how you
application
for your life
and how to do all this stuff
and those bastards
are behind the scenes
not living it out
and the
the real truth
is in their actions
not their words from the pulpit

The positioning of megachurch pastors in this extract focuses on hypocrisy, although Toby doesn't explicitly refer to any individual pastor at this point, and he even self-repairs 'pastors' to 'mega pastors', making clear that the negative positioning only applies to a mega pastors. Matt describes the hypocrisy through an abstraction of the Perry Nobel story wherein pastors that 'tell you all this stuff' but are 'not living it out'. What exactly the 'stuff' they tell 'you' to do is and how they are not 'living it out' are not clearly explained, although it does occur in the context of discussions of pastor salaries and wealth. Toby is particularly negative in his positioning of these pastors, calling them 'bastards' and following a storyline of 'not practicing what you preach', a common storyline of hypocrisy, one that he presents as being literally true of the megachurch pastors.

The potential hypocrisy of religious authorities as a delegitimising force has been absent in the discussions we have so far analysed, where the authority of the figures focused on their learning (in the case of the Kibar al-'Ulama) or their ideological purity (as in the case of Bruce Metzker). Toby's comment suggests that the particular claims of authoritative figures might be undermined by their own lack of piety. The criticism also touches on the complexity of celebrity as it relates to church authority, as in many cases the megachurch pastors are relatively famous figures in communities and can become celebrities like televangelists in previous decades (Saunders, 2015). The authority of the particular individual in the community, in an era of mediatisation of teaching and collective worship and where church congregations grow well into the thousands, is subject to public scrutiny in a way that local church pastors would not have been in the past. This is often a public scrutiny that comes through media channels rather than localised events among people who regularly meet with and know others within their community and therefore behave s more like scandals around celebrities than contained issues with local religious leaders.

Perry Noble becomes a particular focus of the hosts' ire as they criticise Noble's decision to give a guest sermon at a church pastored by Steven Furtick only a month after having been removed from his role at NewSpring. The hosts refer to Noble's return to ministry so soon after being removed from the church as 'a big joke' and 'circus', claiming that the example shows 'you can do whatever you want – there are no rules'. Matt says,

Extract 4-19
> We're in a zone now
> where
> just the wool is pulled back
> the veil is
> lifted
> you
> you just see this stuff as kind of a circus
> like the whole thing's a zoo
> or a clown show
> or something
> like the whole thing
> is it coming unravelled
> or is it just me
> I don't know
> I know some other
> somebody else feels like me
> I'm not saying it's everybody
> but
> the whole thing
> seems like an obvious joke
> and

uh
to me
it's like
uh
I'm pretty sure
it's all wrapped up in just
you know
power and
and money

Matt's description of the position of the pastor within churches suggests that a change has occurred and that this change is finally being rejected. Saying that 'the wool is pulled back' implicitly references Matthew 7:15, where Jesus warns of 'false prophets, which come to you in sheep's clothing, but inwardly they are ravening wolves'. This is followed by another potential biblical reference to 2 Corinthians 3:16 which states: 'But whenever anyone turns to the Lord, the veil is taken away.' Using the biblical language of revelation, Matt positions the megachurch pastors as false prophets and people who are only interested in 'power and money'. Matt is careful, however, to say, 'I'm not saying it's everybody', suggesting that not all megachurch pastors are corrupt, but rather 'the whole thing seems like an obvious joke', using a more abstract storyline. The problem is not necessarily individuals acting within particular churches, but the whole system of megachurches.

The storyline of false prophets exploiting believers for 'power and money' draws analogies to the gospel accounts of Jesus and particularly his opposition to religious leaders. The positioning of the megachurch pastors in the way that Matt does creates an implicit comparison with the Pharisees who are religious leaders whom Jesus explicitly and regularly challenges throughout the gospels. These stories of Pharisees exploiting their religious believers can be abstracted and reapplied to the contemporary world. The caveats also allow for plausible deniability, so that the condemnation is not applied to every megachurch pastor, but rather 'the whole thing'. By making his argument through these positionings of figures and implicit references to the biblical text, Matt draws on the authority of the Bible and the teaching of Jesus without explicitly doing so. Listeners can then draw the comparison for themselves at different levels of abstraction, whether it be generally that megachurch pastors are Pharisees, or whether specific pastors who are named in the podcast are Pharisees. Matt, however, does not need to explicitly 'call out' any individual but rather tell a story that positions the pastors in a storyline of exploiting believers. The entailments for the Evangelical Christian believer are then clear.

Although there are, with some notable exceptions, few places where the hosts can be observed suggesting that they should be heard as anything other than lay Christians, the particular authority of the megachurch pastor, drawing on popularity and audience reach, does have some analogy to the hosts of the podcast. Implicit in their discussion about how authority is or should be enacted is their own position: they too might be seen as exploiting their own influence gained through popularity. The hosts inoculate against this by regularly explicitly and implicitly positioning themselves as regular people, without authoritative roles within churches, even though the host Joey is himself a pastor within a large megachurch. Rather, the ongoing theme of the *Bad Christian* podcast is one of challenging authorities. At the same time, and despite their own positioning of themselves in a storyline of rebellion against church authority, the hosts are aware of their own influence and position themselves in roles of leadership. For example, Toby at one point (BC5, see Appendix) advertises a men's meeting which he is organising called 'True Man Experience'. He introduces the meeting and his impetus for it saying,

Extract 4-20
And basically
it's
men don't get together anymore
to just
have real conversation
we'll get together around the football game
or we get together around
you know
cause our wives bring us to a party
or bring us to church
but men used to
really
get together
and have real conversation
and challenge each other
and we don't do that anymore
so this is basically like
like a male
small group
where we're gonna go
in-depth
uh
about relationships
what you think about yourself
your identity
what
your relationship with your father
your relationship with your church
or not church
relationship with your wife
or spouse

and
uh
it gets really
really heavy

Toby begins by bemoaning the fact that men don't 'have real conversation and challenge each other' and the impetus for his plans as a way of 'putting my money where my mouth is'. The focus of the criticism is not on the structure or teaching of the megachurch as an institution, but the lack of relationships among men in particular within the church. The True Man Experience is described as a meeting of men to simply talk in a way that doesn't focus primarily on a Christian or church identity. The group's focus is also not explicitly on teaching or learning, and the language of discussing relationships positions the group using the language of self-help and personal development rather than right belief and practice. Indeed, there is nothing in the description of the event that focuses on how Christians should believe and live.

The description of the 'True Man Experience' also downplays Toby's own position as a leader, and his description of it as a 'small group' suggests a structure within a larger church institution wherein one-to-one relationships and communal reading and study of the Bible are foregrounded over didactic sermons (Atkinson, 2018). The point of the group is not explicitly to develop right belief and practice based on the teaching of the Bible or the church but to 'get heavy' in talking about emotional connections. Toby does not explicitly describe the True Man Experience as a 'safe' space, but the implication is that the group will allow people to speak freely, something that the podcast itself models.

The positioning of the group and Toby's role within it suggests that although the podcast has influence and reach with its listeners, the *Bad Christian* podcast hosts do not position themselves as leaders in a storyline of authority. Instead, they are critics, particularly of megachurch pastors and institutions which they position as corrupt. In this oppositional storyline, their own authenticity which they highlight in their frank comments about others, swearing, and irreverent attitude gives the impression of a close, intimate relationship among the hosts and the audience, even though the relationship is still decidedly a few-to-many broadcast.

In both the *Bad Christian* podcast and many of Ali Dawah's videos, the positioning of the hosts and those they interact with is informal. This informal approach, however, holds its own kind of influence and authority, allowing the speakers to take positions without having to also make a case for their own relevance. In the podcasts and the YouTube videos, the hosts position themselves as regular people like their own viewers and listeners. This allows them to appear authentic and contrast themselves, in particular, against those who are positioned as overly pious and therefore subject to scrutiny as potentially being hypocrites. The storyline of authentic religious belief and practice then allows for influence to be exerted implicitly, both challenging institutional religious structures and traditions and making suggestions for the development of religious belief and practice.

The analysis has also shown the limitations of presenting novel positionings and storylines within religious traditions and the opposition that can be faced in attempting to challenge thinking. The speakers continue to act within the accepted ways of interpreting scripture and follow the positionings and storylines generated from the texts, even when offering interpretations that they recognise could be viewed as outside traditionally accepted ways of believing and acting. The authority of sacred texts and the long traditions of Christianity and Islam must still be recognised and the interpretations from valid authorities apart from one's self must be presented. Those authorities and their ideologies are also subject to the same constraints and must be presented in ways that are acceptable within the agreed structures of authority.

At each point of the analysis, although the discussion of right belief might be the focus of any particular argument – is or is not the Bible inerrant, is or is not the Qur'an the word of God – the consequences of belief have never been far behind. For the religious believers we've observed here, the discussion about whom to believe has profound effects on how they, and subsequently those who claim the same categorical label, are viewed in the social world, and what actions they may and may not take. Ultimately, religious discourse serves as a way of making sense of one's actions in comparison and contrast to those in the same social context, so that the beliefs and practices they claim are viewed as coherent and morally acceptable by both themselves and those they seek to influence. It is not simply enough for the religious believer to believe for themselves; they must be able to articulate and defend that faith to others, and that articulation and defence must be based in authority structures that are recognised by others.

5   Living Belief and Practice

As social networking sites and social media came into prominence in the late noughts, attempts were made to describe how self-presentation was potentially affected by the presence of multiple audiences in the same online platforms. Marwick and boyd's (2011) 'context collapse' has been a particularly useful way of describing the challenges users of social media sites face when presenting themselves in an authentic way on a Facebook page that might, for example, be seen by their colleagues, friends, and family at the same time. Given the multiple identities that any individual takes on in their day-to-day life, the world of social media can confound that. Subsequent work by Tagg, Seargeant, and Brown (2017) has shown that users of social media are actually quite adept at presenting themselves to different audiences in different ways and at different times on these sites, using a variety of affordances in a process of 'context design'. It is not simply a matter of a multitude of people viewing the same content at the same time; users can and do speak to selected audiences even when their content is visible to everyone.

Although social media sites present particularly complex spaces, many of the same pressures of self-presentation, authenticity, and multiple audiences are features of social life generally (Goffman, 1959). Brown and Levison's (1987) description of positive and negative face – being appreciated and liked, and not being imposed upon by those around us, respectively – is particularly salient in considering the world of religious believes in contemporary society. The speakers, in a variety of different contexts, are often explicitly aware of how their beliefs and actions might be perceived by others, both within their own groups and by groups to whom they might be opposed. The balancing of these different pressures in talking about one's own belief is constantly present.

The place of the religious believer in contemporary life and how they should believe and act present a novel set of challenges. The religious believer can now be contrasted more often and strikingly with the growing population of non-religious individuals, in social contexts where the role of religion in public life may be increasingly viewed negatively. Moreover, the challenges are not uniform, with some religious traditions enjoying powerful positions within certain sociopolitical contexts while others are marginalised and stigmatised.

Right religious belief and practice are now not only subject to the judgements and pressures of your own immediate, physical community but also a worldwide audience to which you have access and which can be present in welcome and unwelcome ways in your religious practice.

5.1   Faith in the Market Economy

Despite a sense amongst some religious believers that there is a marginalisation of religion in contemporary life, the discourse analysed so far shows its continued presence and influence. The arguments, for example, about mega-churches and their minor celebrity pastors who can generate millions of dollars in personal income is clear evidence that religious leader remains a viable and potentially lucrative public position to hold. The popularity of figures, both Muslim and Christian, as media personalities creating content that is of interest for large audiences shows that religion is still very much present in public spaces and interacting with secular ideologies.

For people speaking about religious belief in public contexts, the presence of the market economy is implicit in how religion is discussed and presented. Clack (2018) notes that in contemporary life, economic accounting for value – in private property rights, free markets, and free trade – is the dominant way we construct being human. This orientation towards value has, Clack points out, consequences for how religious believers view them-selves in society because to be a person of faith – be it a Christian, or Jew, or Muslim – is to be a person of faith in a particular context wherein the affordances, the action possibilities for any individual, are limited by society. Faiths are subject to contemporary ideologies and uses and abuses of reli-gious belief and practice to meet goals beyond what might be the stated belief or focus of any individual faith. In market economies, where human activity is increasingly monetised on every level, religious belief and practice are one more way to create value.

Neoliberalism, the political and economic theory which foregrounds indi-vidual, entrepreneurial freedoms and skills in free markets (Harvey, 2007), is the organising philosophy of YouTube and podcasting apps and services, as well as other social media sites. In neoliberal contexts, the content of discourse is irrelevant – the focus instead is on whether a service can profit from its distribution either explicitly through the selling of some service or product or implicitly through the collection of data about users. Both Einstein (2007) and Carrette and King (2004) highlight how religion and spirituality increasingly have become products to be sold in a variety of different contexts; however, importantly for this investigation, the religious discourse itself becomes a consumer commodity. Simply using social media platforms, which for many have become essential for communication and spreading messages in the contemporary world, creates monetary value for companies which use measures such as time users spend on a platform to determine value.

The market economy is perhaps most explicit in the recurring advertisements that appear in the *Bad Christian* podcast. While the YouTube videos may or may not include some passive advertising in the form of banner ads on the video pages, within the *Bad Christian* podcast, the hosts read ad copy for a variety of goods and services, including mattresses, flowers, website hosting platforms, and an online sex shop ostensibly for married couples. The times this copy is read represent clear moments of implicit agreement among the hosts, times when they do not speak over one another and one host reads the ad copy without interruption. The ads are both read during the interaction of the hosts and pre-recorded and inserted into the discussion.

The ads themselves are very rarely the topic of discussion outside of the time in the podcast when the ad is about to be read and immediately after the ad is read. The hosts can at times be heard mixing the reading of the ad with their own experiences of a particular product. In one discussion about sex (BC5, see Appendix), the reading of the ad becomes a part of the interaction between the two hosts:

Extract 5-1
Matt: well you bring up the pre
premarital sex thing
and
that's an important one
and here's the thing
I don't think you should have premarital sex
but if you did
I would do it on a Casper mattress
and let me tell you all why
<general laughter>
Toby: oh my god
Matt: because
Casper
Toby: I would've killed to have a Casper
back then
Matt: ah
you know
this is
I know I'm supposed to talk about my personal experience
but
I don't want to give too many details away
on this one
but
the Casper mattress is awesome

In this episode, the conversation has naturally developed into a discussion of premarital sex, but the introduction of the ad is marked in Matt's use of the brand name 'Casper' in describing the mattress. Toby's exaggerated approving response of 'Oh my god' and the relative lack of negotiation around turn taking (particularly compared to the rest of the podcast when the floor is constantly being negotiated). The Casper mattress ad is the one portion of the podcast that is completely scripted, and there are no interruptions once the reading has begun. The ad, however, is not only meant to be read out – the hosts are given instructions to improvise some elements of it. As Matt reads the ad, he notes, 'I'm supposed to talk about my personal experience' – the ad copy is meant to be experienced by the listener as, in some way, an authentic part of the natural discourse of the podcast, even though it is clearly not.

Authentic support for products one is advertising is a key part of social media advertising more generally (Hunter, 2016) – social media users must project the sense that their content is 'real', even when promoting products that they have been paid to endorse. Matt's subsequent praise of the mattress in this ad and with other ads includes insistence that his enthusiasm for the product is not only because they are being paid to advertise it but also that they personally like the product. The presentation of selling ads on the podcast is described in positive ways, with Toby saying in another episode, 'I love that we are sponsored by companies that I really do think just offer great products' (BC3, see Appendix), positioning the selling of ads as something positive, as a partnership between the podcast makers and the companies buying ads.

The selling of ads by companies like Casper Mattresses on the *Bad Christian* podcast where there is a predominant focus on discussion of religious belief and practice, and indeed controversial positions stated, first suggests that the *Bad Christian* podcast exists within mainstream culture, at least in the United States, and offers clear counter-evidence to claims that religious content or religious believers are marginalised in public life. The fact that companies which are not explicitly religious or affiliated in any way with the hosts see the podcast as a way to spread their message to customers, despite what might be the controversial elements of the show, suggests that the Bad Christians are not necessarily that 'bad', at least in terms of what companies see as needing to avoid. The podcast has a large audience of potential consumers, and companies that are not explicitly religious are clearly not concerned about being affiliated with shows that engage primarily in religious discourse.

The hosts represent the selling and buying of ads as a means of supporting the show, but this model of selling advertising is a shift in the model for public religious discourse which in other institutional contexts is supported through the patronage of members of institutions, through monetary giving and voluntary labour. The shift to ad-supported public religious discourse positions the podcast as a vehicle for not only discussion of religious belief and practice but also consumerism. Corporate sponsorship then represents an emerging force in religious discourse going forward. Matt says at one point, 'So do yourself a favour and help our show by supporting Proflowers.' To buy the product that the show sponsors is to both 'do yourself a favour' and support the show, but this creates a complicated relationship between belief and the market. Whereas the hosts are acutely aware of the issues of consumerism in the megachurch context where there are monetary consequences for supporting LBGTQ+ Christians for example, the role of corporations is not, beyond the claim that there is no conflict of interest because the hosts only sell ads to products that they themselves already enjoy and endorse.

This model of selling advertising is actually praised and contrasted with the traditional model of support for churches. Toby says (BC5, see Appendix):

Extract 5-2
> You know
> they've signed up for more
> to do ads with us
> because they like what we're doing
> they're not
> Christian
> church
> churches
> they're companies
> you know what I mean
> that go
> hey
> these guys are just being honest
> and we
> we can appreciate each other
> and we get to work with companies that we
> this thing's going
> amazing to where
> because we're telling the truth
> we work with ad
> companies
> and
> and companies that
> we
> actually like
> and use

In this extract, 'honesty' and 'telling the truth' are represented as important values for the hosts, and values that allow them to monetise the podcast. The hosts position themselves as authentic, regular guys who are simply talking about the products they already use and like. Advertisers are then attracted to them and eager to 'work with' them. The hosts downplay what seems to be the obvious attraction of advertising on their podcast: the size of their audience. Instead, the success the podcast has achieved and the interest of advertisers are positioned as the result of 'telling the truth'. Matt reinforces this authenticity by saying that they only advertise companies and products that they 'actually' like. This positioning of advertising in a storyline of authenticity also implicitly contrasts with the negative positioning of megachurches and megachurch pastors, which includes storylines of corruption and deception in pursuit of money.

The hosts position the selling of ads as a positive thing for themselves and for their community, because they claim it requires no changes to the podcast or their own positions on issues and products and is a part of what they are already doing on the show. This positioning, however, doesn't acknowledge the commodification of the audience and audience labour (Caraway, 2011). The selling of advertising within podcasts often includes some exchange of information about the audience and their listening habits, in an effort to better match advertisers and content producers and audiences. Moreover, although the audience of the podcast doesn't have to pay money to hear the show, the show is not free. In addition to the ads, the production of user data on podcasting apps and Facebook produces value for these companies in a way that is often invisible to the users of the sites. The hosts position ads in the podcast in a positive way, but listeners exchange their time for the 'free' content.

The *Bad Christian* podcast does also organise a Bad Christian Club which offers additional content and access for a fee of $7USD (in 2019). Members of the club have access to additional show content, a private Facebook group and different private online events with the hosts, and digital content. New members of the club have their name read out at the end of podcasts, following a model popularised by the service Patreon (www.patreon.com), which allows content creators online to collect contributions from consumers, often in exchange for some manner of exclusive content or access to the creators. The hosts regularly publicise the club and present it as 'our online community', a way to not only support the show monetarily but also engage with fans. The presentation of this as a 'community' suggests that the monetary support includes not only the 'perks' of access but also a shared group identity with others.

In physical spaces of devotional practice, the means of support for pastors or vicars or imams are often explicitly stated and giving to the work of a church, mosque, or religious charity is an intentional and explicit act. The social media economy, however, has fundamentally changed how content is paid for and how creators are supported, including those who create religious content. Ali Dawah's videos did not include, at any point, an indication of how his work is supported; when the videos for this study were collected, he did not regularly make an appeal for video viewers to make contributions to his work. The lack of transparency around the funding for his work produces a different set of complications compared to the *Bad Christian* podcast, wherein the viewer of Ali Dawah can't know from where the support for the channel is explicitly coming. This also marks a shift in how religious discourse and authority are represented in public spaces, where the viewer might not be aware of the means of support that each individual figure is enjoying.

Issues of support and monetisation complicate the presentation of religious belief and practice in the contemporary world. Even free devotional apps like 'Jesus Calling' (Trammell, 2015) produce data about users which can be bought and sold without the user being explicitly aware of it. For any digital content, monetisation of data is a constant factor in how app creators are supported. Regardless of whether or not an app creator or content producer themselves is profiting from or even aware of the information being produced by the product's use, the user and their devotional practice are monetised. The discussions of the contemporary world focus on more explicitly obvious questions of adapting belief and practice to changing societal norms. However, the production of religious discourse as 'content' shows that religious discourse has been and will continue to be a part of the market economy. Profiting from religion, the rich televangelists using religious content to develop their own personal wealth (Schultze, 2003) or other ways of monetising religions as brands through selling services or products (Einstein, 2007), is certainly not new, but how mediatised religion is now always implicitly monetised is likely to influence how religious practice and belief are presented to people as consumers, not simply believers.

The collecting and selling of data for the purpose of increasing time spent by users on platforms also have consequences for the development of 'filter bubbles' (Pariser, 2011), wherein the content that users see is actively curated to their own preferences. This curation of content happens automatically as users engage with technologies that collect data about them and provide content that machine-learning technology predicts will more likely be of interest to a user. The filter bubble then leads to people increasingly being presented with information that they find agreeable and avoiding information and content that might challenge their preconceptions. The result is groups that are not only increasingly isolated from one another with their own information streams feeding their own preferences and ideological positions but also with mechanisms in place whereby product and service providers profit from this isolation. Of course, individuals avoiding opinions and perspectives they disagree with, often times without knowing it, is not new and happens in the physical world, with individuals choosing which media to consume and where to live and go, often without an explicit intention of being surrounded by those with whom they agree. However, the increasing ways in which technology allows for these controls to emerge without user awareness are perceived as dangerous, particularly as they have been used to spread 'fake news' and manipulate democratic processes (Bakir & McStay, 2018). Absent other contextual cues, poor social media literacy can be dangerous when users aren't aware of the processes that lead to information appearing on their screens.

At the same time, when market forces encourage growth, religious belief and practice in public spaces may be moderated to appeal to broader audiences, with content focusing on what people find to be most click worthy rather than what is most useful or beneficial for their own development. The Bad Christian hosts are critical of megachurch pastors and ministries for producing entertaining content and monetising church ministry, but the consumer principles that drive interest in megachurches are equally at play in the production of content in online spaces. What counts as disagreeable is different in both places – the megachurches may avoid discussion of issues seen as controversial to conservative members, while the Bad Christian hosts explicitly avoid talk which is seen as too religious – indeed, Toby describes feeling more free to be 'super spiritual' or 'talk more Jesus stuff' (BC4, see Appendix) in the episodes which are created for subscribers to the Bad Christian Club (presumably because the supporters are more likely to be religious believers) than on the publicly available episodes.

An additional effect of marketisation on public religious discourse in public spaces is the focus on competition. One consequence of this orientation to debate is the development of arguments over time, as people become more adept at producing content to match the interests of those who might hear them. Speakers show an awareness of a multitude of audiences, and this awareness inevitably has an effect on how individual beliefs are presented and potentially on how and what individuals actually believe, an argument I have previously made in relation to Evangelical religious talk online (Pihlaja, 2018). Positionings are not static but have been observed to change over the course of conversations, debates, or interviews – the representation of belief is, like any other utterance, a moment of Bakhtinian convergence where the potential to say something creative and new is constrained by what has been said before, what is possible in the 'slender opening' (Foucault, 1971) of the individual utterance.

Awareness of the positioning of the religious believer in the contemporary social world and questions about the durability and legitimacy of faith frame discussions about belief and practice. Key to the debates between Shabir Ally and his Christian opponents is how argument and evidence are balanced with faith – indeed, the presence of an interlocutor of a different faith requires some means of differentiating between the claims of both. Importantly, in these debates, the positionings of Ally and his opponents are always subject to the response of the other and claims are met with counterclaims. This affordance of debates means that getting the 'last word' in the debate is an often impossible task that leads to the development of endless counterarguments (Billig, 1996) and a lack of resolution – no one ever really 'wins'. At the same time, they do highlight the uniqueness of religious belief and practice in the contemporary world insofar as how about religious belief, rather than other arguments or debate in which empirical evidence might be presented to discount the other, is accepted among religious believers.

The clearest example of this focus on uniqueness is the categorisation of religious faith, regardless of what that faith is, as being distinct from a secular or atheistic perspective. In the debate between Richard Lucas and Shabir Ally (D3, see Appendix), focusing on the supposed mathematical miracles of the Qur'an, the issue of faith and how it must be balanced with reason is particularly clear because the focus of the debate is on miracles, a claim that supernatural occurrences in the world both exist and can be accounted for using spiritual or religious explanations. For both Ally and Lucas, the starting point of the argument is a shared belief in the interaction of a god in the natural world. Shabir Ally says:

Extract 5-3

Part of our discussion tonight
is to get to the question of
how you evaluate Christian
miracles
because
uh
I didn't come here to debate with an atheist
and
much of what you presented
is the kind of
uh
critical scepticism that an atheist will bring to such a discussion
uh
but as a Christian
I take it that you believe in some miracles
like let's say the virginal conception of Jesus

Ally's criticism of Lucas at this moment in the debate shows how belief is positioned in a positive way and suggesting that Lucas's use of 'critical scepticism that an atheist will bring to such a discussion' might be positioned in a negative way. Ally's statement positions Christians and Muslims together in a storyline of faith by suggesting that both accept 'miracles'. Ally refers to the evaluation of 'Christian miracles', suggesting that some miracles are specific to particular faith traditions – the statement implies that there are also 'Muslim miracles' that one might evaluate. However, the distinction is removed in the example of the 'virginal conception of Jesus', a miracle that both Christians and Muslims historically accept. Ally positions Lucas as taking a position that is outside the storyline of faith and therefore more similar to an atheist position than a Christian one. For Ally, having faith requires accepting that some things occur in the natural world that can only be accounted for as miracles, and Lucas, regardless of the position he takes in the debate about miracles in the Qur'an, must accept this point.

Miracles are problematic, because, as Ally points out, the criticism of miracles is essentially a criticism of faith generally, not just specific faiths. Presenting a miracle that both he and Lucas believe to be real implies a higher level of abstraction about miracles. It's not the particulars of individual miracles that believers in each tradition might accept (i.e. Muslims believe in particular 'Muslim miracles' and Christians believe in 'Christian miracles'). Rather, there's actually a more abstract storyline, one in which religious believers accept miracles. This storyline contrasts with that of atheism or secularism, wherein non-believers don't accept miracles. When comparing thinking at this level of abstraction, both Ally and Lucas are positioned together. They both believe in the same miracle of the virgin birth, and more abstractly, being religious believers who accept that miracles occur, they can be positioned together in a larger secular world.

The exchange shows the potential moderating effect of inter-religious dialogue even in contexts where the two are ostensibly arguing with each other about the validity of claims in sacred texts and attempting to undermine each other's beliefs. Although they may disagree about the specific stories that appear in each text, on a higher level of abstraction, they both position themselves as religious believers who believe in miracles, and this storyline can be understood in contrast to another storyline of atheists who do not believe in miracles. At this level of abstraction, the difference between the specifics is less important than the shared position of 'people of faith' because both share the consequences for believing in miracles and how evidence can be used to support these claims.

The level of abstraction of storylines about faith shows how differences can be hid or highlighted depending on the moment-to-moment focus of discourse and the level of abstraction. Although the overall debate focuses on differentiating between Christianity and Islam, one can imagine contexts wherein the level of abstraction is more specific, say between an Evangelical Christian and a Roman Catholic Christian, or, more broadly, say between a person arguing for the existence of God with an atheist. Ally's statement about miracles and shared beliefs, at this point in the debate, suggests that finding common ground might be less problematic than the debate framing allows and is indeed a key part of Ally's discourse, emphasising where Christians and Muslims share beliefs, in contrast to a secular world that rejects them.

Ally's positioning of himself in comparison to Lucas highlights the importance of faith, particularly in response to a claim by Lucas that because there is a 'massive degree' of complexity in creation, there must be a creator. Ally says, picking up on a point that Lucas has made where he rolled some dice and tried to show that patterns could be identified in any roll of the dice:

Extract 5-4

I don't want to
I don't want to deny you on that [argument that complexity shows design]
and sound like the atheist myself
but I want you to
just remind you
that atheists do have a comeback to all of this
they will say that no matter what designs you're looking at
if you're dealing with a universe as vast as it is
then you are going to find
uh
evidence of design
but again
they're saying that
you-you
we faith believers are doing what you did with the dice
where you just
roll some dice
and you just pick the ones
that give you the
the result that you
that you desire
uh
and
and I would say
that's not what we have done with the Qur'an
if you study these uh
documents in depth
you will see that that's not actually what has been done with the Qur'an

Ally again positions atheism in a negative way, particularly rejecting a position that makes him 'sound like an atheist' – his response suggests this has a negative valence. Ally's statement that atheist positioning of 'faith believers' together has consequences for who affiliates with whom, and in a telling moment of self-repair, he shifts from the perspective of an atheist ('but again they're saying that you-you') to speak again from his own perspective, saying, 'We faith believers'. In these two lines, Ally shows how Christians and Muslims can be positioned together as 'faith believers' in contrast to atheists, and the problematic nature of the argument of design is not one that is unique for Muslims or for Christians. Because of this positioning, Christians and Muslims must both address the issue of 'evidence of design' from the same position in a storyline of faith believers who argue that God has created the world.

Although Ally voices the atheist positioning and criticism of Islam as the positioning of faith more generally, he doesn't continue to defend himself as a 'faith believer'. Instead, he reasserts his positioning of himself as a Muslim saying, 'That's not what we have done with the Qur'an.' The 'we' in this line includes only Muslims and implies that the atheist criticism of 'people of faith' is really a valid criticism of Christians, not Muslims. Muslims don't in Ally's positioning simply 'roll the dice' and try to make sense of patterns that they see, a reference to an argument Lucas made using the dice to illustrate the arbitrary nature of numerical patterns. Instead, he positions himself and Muslims more generally ('we') as looking at 'documents in depth'. The storyline suggests that Muslims don't simply believe in miracles, but that their faith is logical and the result of 'in-depth' study. There is, however, no suggestion here that Christians as fellow 'faith believers' are doing the same thing and Ally implicitly positions Lucas, and by extension Christians more generally, as engaging in the activity that atheists claim they do. Ally essentially accepts the atheist storyline, but in a way that shifts the positionings. It is no longer about religious believers in contrast to atheists, but people who seek truth and evidence and those who don't. In this storyline, Muslims are implicitly positioned with atheists rather than Christians, because they are truth seekers. Faith is no longer the focus, but rather how individuals interact with evidence and the scrutiny they apply to it.

The response also suggests an awareness of different audiences for the debate, both those in the physical location and those who might view the recording. Although Ally's immediate interlocutor is a Christian who doesn't view miracles in a negative way, Ally is careful to not simply accept a storyline wherein religious believers are positioned together as accepting miracles, in contrast to atheists. Although Ally's point about miracles suggests that the problem is one for both Christians and Muslims, his shifting positionings construct a different storyline that includes a change in how beliefs and practices are judged. For Ally at this moment in the debate, Muslims have more in common with atheists in a storyline of seeking truth and evidence than they do with Christians like Lucas.

Religious believers in the contemporary world must account for the different perspectives that people might take when hearing their arguments. The concept of 'context design' (Tagg et al., 2017) from social media analysis is useful here. Within the context of the debate, Ally and his opponents are carefully presenting messages that can be heard and judged by different people in different ways. For Muslims, that means accounting for Christian storylines about Islam, as well as secular storylines about religious believers more generally. Any given argument or positioning must take into account this variety of perspectives and, to the extent possible, make them coherent from point to point within the discourse event.

The awareness of different audiences and the pressure to present controversial beliefs in a way that accounts for public disapproval is then always a part of religious discourse, particularly when what one says about one's faith might be heard by a broader audience. The *Bad Christian* podcast discusses the consequences of particular beliefs in relation to the Christian doctrine of hell (BC8, see Appendix), part of an ongoing theme across the episodes in which the hosts discuss Joey's apparent decision to no longer believe in a literal hell, and the consequences of this change. One particular conversation begins with Matt discussing the difference between people's stated beliefs and their actions, saying,

Extract 5-5
Do most people think
that God is going to send somebody to hell
forever
if they were to
use the word fuck
or shit
I don't think
most people's actions
would prove
they don't really think that

In this section of the podcast, the hosts discuss the consequences of belief on practice and whether belief in a particular doctrinal position actually impacts how they live their lives. For Evangelical Christians who accept literalist interpretations of the Bible, hell is meant to be understood as a literal location of eternal suffering. This belief requires positioning all wrongdoing or sin as equally offensive and requiring punishment, but Toby points out the practically: Christians don't act as though they believe this point. He poses a rhetorical question asking if 'most people' think that using offensive language actually deserves hell, saying the expletives to emphasise the absurdity of believing that simply saying the words would lead to eventual judgement, and to make the point that 'most people's actions' don't comport with the belief. A belief in hell may be an important marker of faith, but it might also be one for which there isn't any practical evidence.

The complex relationship between faith and categorical religious labels comports with empirical research, wherein participation in a religious tradition creates a sense of spiritual identity (Ammerman, 2013), but how that religious identity is worked out, how it is lived in one's day-to-day interactions with others, is a different issue – saying you are a Christian and the consequences that has for how you live your life are two different things. This is particularly difficult with beliefs that don't have clear, incumbent actions. If being a Christian requires a belief in a literal hell, but there are no incumbent actions as a result of that belief, the only evidence is a person's claim to the belief. The process is entirely discursive and therefor problematic because no one can produce evidence that they actually believe in what they claim to believe.

The discussion also highlights how particular doctrinal beliefs can have little to no effect on how people actually live their lives. Matt says the following, in relation to Christian belief in hell and the ongoing discussion on the podcast about the centrality of different beliefs in Christianity:

Extract 5-6
> Do you believe in hell
> as an abstract
> most people believe in hell as an abstraction
> and as a doctrinal truth
> and
> the Bible says there's hell
> and I believe it
> and that's fine
> that's me
> that's basically what I think
> but I promise you
> I don't behave
> as if I think people are in hell

In this extract, Matt builds on the earlier point parsing the difference between beliefs and actions. He takes up the argument that hell is something that 'most people' believe as an 'abstraction', first affirming his own belief, but in a way that minimalises its consequences and therefore its importance for him. It's something that he says he 'thinks' while he 'promises' the other hosts and the audience that 'I don't behave as if I think people are in hell.' The two statements position Matt as both an Evangelical Christian, accepting its core beliefs, and a hypocrite, a positioning that is both understandable within Evangelical Christianity and also softens his position in relation to audience members who might find a belief in hell offensive, something that is reinforced by his use of swear words to further position himself as not following a fundamentalist storyline.

The discussion of hell provides a clear example of the difficulty for religious believers positioning themselves in a contemporary context, and their ability to simultaneously position themselves in different ways before a variety of audiences. Throughout the episodes, the hosts rarely take positive positions on particular issues but regularly position themselves as questioning what others are doing or 'deconstructing' different parts of Evangelical Christian culture. Matt's description of his belief positions himself as both adhering to a key belief in Evangelical Christianity while also still rejecting that same belief. The parsing of belief and action allows different storylines to be heard depending on the audience's own beliefs. Matt goes on to say:

Extract 5-7

I look at the Bible
I think about hell
if
if somebody asks me
do I believe in hell
I'd say yes
I mean
you know
but I just
I must not
believe
if you get down to any specifics
I won't
I will never
be anywhere close to
committal
or even probable
that some individual is in hell
I
I don't think they are
I must not think they are
because
it doesn't bother me
I'm not worried about it

In this extract, the belief in hell is presented as something that Matt simultaneously believes and doesn't believe. Although logically this positioning can be understood as a differentiation between professed belief and what one feels or how one acts, pragmatically it allows Matt to position himself in a way in multiple storylines of faith. In the storyline of Evangelical Christianity, professing a belief in Jesus is the key marker of an individual's faith. At the same time, right belief and practice also include continuing to be a 'sinner', so Matt's admitting that there is a disjuncture between his belief and actions is understandable in a Christian storyline of faith. By saying 'I must not believe', Matt hedges his potential disbelief as an external positioning of himself and his actions. It is not something that he himself necessarily thinks, but the result of a logical evaluation of his actions and what he says.

Matt's statement about his belief might also be heard as Matt positioning himself as distinct from Evangelical Christians who hold a strong belief in the so-called reality of hell and the importance of that belief. By saying that his actions don't support his professed belief, the positioning could also be heard in a storyline of moderate Christianity, positioning Matt as someone who rejects more fundamentalist readings of the Bible and accepts interpretations of the Bible and Christian faith that don't necessarily require a belief in a literal hell. This positioning and storyline might be heard by audience members who view a belief in a literal hell in a negative way and understand Matt's description of himself and his beliefs as a way of distancing himself from more fundamentalist interpretations of the Bible.

The frank, but ambiguous, discussion of hell here shows the complicated nature of professed beliefs, particularly when it comes to problematic concepts in the contemporary world like a literal, eternal hell, which could be seen as an incumbent belief of biblical inerrancy. Belief in a literal hell shows group membership, an acceptance of a 'doctrinal truth', as Matt says. Analysis of discourse, however, shows how these professed beliefs can be positioned within different storylines depending on what the audience might be inclined to hear. Matt's and the other hosts' reticence to position themselves as positively affirming a doctrinal stance allows for the possibility of different and even contradictory storylines to be heard.

The same could also be said of moments in the Ali Dawah videos I've presented, where Ali Dawah interacts with sheikhs about potentially controversial topics. Both Ali and the sheikh present what might be consider ideal beliefs and then discuss the difficulty of putting these beliefs into practice, often avoiding judgemental language and highlighting the ambiguity of individual choices, for example, when trying to decide whether or not one 'needs' car insurance. Using examples that are ambiguous and representing several positions while encouraging the audience to not judge those who don't follow the same practices allows for multiple positionings and different storylines to emerge. Speakers are then also able to present and discuss controversial beliefs and practices in a way that acknowledges their problematic nature and accepts that different beliefs and practices are, if not necessarily right, understandable.

The religious discourse we've discussed here presents a good set of examples of context design (Tagg et al., 2017) and how it operates in these contexts of public discourse about religious belief and practice. Believers can present themselves simultaneously to multiple audiences who hear and position them in different storylines depending on the individual audience member's own understanding of their beliefs and practices. The self- and other-positioning in which Matt, Toby, and Joey engage on the podcast shows how fundamentalist religious belief in contemporary contexts can be positioned in storylines that allow for the hosts to both retain fundamentalist positions and also be seen as challenging these positions. Because they do not explicitly take on authoritative positions as religious or spiritual leaders, they can speak about religious belief and practice in a way that allows for multiple interpretations, growing a more diverse audience.

5.2   Debate within the Faiths

Considering the role of market forces in contemporary religious discourse, debates within faiths, particularly those that focus on developing right belief and practice within a particular tradition, are inevitable because individual choice is valorised. At the same time, continuity within faiths is essential for communities to remain cohesive. How disagreements are managed and whose ideas should be followed are therefore perennial issues within discussions about religious belief and practice. As the preceding chapters have shown, religious authorities, sacred texts, and scholars cannot simply resolve disagreements among people, and discussions about these disagreements are inevitable. Debate, as the moderator Michael Coren says, is 'one of the great triumphs of democracy'.

In the debates among Christians and Muslims, discussions among Muslims in YouTube videos, and in the *Bad Christian* podcast, disagreements have been present at every point, with a repeated focus on showing respect for the opinion of others, even in cases where opinions are cast as being diametrically opposed, for example, in using the language of competition – the Bible *versus* the Qur'an – in the debates between Ally and his opponents. Ideas are simultaneously presented as opposed to one another, with only one possible true outcome, while the different opinions that individuals represent must be treated with respect at least stylistically. Still, there are few if any examples of genuine insults of others or attacks attempting to completely delegitimise another's position.

For the *Bad Christian* podcast hosts, the market economy as a driving force is unproblematic in terms of resolving good and bad ideas. The hosts seem the most comfortable with the discussion of the pressures of the market economy, even drawing that explicit comparison in the episode entitled *Church shopping vs. Car Shopping* (BC2). The analogy of believer as consumer is a key part of their discussions about the megachurch and their frustrations with the behaviour of megachurch pastors in relationship to money. The consumer economy in American Evangelical Christianity is, for them, expected when attending church, with some churches being more effective than others in producing a good consumer experience, and their evaluations of experiences at church are framed in the language of consumer satisfaction.

The market economy's relationship to theology and belief is also explicitly discussed around the development of ideas in the contemporary cultural context (BC5, see Appendix). The hosts specifically discuss the role of the 'economy of ideas' in talking about biblical inerrancy and whose position on the Bible is likely to dominate Evangelical Christian faith going forward, mixing thoughts about consumer culture and right belief and practices with the key question of how Christians should position themselves in relation to new knowledge, particularly when new knowledge could be seen to undermine core parts of one's faith. Matt, in discussing this issue says:

Extract 5-8

I've heard people throwing around
the phrase
a lot lately
just the economy of ideas
and beliefs and stuff like that
and that
and the idea there is just that it
uh
if
there's a good idea
it will make it
and a bad idea
it will go away
and you don't have anything to be worried about
you know what I mean
like if the
if there's good ideas
that should
bear fruit
and show
that
they make sense
or are functional or
can be utilised
then they will survive
and silly
and goofy ideas
will just be
more and more pushed
to the wayside

This positioning of argument among religious believers is explicitly oriented to a neoliberal economy of ideas with a belief that it is the natural course of the world for 'good ideas' to 'make it' and 'bad ideas' to 'go away'. Matt goes on to describe these 'good ideas' as 'bearing fruit', taking a metaphorical description of good outcomes from a Biblical parable. What is 'good' in this description is explicitly ideas that 'make sense', are 'functional', and 'can be utilised'. These ideas are contrasted with ones that are 'silly' or 'goofy', with Matt arguing that those ideas are 'pushed to the wayside' naturally through the forces of the economy. Matt goes on to say that the 'interconnectivity' of the world makes it impossible to avoid the ideas facing criticism and that if someone is 'confident enough in their faith', they should be willing to see 'how it just all shakes out'.

Matt suggests that 'if God is real', there is no need to be 'fearful' of ideas like evolution that might appear to challenge long held beliefs. Matt explicitly criticises the attempts to 'squash' evolution as not being 'capitalistic', because the economy will decide whether it is 'stupid and not true' or whether it is 'fruitful'.

The analogy between the market economy and the survival of good ideas as the ones that 'bear fruit' implies that the mechanism of the economy is an efficient way to evaluate belief and practice. 'Good fruit' and 'making it' are understood as analogous and reflect a larger understanding about what success in the world should look like. If materially good things come from the market economy and one agrees that it is the best mechanism for producing goods, the same potentially can be said of ideas. The argument shows how ideologies can and are driven by material concerns and the working of the physical world can be used to understand concepts like 'right' and 'wrong'. Matt describes this as a natural mechanism, one in which individuals do not play an active role. Instead, the bad ideas are 'pushed to the wayside' by forces that are inevitable and not explicitly identified as acting with agency. It's simply the way the world works.

The ambiguous language around this discussion is potentially problematic in that what Matt believes would be a 'fruitful' idea rather than one that is 'stupid and not true' is not clearly delineated. The argument hinges on the point that bad ideas 'go away' eventually and that good ideas persist, but examples of this being the case are not necessarily presented. Moreover, Joey, in response to Matt's argument, identifies how opposing arguments can be made, also referencing the Bible:

Extract 5-9
I think
I think the only problem
the only potential problem
with that
and where
a stalemate would
happen with
with Christians
would be
yeah
that's exactly what the Bible says
is
there's an enemy
that wants to
make foolishness out of
you know
the truth
and make truth
out of the foolishness of this world

The argument against the economy of ideas is the argument of supernatural forces in the world and that the 'world' is the domain of the 'enemy'. Joey points out the juxtaposition between the 'truth of the world' and another truth which is not named but appears to be a supernatural or Godly truth that supersedes everything else and indeed makes the truth of the world 'foolishness'. In this case, the very opposite could be true: the ideas that appear to be successful in the world are actually foolishness because they are successful as the result of the work of the 'enemy'. In this storyline, God and the enemy are each attempting to undermine the other's truth by making it appear foolish, and the believer, in this case Christians, must be on guard to avoid being manipulated by things that appear to be true, but actually aren't. The concept of an 'enemy', and particularly the enemy's deception in undercutting belief in Jesus, is a powerful concept in controlling what people believe. The word makes clear that the positioning that Toby represents sees the acceptance of the 'foolishness of the world' as a serious problem in Christian belief and practice, beyond simply making a choice between two options and accepting the more durable of the two, because one must take into account the possibility that they might be led astray.

Joey's response challenges the idea of the market economy as being too materialistic in its approach to belief and practice, because it argues that an understanding of the spiritual world must supersede the economy and in that what might appear good in terms of the market or the world more generally could actually be wrong. This vision of religious faith sees right belief and practice as subject to what 'the Bible' says, an authority that goes beyond what the economy promotes. Toby doesn't quote the Bible directly but makes allusion to the 'foolishness of this world', a reference to 1 Corinthians 1:18–27, where the Apostle Paul writes:

18 For the preaching of the cross is to them that perish foolishness; but unto us which are saved it is the power of God.
19 For it is written, I will destroy the wisdom of the wise, and will bring to nothing the understanding of the prudent.
20 Where is the wise? where is the scribe? where is the disputer of this world? hath not God made foolish the wisdom of this world?
21 For after that in the wisdom of God the world by wisdom knew not God, it pleased God by the foolishness of preaching to save them that believe.
22 For the Jews require a sign, and the Greeks seek after wisdom:
23 But we preach Christ crucified, unto the Jews a stumbling block, and unto the Greeks foolishness;
24 But unto them which are called, both Jews and Greeks, Christ the power of God, and the wisdom of God.

25 Because the foolishness of God is wiser than men; and the weakness of God is stronger than men.
26 For ye see your calling, brethren, how that not many wise men after the flesh, not many mighty, not many noble, are called:
27 But God hath chosen the foolish things of the world to confound the wise; and God hath chosen the weak things of the world to confound the things which are mighty.

This passage describes the 'preaching of the cross', or the core message of the Bible as meant to destroy the 'wisdom of the wise' and to make 'foolish the wisdom of this world', itself a reference to the Old Testament passage of Isaiah 29:14. Although Joey himself doesn't take the position, he makes clear that negatively positioning 'wisdom' as it relates to scientific discovery or contemporary norms is a common Evangelical Christian argument. The 'wisdom of the world' is actually a strategy of the 'enemy', in a storyline of war between God and Satan. To acquiesce to ideas that appear to be the best can lead to serious consequences for Christians, including leading them away from right belief and practice and risking not being saved. Verse 22 suggests that being saved requires going against the 'wisdom of the world', creating a further, serious consequence for those who reject the 'foolishness of God'. To follow the 'wisdom of the world' is to potentially jeopardise one's salvation.

The listener is essentially given two opinions on how they might decide what is and is not right, with neither essentially being championed by the hosts. Joey, in describing his own solution to the problem of what someone should or should not believe foregrounds his faith in Jesus, who is presented as being separate from the Bible, with the ability to dynamically relate to every social context. The foregrounding of Jesus, however, doesn't resolve the issue of whether Christians should accept developments in science and if, indeed, the 'economy of ideas' is actually the best way to decide which ones are the strongest. The representation of both approaches to the world doesn't value one over the other and by re-establishing the centrality of Jesus, listeners from both positions can hear their own storyline reflected in the hosts' words. The listener to the podcast, regardless of what they believe, could come away from the particular episode feeling as though the hosts support their position.

These extracts again highlight the plasticity of religious belief when it is separated from practice and show that belief can be positioned in a variety of ways depending on how the listener sees themselves within the social world. In this context of pluralistic beliefs, including within one's own faith, the issue is resolved by positioning the two opposing positions as legitimate and based in a reasonable disagreement, before appealing to a superseding belief to which both parties can agree, in this case the centrality of a belief in Jesus, something that both moderate and conservative Evangelical Christians can accept. The same pattern might also be observed in the debates where disagreements about the particulars of the different faiths are superseded by an appeal to a shared value of decency or humanity. What are most important, at least rhetorically, are the things that bring people together rather than those that pull them apart.

At the same time, the trajectory of the discourse from the representation of disagreement within the faith to a resolution where belief in Jesus is a neutral, shared storyline negates the potentially quite heated rhetoric of disagreement, particularly the positioning of the force misleading Christians as the 'enemy' in a storyline of war. Although a shared belief in Jesus might resolve the conflict in the context of the podcast, the danger of this positioning and the storyline that emerges from it suggest that the same forces that lead to contemporary violence between Christians and Muslims (which is rhetorically defused in appeals to shared humanity) is also latent in these storylines. Richardson and Pihlaja (2018) have made this observation in representations of Muslims by Evangelical Christian apologists, showing that activating violence in negative positioning of others, particularly when the positioning is malignant and the voice of the other is removed from discourse, has the potential for positionings to not be resolved in positive ways. This should not be ignored, particularly in contemporary contexts where violence against religious believers has been well publicised in attacks on places of worship by individuals who come to see those of differing beliefs as enemies who need to be physically destroyed.

For the *Bad Christian* podcast hosts, the challenge is resolving questions about biblical inerrancy as they relate to scientific developments, but these questions remain largely intellectual with the exception, perhaps, of the issues surrounding sexuality and whether a church will 'affirm' same-sex couples. For Muslims, however, the question of living in a halal, or right, manner in the contemporary world often requires making decisions about the extent they should take part in what are considered normal activities for people living in non-majority Muslim societies. Living a life as a person of faith where one's religious beliefs and practice are in the majority and largely understood, even when others don't necessarily follow the practices, is far simpler than living as a pious Muslim in the United Kingdom or the United States, where one doesn't enjoy this same acceptance. Discussions about how contemporary religious life and what should and should not be accepted are then more pressing, because they potentially have serious consequences for how an individual is viewed and how their actions reflect on Islam more generally.

We have seen how different authority figures, particularly sheikhs, play a crucial role in Ali Dawah's videos, in helping resolve questions about the faith. These questions are often positioned as coming from young people who are attempting to live with an underlying concern for the commitments of right belief and practice but meet the expectations of, for example, a regular worker in a supermarket. Like the tension of belief in biblical inerrancy and scientific discovery, the questions to Ali Dawah often suggest a tension between the requirements of a religious belief and a changing world where the practice of faith might not be understood, particularly when Islam is a minority religion as it is in the United Kingdom where Ali Dawah makes a majority of his videos. The process for making these moral judgements is necessarily discursive (Jayyusi, 1984), because it involves taking concepts from sacred texts and institutional authorities and applying them to contemporary contexts. The question, for example, around nasheeds and what counts or doesn't count as music requires discursive work to establish and maintain boundaries, because the questions are not empirical ones.

In Ali Dawah's videos which feature the physical presence of sheikhs or where their opinions are represented in discourse, he is deferential to their opinion; while he may question them or ask for clarity, the participants in the discussions are not positioned as equals. Ali is seeking the advice of the sheikh, and at the end of the video, the opinion of the sheikh is presented as the final word without Ali's own interpretation. Even when there is disagreement about what is right belief and practice, Ali and in the case of the discussion of the nasheeds, his co-host Musa present themselves as being deferential to the authorities, even those with whom they disagree.

Disagreement between Ali Dawah and his peers, however, is positioned in a different way. When Ali and his friend Musa discuss their decision to promote a nasheed artist in the video *ARE NASHEEDS REALLY HARAM??* (A8, see Appendix), the complaint about their use of nasheeds doesn't come from an authoritative figure, but an unnamed group of people who are described as 'brothers' (that is, Muslims), but these brothers are not represented as holding positions of authority. Ali and Musa address the criticism they've received, and Ali introduces his position by saying:

Extract 5-10
Obviously
as you guys know
we released a Nasheed video
uh
and in this Nasheed video
um
a lot of people start getting a panic attack
or should we call it
a piety attack
uh
basically
saying
it's not permissible
you know
it looks haram

you know
you guys are you are
imitating the Kafir [non-Muslims]
with your hand movements
you know
[...]
he's trying to make his
voice sound like a woman
that's imitating the woman
which is backbiting
cause you don't know if he's
he's doing that
just got his voice a certain way
um
and
all these kind of mannerisms going on
like you use music
uh
blah blah blah blah blah

The presentation of the pushback that the video received from 'a lot of people' is at first described as a 'panic attack' that Ali then changes to a 'piety attack', positioning those who have criticised their nasheed video as being reactionary in an emotional way that includes a religious rational for the reaction. The positioning of those critical of the video delegitimises their complaints from the outset and positions Ali and Musa as magnanimous in responding to them. Their complaints about the nasheed are further expanded with Ali saying people have taken issue with different elements of the video because it 'looks' haram. Ali notes a couple of complaints about the specifics of the video including the 'hand movements' and that the performer is trying to make his 'voice sound like a woman', and a more general complaint that includes 'all these mannerisms'. Although the complaints are voiced, Ali positions himself as having stopped listening and ends saying 'blah blah blah blah blah' to emphasise his feeling that the complaints are not valid nor genuine.

Key to this particular argument is to what extent the video that Ali has supported falls within the boundaries of acceptable behaviour for Muslims. Although Ali doesn't explicate specifically his understanding of what is acceptable, the voicing of the complaints shows the perceived problems in the video: primarily that it could be seen as imitating the *kafir*, and therefore not acceptable for Muslims. However, the grounds by which the video could be considered an imitation of the *kafir* are less clearly defined, with judgements about mannerisms and whether the singer was 'imitating a woman', and even what exactly constitutes 'music'. Each of these complaints against the video involves some question of the degree to which an action may be acceptable and what one's intentions were, all of which require some moral judgement and interpretation on the part of the person making the complaint.

The judgement about intention seems to be the most troubling one for Ali in his positioning of himself, and his response suggests a need to not only defend the actions in the video itself as halal but his own intentions in making the video as also being good. The video represents an implicit contradiction between two positions that Ali takes within it. First, he positions the people complaining about his support for the nasheed video as not legitimate and not made in good faith. Second, the complaints against the video and the use of nasheeds in general represent a legitimate concern and are serious enough to warrant a response from Ali and Musa. How they respond suggests that the complaints about the video, even if they are not presented in a way that Ali feels is legitimate, do represent a topic that should be addressed. The positioning of the complaints and the people making them however as over-reacting does contribute to an implicit positioning of Ali as simply trying to do what is right while others attack him for what are essentially trivial issues.

The discussion of whether nasheeds in general, and this video in particular, are acceptable within Islam is at times positioned as a legitimate concern, but Ali talk about those making complaints about the video does not represent them as voicing a legitimate concern, but instead as manipulating religion to attempt to delegitimise Ali. As he progresses in the video, the argument against those complaining about it becomes more serious, as he says:

Extract 5-11
Ali: You make what Allah's made halal [acceptable]
haram [unacceptable]
it's like me sitting here in front of you
brothers and sisters
this is halal
I have no qualification
whatsoever to tell you this is halal
that's why I'm giving you evidence
[Musa: yes]
Ali: these same brothers
it's haram bro
it's haram
[Musa: yeah]
Ali: and if these scholars came and said it's haram
we will put hands up
we put our hands up

This extract presents the problem as much more serious than the initial positioning of 'a lot of people' complaining about the video. Instead of simply having a 'piety attack', Ali positions those criticising him as making 'what

Allah's made halal, haram' and doing so despite Ali 'giving you evidence' that it is not in fact haram. Ali further contrasts himself with his detractors, as he is logical and using evidence while his opponents use surface-level criticisms about how something may or may not look. His positions his actions as being motivated by right intent, because he has thought through the video and the potential concerns that might arise from doing it. Even if the video is eventually judged to be wrong, he has acted only after taking proper precautions. By contrast, in the description of the brothers contradicting Allah, the positioning of his critics goes beyond the 'blah blah blah blah blah' description of the earlier complaints. They are now not simply criticising a YouTube video but acting in opposition to Allah and contradicting Allah's commands.

Ali also positions himself as having 'no authority' and 'no qualification' to decide what is or is not halal, drawing an implicit contrast with the brothers making the comments. Ali instead positions himself as acting after having looked carefully at evidence, but also being will to change his mind if he is presented with new evidence. What this evidence is precisely is not clearly defined and it's also not clear what Ali might accept as a legitimate complaint against his actions. A key part of this positioning is to present himself as under the authority of 'scholars' and willing to accept their judgement about his actions, although he is not clear in this part of the video which scholars to whom he sees himself as being subject. He positions himself as eager to take advice and says 'we will put hands up, we put our hands up' showing a sign of surrender and making clear that he is willing to stop making the videos if they are indeed haram. The complaints against him are then positioned as not being illegitimate because they are complaints, but because they don't have the required support that Ali argues is necessary to stop him from making the video – those complaining about him are not providing 'evidence'.

This positioning of those complaining about the video is an attempt at re-telling the same story, with the positions of the actors reversed. Whereas the initial complaints positioned those making the complaints as righteously opposing a negative, diluting force in the belief and practice of Islam, Ali's response positions those making the complaints as being the negative force in the religion. In both the comments opposing Ali and Ali's own discourse, the same abstract storyline of Muslims going against the will of Allah is present, with the actions and words of those to whom one is opposed taking the position of the person acting wrongly. The extract again highlights how the same storylines can be told in symmetrical ways, with no disagreement about what the problem is conceptually – both sides agreeing that going against the will of Allah and trying to make rules for right behaviour for oneself are unacceptable. Instead, the argument is about the interpretation of particular actions and their motivations. Because these are not empirically observable phenomena and require making sense of why people are doing what they do, there is always space to disagree over the meaning of any ambiguous action.

Ali takes care to position himself and his intentions as good, particularly his own ability to take criticism and consider what people say about what he does, while implicitly questioning the motives of those who are criticising him. Ali says:

Extract 5-12
> We respect your opinion
> respect our opinion
> we will carry on doing what we're doing
> you can do backflips
> yeah
> you can do front flips
> do somersaults if you like
> yeah
> we will
> we've got evidence behind it

Despite the initial positioning of those making complaints against him as having a 'panic' or a 'piety attack', Ali makes clear that 'we respect your opinion'. At the same time, he positions them as doing 'backflips', 'front flips', and 'somersaults', suggesting that their arguments require a great deal of performative effort, while his argument is simply supported by 'evidence'. Addressing the people who have voiced complaints against the video as the audience with the second-person address 'you' suggests that Ali assumes that the same detractors are watching his videos regularly, similar to evidence I have shown in previous research about ongoing 'antagonistic' relationships on YouTube (Pihlaja, 2014a). The opinions of those who have made comments about the video aren't treated as legitimate complaints in the same ways as the disagreements among scholars. Ali's response to the critics shows that the complaints against him represent a different kind of criticism, one that is based in trying to undermine him as a YouTube and social media personality, rather than to have a legitimate argument about the rightness or wrongness of his beliefs and actions. His video shows that he intends to continue acting in the way that he has, regardless and in spite of the criticism that he has received.

In terms of the actual disagreement about whether nasheeds should be considered halal, Ali's response is, as we have seen in the previous chapter, to claim the authority of the Kibar al-'Ulama, the council of judiciary scholars based in Saudi Arabia. The evidence is simply that scholars have looked at the issue and made rulings that agree with Ali in this case, they have looked specifically at the video that was made and agreed that it should be considered halal. Importantly, no criteria are given for the ruling, simply that the authorities that Ali claims to be following have accepted the video. In this way, the resolution to the argument follows a traditional path, wherein lay members of religious communities appeal to scholars and religious authorities to give judgements about right belief and practice and deference is shown to them.

The response to the criticism that he receives about the videos highlights the problematic nature of presenting religious content in public spaces, particularly on social media, where the arguments about right belief and practice are intermingled with other issues about Ali's personality and his presentation of Islam. How the bulk of his audience sees him, however, and whether his positioning of himself and his status as an influencer rather than a religious authority are hard to judge. The questioning of his authority opens up a series of larger issues about the extent to which individuals who have been successful in representing themselves in media contexts are and should be seen as authorities on questions of theology. What social media allows is the immediate presence of those detractors in the conversation about the content that Ali is producing and a perceived need to respond to their arguments against him to maintain his authenticity as a social media person.

The 'Ask the Sheikh' videos which focused on discussions over whether working at a large supermarket (including selling alcohol and pork) and buying car insurance should be considered acceptable also include the difficult nuances of how young Muslims in particular should make moral decisions when confronted with aspects of contemporary life. Regardless of how the videos position the sheikh and Ali as trying to help young people navigate the difficulties of contemporary life, they faced clear resistance in the video comments. Although Ali does at points press the sheikh on specific positions, there is little open disagreement with him and Ali maintains a respectful demeanour and eventually accepts the sheikh's ruling. Commenters, however, show less deference to the sheikh and disagreements which voice traditional positions against alcohol can also be viewed in the comments.

In the video *CAN I SELL ALCOHOL & PORK AT WORK? (SPECIFIC FATWA) || Ask the Sheikh* (A7, see Appendix), commenters take issue with the sheikh's position that people working in supermarkets are not necessarily 'selling' or 'serving' alcohol when they scan items. The video had 438 comments at the time of analysis, including both supporters and detractors of the sheikh. Of those disagreeing with him, a level of respect for his position can still be observed. The following exemplar comments come from this specific video:

Extract 5-13

Narrated from Ibn 'Umar that the Messenger of Allah (ﷺ) said: "Wine is cursed from ten angles:
1   The wine itself, the one who squeezes (the grapes etc.), the one for whom it is squeezed, the one who sells it, the one who buys it, the one who CARRIES it, the one to whom it is carried, the one who consumes its price, the one who drinks it and the one who pours it." Sunan Ibn Majah.
2   It doesn't take a scholar to know that alcohol is haram. So in this case as I not drinking the alcohol I can work in a pub and work in nightclubs where alcohol is present as I am not drinking it. Also I don't think that that is the only answer. Go to the job centre a seek job seekers allowance. They is not excuse on the matter of alcohol. Alcohol is the mother of sins.
3   Sorry sheikh but your information is wrong. We are not even allowed to touch alcohol. Also even if someone is 'scanning' the alcohol (I personally believe it's selling) he handed it to someone who drinks it and we all know what alcohol can cause. That person is basically responsible for that.
4   Im sorry but I disagree. ANY handling wich helps facilitate the selling of alcohol/pork is haram. It's the like working at a bank while you don't own the money you do take notes about riba and the Prophet (pbuh) said in a Hadith it is haram to receive, to give AND deal with Riba!

NB The Arabic 'ﷺ' means 'Peace be upon him.'

In disagreeing with the sheikh's opinion, commenters employ different strategies which appeal to different authorities in different ways. The first commenter uses a quote from hadith to challenge the specific point from the sheikh about whether simply touching the alcohol is haram, by putting the word 'CARRIES' in all upper case to highlight the point that it is not acceptable. This same strategy can be seen in other comments which quote from hadith and expound on the positions or simply copy and paste large portions of text, suggesting that the position of the sheikh should be disregarded. Many comments also argue that the reasoning Sheikh Haitham has used could be potentially problematic, as seen in comments 2–4: first, on account that the scanning of the alcohol is not selling, and second, whether there is some level of 'necessity' for certain people in having to work in supermarkets. The fourth comment makes an analogy to working in a bank, arguing that the same reasoning the sheikh has used could be applied to a different context, one which they all agree is haram.

These different strategies show that disagreements about religious belief and practice cannot be simply resolved with appeals to a single authority, and differing opinions will arise when attempting to apply religious law in the contemporary world. However, the comments do not appear to be critical of the sheikh's or Ali's intentions in making the videos, and deference to the sheikh is prominent. Two of the comments also begin with 'sorry', marking their politeness in the response, rather than simply attacking either the sheikh or Ali. Another commenter hedges their disagreement with the phrase 'No personal disrespect to the sheikh or ali' while another writes 'I humbly Disagree with sheikh.'

These responses suggest that disagreements with people in positions of authority are different from responses to others in the comments, where the users can be much more aggressive. At the same time, the authority of any individual commenter is not established in the same way as Sheikh Haitham's authority. Commentators even take issue with the notion that anyone online can voice their opinion and try to act as an authority, with one user bemoaning 'self-proclaimed (internet) shuyukh [sheikh] who probably don't even study the religion and don't even go to most of the lectures and study group'. Commenters supporting the sheikh's position make the repeated point that those disagreeing with the sheikh do not have his level of 'knowledge'.

In addition to arguing with the sheikh himself, of the more than 438 comments, 41 receive at least one reply and 10 comments received 10 or more replies, mostly in cases where an argument about the original comment develops. Of these most discussed comments, 5 focus on the topic of the video – what should be considered forbidden as a part of one's normal work. In these arguments back and forth between commenters, the issue of the sheikh's authority does come into play when commenters respond to one another. The third comment in Extract 5–13 results in a back-and-forth discussion:

Extract 5-14
User 1
where have you studied o noble scholar?
User 2
Neesha sessions [popular YouTube dawah preacher] are going to clarify this matter with the truth. Anyone who takes these guys seriously who are passing baseless fatwas left and right, is either ignorant or upon their desires or both. I don't even understand what Ali is doing giving Hadad such a platform where he can announce to the masses that Uni loans (interest/riba) are halal and carrying alcohol is halal etc. Astaghfirullah.
User 1
USER 2 NAME who are they? what scholars have they studied, I don't take my religion from a bunch of children from Neesha sessions loool
User 2
You don't have to have in depth knowledge to understand the basics of your religion. And people who are actual students of knowledge will tell you the same; this ruling that Hadad pulled from the back of his pocket, is baseless. Quotes a vague

Aya from the Quran as evidence. Narrated from Ibn 'Umar that the Messenger of Allah (ﷺ) said:
'Wine is cursed from ten angles: The wine itself, the one who squeezes (the grapes etc.), the one for whom it is squeezed, the one who sells it, the one who buys it, the one who CARRIES it, the one to whom it is carried, the one who consumes its price, the one who drinks it and the one who pours it.' Sunan Ibn Majah.

User 1
USER 2 NAME so sheikh doesn't know the basics LOOOL wallahi listen to yourself and fear Allah. salam

User 2
'I have never debated with a knowledgeable person, except that I won, and I have never debated with an ignorant person, except that I lost.' – Imam Shafiee. Wa-Alaikum-Salaam

The argument here starts with a reference to the user who made the first comment but who doesn't respond. Instead, as User 1 and User 2 respond to different points in the comments, they eventually come into dialogue with each other specifically and their argument devolves from one about the topic of the video to whether either of them is knowledgeable enough to argue with the other. User 2 ends the exchange by implying that the argument is pointless because the other users are too ignorant to be debated. The two position each other as not having enough training and knowledge to engage in the argument, making the opposing position illegitimate without necessarily questioning the motivation or religiosity of the person with whom they are arguing.

In many ways, this represents an exemplar YouTube comment exchange between users of the same religious belief. They argue with each other and question each other's evidence, becoming frustrated and disengaging, and then ultimately offering some concession to position themselves as acting in good faith. Users write and delete comments and the resulting discussions can be fractured and disjointed. Here, User 2 later comments 'may Allah increase me in patience because I get a little zealous with issues of such', and User 1, responding to another user writes, 'we can agree to disagree on which scholars we follow, thanks :)'. Despite the disagreement among the users, positioning oneself as being magnanimous even when rejecting the opinions of others in harsh ways appears important to maintaining a respected position.

Notably, of the ten comments that receive at least ten replies, two are not on the main topic of the video, and two focus explicitly on the issue of gender and whether the video is misogynistic. A minor point in the video that the sheikh makes in addition to his fatwa on whether the scanning of alcohol should be considered selling revolves around whether the woman should be working at all. He comments that the 'real career' of women is to be mothers but moves on from the topic because the focus of the question in the video is on the necessity of the work. However, because the discussion of gender roles is a prominent contemporary issue, the commenters ultimately move away from the specific fatwa about the selling of alcohol to related disagreements.

The comments and how they develop into different arguments is perhaps unsurprising in one sense – Ali has explicitly taken on a topic that might be seen as controversial because it is, he shows, a genuine concern for one of his viewers. Because the issue is not a clearly settled one, the idea that a fatwa, or judgement, is needed is a part of the practice of Islam; however, because the video is done publicly and the video page provides an affordance for users to comment on anything, from the physical context of the video, to criticising Ali's haircut, to asking whether it's haram to monetise YouTube videos. The forum creates space for a range of different opinions and judgements about Ali and the sheikh.

The introduction to the video *IS CAR INSURANCE HARAM? Ask the Sheikh* (A2, see Appendix) discussing the issues of car insurance shows the pressure that Ali and Sheikh Haitham received from those within Islam claiming that they have 'made alcohol halal' with Sheikh Haitham's fatwa that the woman should be allowed to continue to do her job, even if it requires touching alcohol and pork. The original video title is amended to say '(Specific Fatwa)' and Ali is even more explicit in his rejection of a particular kind of criticism of his work. He posts the following statement on the screen, responding to critics:

Extract 5-15
Some people have the disease of critising [sic] all the time. They forget the good about others and only mention their faults. They are like flies that avoid the good and pure places and land on the bad and wounds. This is because of the evil within the self and the spoiled nature Ibn Taymiyyah.

Ali's response to the criticism from others, in many ways, is to respond in kind, similar to the final quote in Extract 5-14, which re-voices an authoritative figure's statement to call the opposing user ignorant. In this posted comment, the statement, a quote attributed to the theologian Ibn Taymiyyah, implies that critics do not always act in good faith, and criticism itself is not necessarily admirable, particularly when it does not include self-reflection. Using the quote, Ali suggests that those who have been critical of him and Sheikh Haitham are not doing so out of pure motives, but to simply make trouble. He again implies that they are evil and their actions are motivated by a 'spoiled' nature, similar to the argument that was made in the video responding to the criticism about the nasheeds. At the same time, the actions are described as being the result of having 'the disease of critising [sic] all the time', which suggests the criticism is something that isn't chosen but infects someone unwillingly. It is the result of 'the evil within the self', again suggesting that the users are acting out of something in their 'spoiled nature' which they cannot control.

This direct criticism of those who attack him is the harshest rebuke in the videos here. At the same time, Ali does not single out specific people and instead makes a blanket rejection of a particular type of response to his videos and one that positions him in a battle of good and evil, where those attacking him are part of a force that is bigger than the individuals themselves. In this sense, the response to the other users is not positioned as being small disagreements between people with differing opinions, but a storyline wherein Ali views himself as a force for good which is being opposed by people with a 'disease'.

Challenges to Ali regularly follow this pattern of questioning his intentions and the advice that has been given in a video, highlighting the problems of presenting religious advice more generally in online contexts. Despite adding the words 'specific fatwa' to the video title, users still hear the advice that is given by Ali and Sheikh Haitham as intended for everyone in a similar situation. The videos and the back and forth between different users show the limitations of context design, and the extent to which users can limit their publicly available messages for particular audiences. Regardless of what Ali says and the caveats, the message is still heard as a rationalisation for touching and selling alcohol, something that other users feel very strongly should never be rationalised. There is seemingly nothing that Ali or Sheikh Haitham might say that will change this perception. Moreover, despite Ali's apparent frustration with the criticism that he receives, it does serve a purpose for him in driving interest in his videos and his positioning of himself as a person willing to take controversial positions and to challenge others, something that increases his social capital online.

The disagreements between those of the same faith suggest different pressures on internal discussions about right belief and practice. Perhaps more so than the debates between Shabir Ally and the Christians, there is a focus on attempting to resolve specific points of disagreement, particularly when the medium allows for long protracted debates, as in YouTube comments. In the debates, many of the points of disagreement were not followed up, with the debaters focusing instead on changing the topic to their own line of argument. In online spaces with a written record of an argument, users are much more likely to continue to follow up specific points and respond to the evidence that was presented, without changing the subject. That said, there seems to be little movement in terms of people changing their positions. The users go back and forth, often citing authorities in the same way, but to opposite effect and ultimately arguments resolve with users accepting that they can't come to agreement, the 'we can agree to disagree on which scholars we follow' response.

Despite Ali's line of defence and suggestion that criticisms are challenging his intentions, questions about his good faith in making the videos doesn't appear to be a frequent feature of comments critical of him. The same could also be said of the debates – there are few obvious moments where anyone engaged in a discussion about religious belief suggests that the person with whom they are arguing is intentionally misleading others. People engaged in arguments – whether they are users in the YouTube comments, Sheikh Haitham and Ali Dawah Shabir Ally and his various opponents, or the *Bad Christian* podcast hosts – generally accept that differing opinions exist and even if one disagrees with someone, they should still treat them with respect. Still, there are moments that make clear people believe they are fighting on the side of good in a battle against evil. In many ways, this stands as the grand contradiction of the religious discourse we have analysed – people position themselves as both engaged in a struggle between good and evil and resigned to accept that there are good faith disagreements and that people must accept this diversity both within their own faiths and with people of other faiths as a part of contemporary life.

5.3   Deciding for Yourself

Neoliberalism and the marketisation of religious discourse affect how particular views become favoured over others and 'liberate individual entrepreneurial freedoms' (Harvey, 2007, p. 2) in making decisions about religious belief and practice. Entrepreneurial freedoms in the context of religious discourse mean that different people can rise as authorities on religious issues, but also that individuals are given the responsibility to decipher truth themselves. In the debates, podcast episodes, and YouTube videos, religious beliefs and practices are positioned as an individual's intentional act, and in making decisions about what is right or wrong, the individual must look at the evidence that is presented to them, consider a variety of different positions, and make their own judgement.

Debate is often positioned as a tool for individuals to decide for themselves what they might or might not believe; however, more often than not, debate can simply function as a platform for people to position their own beliefs in contrast to others'. Central to the discussion of right belief and practice throughout the different interactions we've looked at is a lack of clear commands from religious authorities about what people should or should not do, even when making claims based on sacred texts or authorities outside themselves. At no point in the videos or podcasts do the speakers implore people to simply follow what they have been told; indeed, the idea of belief without reasoning is both implicitly and explicitly positioned in a negative way. Instead, there is a repeated, constant reminder for the audiences to consider things for themselves and make their own decisions, and negative positioning of people who tell others how to act and what to believe.

An explicit expectation of audiences and individuals is that they must make choices about right belief and practice. As with the discussion of hell in the *Bad Christian* podcast, speaking about faith in a public space without taking an authoritative position not only allows the speaker to avoid being seen as dictatorial, but it also can result in hearers of that message positioning the speaker in storylines that are amenable to the hearers' own beliefs about the world. Because positionings are dynamic and the storylines that emerge around those positionings are abstract and embedded in particular ideologies, audience members can understand even evidence that might be seen as contradictory to their beliefs in a way that fits a particular storyline. Whether Matt, the *Bad Christian* podcast host, believes or doesn't believe in a literal hell depends on how you hear his own positioning and what storyline emerges from it based on the way that you perceive both his actions and what he says. It's not simply a matter of being right or wrong, but how speakers and hearers make sense of what others are saying.

The importance placed on the individual to make a decision about particular truth claims is also at the core of the rhetoric of debate, albeit often with the heavy suggestion that one position is right while the other is wrong. In the end of his debate with Shabir Ally (D2, see Appendix), the Christian apologist James White says:

Extract 5-16
    I'm here to talk about truth
    and if you walk out of this room tonight
    and you have not thought about these things
    if you did not take
    if you're a Christian
    and you didn't listen to Shabir
    shame on you
    but if you're a Muslim
    and you're not listening to me
    shame on you
    we need to listen to what each other says
    that's the only way
    we're gonna make advancement
    that's the only way
    that we are going to
    really grow
    in understanding

Analysis has shown that the debates serve as a way for Christians and Muslims to present their own beliefs, but the positioning of debate as a way of thinking about differences and seeking truth follows a different storyline, one wherein it is not enough to simply attend the debate in support of the debater who shares one's own beliefs – the audience must think about both positions and decide which one to believe. In this extract, White positions the audience members as failing and acting shamefully if they don't 'think about these things', after reminding them of the main argument he has made in the debate about why the early followers of Jesus believed Jesus was God, but also after listing what he perceives as the problems inherent in the Qur'an's representation of Christian theology. White's final statement foregrounds the agency of the audience members and positions them as needing to be actively engaged with their own belief. It's not enough to simply believe what one already believes – the audience must also believe what they believe with full knowledge of what others believe. Belief requires intellectual labour and 'thinking about these things' is a prerequisite for a faith that is not shameful.

White speaks in the same authoritative tone to both Christians and Muslims and positions the audience as needing to engage with one another and 'listen to what each other says', suggesting not that listening to an opposing side might result in possible changes to one's own beliefs, but that it results in 'advancement' and growing in 'understanding'. This meta-phorical description of understanding as advancement and growth applies to 'we': White says, 'We're gonna make advancement' and 'we are going to really grow in understanding'. This could be heard in several ways: the communities of Christians and Muslims move forward when they listen to one another, or it could be heard as each individual including White and Ally making progress and advancing when they listen to what others have to say. White positions the audience with himself and Ally as working towards an ambiguous outcome, an 'understanding', but it's not clear what the object of the understanding is.

White's vagueness at this point in the debate, where he has his final chance to assert his main argument is illustrative of the difficulty of arguing for a particular religious belief in a multifaith context, particularly when there are believers from both religions present. Neither White nor any of the other debaters make a concerted effort to convert others; the explicit focus of the debates remains on logical arguments, with the debaters and moderators fram-ing the disagreements between religious believers as questions of facts and evidence. The debaters then carefully position the need for finding 'truth' as the ultimate goal. Their apparent reticence to say explicitly that they are right and their opponent is wrong in general terms also contributes to the sense of responsibility for decision-making placed on the audience. White can position himself as someone who merely wants everyone to have all the information that is available so that they can make an informed choice about whom to believe – he's not an aggressor actively advocating for his point of view. By encouraging everyone to grow in 'understanding', he avoids positioning himself as an evangelist, while still suggesting that changes in belief are possible as a kind of advancement.

The focus on 'talking about the truth' in White's statement particularly after again presenting evidence that his position is correct, suggests that his goal is an Evangelical one. Rather than attempting to make credible arguments that may cause their debate partners to change their minds, the arguments more often than not just offer further support for an audience of confessional believers who already share the same faith. Despite the rhetoric of advancement and understanding, neither of the debaters appears to be open to changes in their fundamental positions. Because they serve as exemplar members of faith categories for audience members, their own lack of concession also suggests that the stated focus on individual choice and making informed decisions might not necessarily be genuine. Both debaters quite obviously believe that their own 'truth' is the correct one, even while they position themselves in amenable ways and present storylines of mutual understanding. Although they arguably might be modelling understanding, they never present themselves as changing their minds.

The positioning of one's own faith as a genuine individual conviction, however, is also an important part of the 'individual entrepreneurial freedoms' of a market economy. White and Ally both position themselves as following their own religions out of an authentic conviction that they are right. Because of this positioning by both of them, they are limited in the extent to which they can undermine the claims of the other. If both value their own sincere beliefs and position their own sincerity as a hallmark of the truth of what they claim, undermining the other requires challenging the other's sincerity or suggesting that the other's positioning of themselves and their faith is in some way inauthentic. This further limits their ability to conduct a genuine debate about the truth of each other's claims, while still positioning individual convictions and freedoms as a fundamental prerequisite for faith. Debaters (and Ali Dawah and the *Bad Christian* podcast hosts as well) avoid personal attacks as a part of positioning themselves in a positive way, further limiting their ability to completely challenge others.

Following one's own convictions is also a recurring theme in the *Bad Christian* podcast, particularly for the host Joey, a full-time pastor, whose shifting views on hell and biblical inerrancy become the topic of discussion on several occasions. Although all three of the hosts present themselves as struggling with similar issues, Joey's decision to reject a belief in a literal hell becomes an exemplar case of how beliefs can change and how each individual's belief is their own 'journey', a metaphorical description of change that is positive and suggests a developing view of God and the Bible is moving forward towards a goal in one's faith. However, theses developments in faith are positioned as acceptable only so long as they occur as the result of genuine individual conviction and are not the result of personal advancement, which by contrast is something the hosts regularly ridicule when they identify it in others, particularly Christian leaders whom they position as self-serving.

In a discussion of Joey's changing beliefs, the *Bad Christian* host who serves as a pastor, Toby describes Joey's changing belief the following way (BC5, see Appendix):

Extract 5-17
> For example
> like Joey
> you now believe
> most likely
> that it's annihilation
> -ism
> right
> but the reason why you believe that
> is because you like it better
> it could be true
> it could not be true
> God could send people to hell forever
> or he could annihilate them
> but
> the reason that you sought after that answer
> is because you wanted something that was true
> to you that you could accept
> and that you could
> appreciate
> and value
> and go
> God
> this lines up
> with how I want to see God
> and maybe who God is

Joey's own feelings about hell are positioned initially in a negative way. Toby says that Joey has taken this position because Joey 'likes it better'. However, the decision to believe in one thing over another is presented as arbitrary – Toby says simply 'It could be true, it could be not true' and makes the point that the different ways of addressing the judgement of God in hell are equally acceptable. In his interpretation of Joey's actions, Toby sees the decision as primarily one of attempting to make different beliefs align – whether Joey's metaphorical 'view' of God matches his belief about hell. The two beliefs are connected, and Toby continues to use the language of desire and choice, saying that Joey's choice is about making sure his belief about hell 'lines up with how I want to see God'. Although Joey's study of the Bible and theology is highlighted throughout the discussion, the decision is ultimately presented as one that is made because it fits Joey's world view, which includes believing in a God who doesn't send people to hell for eternity.

Toby's subsequent comments highlight how shifts of these kinds are at the root of most belief and Joey's honesty about his own developing belief and his use of evidence to support that shift are to be commended. In this part of the conversation, Toby makes the point that changes in belief are not necessarily about alignment with the teachings of a sacred text or particular church authorities but can be motivated by a personal desire – Joey is described as changing his belief about the nature of hell because he liked an alternative position better and he 'wanted something that was true' that he could accept. Although the positioning of this process isn't necessarily positive in and of itself, Joey's authenticity in making the *decision* in an honest way is positioned positively, particularly given his understanding of theology and his attempt to study the topic in an in-depth way. His authenticity makes the decision to believe one thing over another acceptable.

Toby's representation of Joey's change in belief about hell initially sounds like Joey made this decision primarily because of his own desire, but Toby makes a further analogy between Joey's change in belief and the historic shift in some forms of Christianity from a belief about slavery. Toby continues:

Extract 5-18
But I think
when you were going through all that
I started thinking
you know what
many years ago
in the Bible
slavery was okay
that sure doesn't sit right
what does that mean
why can't I wrestle with God about that
like why
why didn't
more people
or why didn't
some
things
end up
just like you said
true things
end up being true
and that's okay

Toby's analogy of things that don't 'sit right' suggests that moral reasoning about what should or should not be accepted as right behaviour and belief is embedded in the experiences of individuals. The fact that something 'doesn't sit right' elevates the judgement of the individual again in making decisions about what positions should be taken and whether something can be defended in theological terms. Because, in retrospect, the positions that religious institutions have taken can, and in some cases should, be viewed in a negative way. The dynamic nature of interpretation of sacred texts and the ability to see and admit that changes in belief do occur allow the hosts to accept that current shifts in belief might also be ultimately positioned in a positive way.

Toby uses the common Evangelical Christian metaphor of 'wrestling with God' to talk about how to deal with parts of a religion that you find disagreeable, creating a space for arguments with God that are acceptable. The phrase alludes to the story of Jacob in Genesis 32:22–32 wherein Jacob wrestles with a man whom he doesn't know, but who the passages suggests is God. Jacob says, 'I have seen God face to face, and my life is preserved.' Although Jacob wrestles with God in the story and he is injured, his life is spared and he is blessed after the experience. Toby's allusion to this verse uses it as a metaphorical storyline for searching for truth. To question God is not inappropriate even if it includes violent struggle and is implicitly sanctioned by the Bible. Positioning Joey as 'wrestling with God' suggests a positive storyline about Joey's engagement with his faith and with God. By thinking about the topic carefully, Joey, or anyone 'struggling' with God', is positioned as having true belief. Moreover, the metaphor of 'wrestling', although it implies mutual violent engagement, suggests a goal of submission rather than destruction. There is no problem 'wrestling with God' because it will, as it did with Jacob, lead to submission – no person can, of course, cause God to submit.

The tautology underpinning Toby's acceptance of difference in beliefs and practices among people is simply 'true things end up being true and that's okay'. The statement highlights the recurring point that the hosts make throughout the episode, that there is no need to worry about 'truth' winning out. The focus is ultimately on the motives and intentions of each person to do what they believe is right and their attempt to study and understand things for themselves. This storyline and the incumbent positionings can accommodate a wider range of beliefs because audience members, even if they hold differing views on, for example, the 'reality of hell', can accept that ultimately 'true things end up being true', assuming that their belief will be proven to be true while others will be proven false.

This discussion of hell and the mutual positioning of the hosts in both this episode and in others shows how mutually affirming contexts can create conditions for acceptance and development of particular positions. Toby's claim that 'true things end up being true and that's okay' works well in a storyline of religious belief and practice as developing and growing over time and where individual errors are corrected, provided someone is committed to seeking the truth. However, this positioning is not acceptable in other storylines about Christian belief that require a more fundamentalist adherence to tenets of belief. Those opposing views are very occasionally voiced in the interaction on the podcast, but none of the hosts adhere to those beliefs and the storyline of authenticity perseveres.

Toby tells a similar story about the development of individual faith, discussing his relationship with a friend who came out to him as a lesbian (BC7, see Appendix). Toby says:

Extract 5-19
What has really brought me over the edge is
is a
is a girl that I know specifically
and she
actually
came to me for counsel
years ago
and basically said
I'm struggling
uh
with
with lesbian tendencies
and this girl
has been brought up in church
uh
you know
hardcore conservative
and she's coming to me because she's like
this is a sin
and I don't know what to do
well I have like
watched her
process this
this girl
I mean
I'll just
it sounds cliché but
I feel like she has
more of a heart for God
than I do
wants to do the right thing
more than I do
seeks God
more than I do
and here she is now
and she's like
I think this is okay

and if God told me otherwise
I wouldn't be a lesbian

As in the discussion of hell, the woman who Toby talks about is positioned as 'struggling', in this case with 'lesbian tendencies'. His positioning of her focuses again on her motives by saying she was 'brought up in church' and is a 'hardcore Christian'. She is further described as having a 'heart for God', someone who 'seeks God', and wanting 'to do the right thing'. This positioning builds up the woman in a way that suggests whatever she is doing is fundamentally done in a pure way, and she is someone who is not, as suggested in other places, 'cherry picking' from the Bible or attempting to get away with a negative behaviour as Perry Noble, the pastor who 'struggled' with alcoholism, was positioned. Instead, she is positioned as a person who is both acting from pure motives and willing to accept anything required of her, even if it goes against her desires.

Toby reveals that the woman believes that being a lesbian is 'okay', but he is still very careful to hedge his statements about his position. He says presumably in the voice of the woman thinking about her decision to accept her homosexuality, 'This is okay', even though what 'this' stands for is not explicitly clear in relation to what he has said previously. In revealing her decision about coming out, she says not that God told her it was okay, but rather 'If God told me otherwise, I wouldn't be a lesbian.' The structure of the positioning shows Toby's own reticence in talking about the issue and how what she claims as right for her does not align with orthodox thinking about sexual orientation within Evangelical Christianity. Toby cannot simply say that she is both a Christian and a lesbian – he must highlight and foreground her piety as a Christian first. However, that piety allows for her actions to then be understood as sanctioned by God, because it is impossible for her to be both a pious Christian who is seeking God on this particular issue and also acting in bad faith or making the wrong decision.

Toby's talk about the topic shows how personal freedom with pure motives is the ultimate arbitrator of whether an individual's actions should be considered right or wrong when there is a 'grey area' of faith, something that can be seen in storylines constructing gay Evangelical Christian identities (Thumma, 1991). Toby's storyline implies that it is possible, at least from Toby's point of view, for homosexuals and lesbians to be Christians, provided that they have carefully considered their 'choice' and made a visible and obvious effort to do what they believe is right. This moral reasoning is implicit in the positioning of the woman – Toby doesn't make this an explicit prerequisite for the validity of the choice, but the storyline shows it to be the case. In the process, he shows the same 'emotional atunement' that Richardson (2017) analyses in Muslim-Christian interaction. Toby accepts the positioning of the woman because he empathises with her and her decisions can be understood in a storyline of wanting to 'do the right thing'.

The extent to which he and the other hosts are apparently uncomfortable discussing the issue and avoid making direct comments suggests that it is not necessarily an easy process or one that is quickly accepted, but one that given the right conditions should be positioned in a storyline of following God. Moreover, this logic doesn't apply to every potential issue of disagreement and the *Bad Christian* hosts particularly focus on areas where there appears to be a shift in culture that is not necessarily reflected in the Evangelical Christianity within which they are active. They position themselves as living in a dynamic environment where the culture develops more broadly and Evangelical Christians must act within that environment. Where there are questions about right belief and practice, the hosts make clear that there are many possible ways that Christians might act; however, when a person is clearly acting in self-interest, their decision, whatever it is, is unacceptable. Alternatively, if a person is 'seeking God' and is, by all accounts, a pious believer, their choice must not only be respected but should also be viewed in a positive way, as a marker of their own authentic commitment to their religious beliefs.

The issue of one's motivation in making moral choices is apparent in Ali Dawah's videos. As I have shown earlier, it was a key part of the rationale for defending the use of nasheeds, which involved arguing that neither Ali Dawah nor the artist in the nasheed videos was trying to bring honour to themselves. It was also a part of the moral reasoning around whether the woman working in the supermarket should or shouldn't sell alcohol. Her need to support her family and her interest in doing the right thing were used as evidence that it was okay, in her case, to scan the alcohol. The issue of authenticity and motivation was also part of the moral reasoning used in offering forgiveness to the woman who had been video recorded twerking on the street in a hijab. The condition of her own thinking and her willingness to admit her mistake resulted in Ali Dawah and Musa positioning her and her actions in a different way, after having been judgemental of her.

At the same time, there is a clearer sense of authority and authority structures in the videos about deciding what is haram, and in particular the use of the word *fatwa* or judgement in describing the sheikh's opinion implies that there are clear right and wrong behaviours that can be decided. However, the discussion of personal responsibility in making decisions about what should or shouldn't be done is also present in the Sheikh Haitham's talks with Ali Dawah In the video discussing whether insurance should be considered haram entitled *IS CAR INSURANCE HARAM? AskTheSheikh* (A2, see Appendix) because it might result in a person making money without working for it. We previously discussed the video in terms of what it says about living in contemporary contexts, and the difficulty of resolving whether a car is 'needed'. Although the issue is presented as one where there might not be an obvious answer, Ali and the sheikh have the following exchange, making it clear that the responsibility for deciding what is or is not haram is the work of 'scholars' not individuals:

Extract 5-20

Ali: Now Sheikh
when you say necessity
is it really a necessity for the car
because we can say
look there is a bus
there is coaches
there is trains
there is taxi
you can walk
Sheikh: yeah
Ali: it's actually better for the environment
if you're walking
Sheikh: yeah
Ali: so
how do we determine necessity out of this
Sheikh: yeah
see
in terms of necessity
this is something
the scholars should
decide
yeah
Ali: so
so not a
any layman
Sheikh: yeah not layman
okay

In this interaction, the point of personal responsibility is backgrounded, but the presentation of the opinion is given first as a logical statement about 'necessity', that it may not actually be a fact that someone 'needs' a car. However, Ali is careful to not make a direct statement about whether any individual person needs a car, stating it as a question: 'Is it really a necessity for the car' before listing other possibilities for transportation. Ending the list with 'walking', Ali further supports it as a good thing to do, saying it's better for the environment. These reasons, however, are given in support of a ruling that is presented as a non-negotiable point that car insurance can only be purchased in situations where it is absolutely necessary.

However, although these reasons are given, the sheikh makes clear that the decision about whether something is necessary should not be left to an individual, particular a 'layman'. Necessity might differ between people, but there are limits to the extent to which individual needs should be taken into account in deciding on right and wrong behaviour. In the case of the car, the decision should be made – and the sheikh suggests has already been made – by scholars. Although the decision about whether to own a car is a necessity is positioned as being a genuine question, the sheikh makes clear that it is not. This does not mean that a situation of genuine necessity doesn't exist, but that exceptions to an accepted ruling can't be used by people to do whatever they want.

At the same time, the sheikh describes his frustration with people who come to him and ask for his approval, in this case about the need to produce a letter of credit to open a limited liability company (LLC) in the United Kingdom. In this case, the sheikh offers a different answer:

Extract 5-21
> **Sheikh:** so it's not about
> many people
> call Sheikh
> I have to do LLCs
> is it halal or haram
> I say Habibi [Beloved]
> can you
> avoid it
> **Ali:** no
> **Sheikh:** they say no
> by the law
> I say then
> why are you asking me
> now
> then Sheikh
> don't take rubber stamp from me
> you need to ask me
> how can I minimize the haram
> or how can I deal with it

Although the discussion of car ownership and car insurance is positioned as something that can and should be avoided, based on the ruling of scholars, the question of whether one can acquire a letter of credit is presented as a genuine area where necessity might not be clear. The sheikh describes his own judgement being seen by others as a 'rubber stamp', but he makes the point that the real question is not whether something is appropriate, because the concept of 'necessity' applies clearly in this context. Here the responsibility is placed on the individual asking for support from the sheikh rather than the scholars, and the sheikh offers a heuristic about whether something is genuinely needed and whether a person can 'minimize the haram' and how they might 'deal with it'. The sheikh positions himself as ultimately being unable to help, with the responsibility lying on the individual and their own conscience.

The discussion of 'necessity' in these videos places more importance on the individual's judgement, but the point that Muslims are positioned in these stories as seeking out the sheikh's advice suggests some reticence to the idea that individuals are capable of making decisions about religious practice for themselves and different scenarios and questions require different responses – there are some decisions that can be made by the individual and some that can't be. People must decide for themselves whether they attain a letter of credit to start a business or work in a job that occasionally requires them to do things that might be considered haram, like touching pork and alcohol, but not in the case of car insurance, which is presented as a settled case, one that the scholars have already decided.

As with the *Bad Christian* podcast, different decisions and different positions are presented as being non-negotiable questions of moral judgement while others are not. However, what is fixed, in the cases we have seen in this chapter, is open for interpretation and because the issues are represented as being confusing for individuals, even where, for example, the sheikh takes a clear position that car insurance is haram, the issue is clearly not resolved. The same could be said about homosexuality in the *Bad Christian* podcast where, although the positioning of the woman who comes out as a lesbian to Toby is positioned in an ultimately positive way, Toby's talk about it and his hedging show that it is not a resolved issue and others will disagree with him. Positioning oneself and others within particular storylines does not then resolve the fact that alternative storylines exist and a part of one's positioning of one's self and others must be some awareness, be it implicit or explicit, of the ways in which others might tell a different story about the same circumstances, internalising that debate, and in your own storyline, accounting for those dissenting voices.

In issues where there is disagreement, speakers also position their choices as the result of study and contemplation, as well as a willingness to be convinced of another point of view. In discussing the appropriateness of the nasheeds, Ali says in *ARE NASHEEDS REALLY HARAM?? ALI DAWAH* (A8, see Appendix) describing their instructions to Musa's friend who takes their video to various scholars to see if it is right says:

Extract 5-22
    Please find out for us
    is it halal
    is it haram
    what's wrong with it
    if it was haram
    me and Ali
    and Omar [the nasheed artist]

we're
we're fully willing to take it down
and never do any of this again

Freedom to decide for oneself what is or isn't wrong is not necessarily seen as desirable; particularly within the videos where people are seeking advice from Ali and the sheikh, there is evidence of a felt need for guidance or confirmation before making a decision. Ali and Musa do not position themselves as wanting their actions to be simply seen as right. Instead, Ali positions both himself and Musa as *attempting* to do what is right, not justifying their choice to make the nasheed video without reasoning. They position themselves as willing to be corrected and to be told by appropriate authorities that what they have done is wrong and then to correct themselves and 'never do it again'. Although implicitly, they may be positioning themselves as having made the right decision and done nothing wrong, the storyline suggests that more important than that is their own willingness to seek out the truth and do what is right.

The discussions about what should be considered haram provide an explicit example of what also appears to be occurring in the *Bad Christian* podcast in a more implicit way. Although there is personal responsibility in making choices about right and wrong belief and practice, there are also clear red lines where this reasoning doesn't apply. Those red lines, however, shift depending on the cultural context. The example of homosexuality in Evangelical Christianity perhaps presents the clearest example of that shift in process and the discursive mechanisms that make it possible for a Christian to move from one position to the next. It is not simply the switching on and off of a belief but a complex interaction between stories about particular individuals in particular contexts, analogies to other shifts in belief over time, and a discussion about personal responsibility and whether someone is acting with selfish motivations.

The evidence from the interaction suggests limitations to a 'truth is truth' model of deciding what is right belief and practice. Instead, it seems more accurate that the speakers are grappling with shifting truths and how to weigh up the teaching of texts and authorities, tradition, and individual piety and intention. Tradition and what is accepted as right belief and practice within a religious community is the most obvious default position, and going against what is accepted as right in a community appears to require the most discursive work even when one is moving in the direction of cultural change. Mediatisation, however, does appear to have an effect on the speed at which change might happen, as fixed local ways of thinking about right and wrong belief and behaviour can be more quickly challenged by evidence brought to bear from other contexts.

At the same time, religious belief and practice don't always or consistently travel in the direction of cultural change, as in the discussion of car insurance, a widely accepted cultural practice in the West. Different issues arise in different communities and how the issues are resolved can vary drastically. A marked difference can be observed, for example, in the role of authority when comparing the *Bad Christian* podcast hosts and Ali Dawah, particularly in how they position themselves in relation to institutional leaders. The differences in how they relate to one another, their sacred texts, and the opinions of those in authority show the ways in which attempts to make meaningful comparisons between different religious beliefs and their interaction with a secular society begin to dissolve under the scrutiny of close analysis of discourse. How Ali Dawah talks about this interaction with the broader society and how the *Bad Christian* podcasts hosts do are radically different. There are, of course, a myriad of factors that need to be considered in thinking about why that's the case and how the different speakers orient to different concerns at different times.

What is clear, however, is that although a simplistic description of context is not a *deus ex machina* (Browse, 2019) providing a catch-all explanation for everything that occurs in the interactions, neither do the identity or beliefs of any individual. The stories that each individual tells and how they position themselves and others are subject to a range of factors embedded in both the broader cultural world and the specific religious and cultural practices of their own communities. Those beliefs are often implicit and appear in the ways they hedge potentially divergent views or offer apologetic explanations for opinions they view as potentially controversial.

Although there are few consistencies in how people make claims to authority or the heuristics they apply for deciding on right belief and practice, across the different interactions we've observed, the motivation of each individual is consistently a factor in deciding whether someone's opinion should be heard or judged more or less harshly. Authenticity and honesty and the sense that one is not acting simply out of self-interest are common factors in showing that one's actions should be viewed in a positive way, even if they are ultimately judged to be wrong. Moreover, simply believing is not enough – the believer must also carefully consider other possible beliefs. Consistently across all the interactions we've observed is the positioning of the individual as central in figuring out their own faith system, and as someone who needs to represent their own belief as the result of a careful, logical examination. Whatever one believes in the end, that belief can't simply be given or inherited, but the religious believer must make an effort to understand what they believe exactly and why, being able to explain it and defend it against people who hold differing views.

6   Conclusion: The Future of Religious Discourse

In his poem *Treatise on Touch,* David Baker writes about watching his wife undergo medical treatment to alleviate her chronic pain. The poem juxtaposes the medical treatment she receives with her memories as a child of a funeral procession at the Catholic school she attended; the children were lined up and told to kiss the body of a nun who had recently died. Baker makes an implicit comparison between two understandings of pain, one from the perspective of science and one from the perspective of religious belief, neither of which is presented as bringing much comfort to the suffering they are intended to alleviate. In the implicit comparison of the two, Baker challenges the certainty and order both might be understood as imposing on the world. The first line of the poem is a question: 'Whom to believe? This is our central task' (1998, p. 65). He asks two more times, 'Whom to believe', but there is no clear answer. The question remains open, unanswerable.

At their core, all the debates, the question-and-answer YouTube videos, and the back-and-forth about what everyone believes and why, revolve around the question of 'whom to believe' and the various ways religious believers answer this question. The practices that people use to provide answers are, as we have seen, varied, depending on the factors at play in any interaction. How any individual works out what is right belief and practice for themselves differs depending on with whom they are speaking, whom their potential audiences might be, and their own individual histories. Some of these findings should be obvious to us – we know that people speak in different ways with their family than they do with their colleagues. What the analysis has shown is how these processes actually work in different contexts and how positioning can be accounted for both in the individual interactions of people and the storylines that emerge. When examined, they reveal how people understand the social world.

The resources that individual faith systems offer are also different but are not necessarily used uniformly – any attempt to identify a 'Muslim Discourse' or a 'Christian Discourse' would require caveats to the degree that the categories themselves start to become meaningless. Instead, the analysis has shown how positionings and storylines about religious belief and practice emerge in and from interaction and how the conditions of interaction can influence what is considered right belief at any given moment. The Evangelical Christian may denounce historical scholarship at one moment when confronted with opinions that do not fit with their accounting of the world but later use the work of scholars to support a claim. The analysis has shown that religious discourse is dynamic, contextual, and shifting, depending on whom speakers are addressing, both in their physical context and those who might be listening remotely or are told of their opinions in other places.

As a discourse analyst, I am interested in both *what* people do in discourse and *how* they do it. Interaction shows the particular beliefs that people hold and what they think about themselves and those around them, but it also reveals the processes by which those positionings are accomplished. They are not structuralist categories applied in mechanistic ways, with criteria applied based on a sacred text rulebook. Instead, in the interaction of people about particular topics, the role of a range of factors comes into play and people can be observed shifting what they say about themselves, their beliefs, and the beliefs of those around them. How that happens differently depends on the topic, the kind of interaction, the interactants, the physical space, the time – the list of factors that might be relevant is difficult to imagine limiting. This suggests religious belief and practice are far more fluid then we tend to believe when we see others or talk about ourselves. With changes to the contextual factors, we might say we believe something entirely different from what we would believe in another context.

Dynamicism and particularities can be, it seems, inoculated against through abstraction, through positioning people in well-known storylines which explain why things happen and why people do the sorts of things they do. As heuristics, these storylines allow shortcuts to solutions that make an occurrence, or an individual action or experience, fit into something that can be understood. This doesn't require faith but falls naturally out of the experiences in particular communities where people tell and retell the same stories to one another and storylines become like ruts in the road of speaking about experience. They become meaningful tautologies or truisms that are vacuous in the abstract but make perfect sense when said to a knowing audience: *Boys will be boys,* or *what will be will be.*

At the same time, shifts in thinking can and do occur, sometimes with or in spite of changes in culture. These changes can happen broadly, for example, when there is a widespread acceptance of homosexuality and Christians must adapt to a changing political norm. Or they can happen for smaller groups, or individuals, for example, when a Pakistani Muslim man and a Somalian Muslim woman fall in love in London, and their families come to accept a relationship they may have earlier rejected. These changes show how abstraction is a two-way street. Particular stories and experiences can be used as evidence to support a different storyline. Which way the abstraction travels is by no means a settled matter, particularly around controversial topics, and the struggle over which storyline is or should be dominant emerges in interaction.

Much of my analysis has revolved around this issue of fluidity in discourse, of abstraction to particularity and vice versa, and how things shift when people start talking: how right practice and belief are represented and constructed in interaction, how religious believers address perceived challenges to their practices and beliefs, and how the presence of diverse audiences changes how people talk about their own faith. The analysis has broadly revealed three recurring ways in which the discourse around these topics is influenced in the contemporary, technologically mediated world: speaking publicly as speaking with authority, the challenges and opportunities of religious belief and practice in an increasingly rapidly changing world, and diversity and community in contemporary contexts.

6.1 Speaking Publicly as Authority

On the face of it, Ali Dawah, some of Shabir Ally's opponents, and two out of three of the *Bad Christian* podcast hosts have little in terms of traditional claims to theological authority. Even the debaters, some of whom had PhDs and published books, were more often than not apologists for their religious beliefs rather than theologians. They are not, in most cases, recognised as religious leaders or authorities within well-established religious institutions. And yet, all of them have achieved a level of recognition – they have been presented by others as authorities on religious issues and have audiences. The podcasts and videos and debates have been viewed or listened to tens of thousands of times; considering their combined audiences, their words have likely been heard by hundreds of thousands, if not millions, of people.

Putting your finger on exactly why any individual is popular or is seen as an authority is more difficult than it appears. For many of the speakers, their authority stems from another strange tautology of celebrity and influence: the fact that many people view their content results from the fact that many people view their content. Their authority is embedded in the fact that they are seen as an authority. This, however, downplays the real skill that each speaker shows in orienting themselves to their audiences, and considering how their words could be heard from a variety of perspectives. Their speaking is laced with the words of first-order authorities (Foucault, 1971), and even when they are not quoting scripture, scripture is present in what they say. They speak to the doubts that people have and show their own confidence in confronting and solving the problems of right belief and practice, whether or not you agree with them.

184 Conclusion: The Future of Religious Discourse

One of the most striking observations from the analysis of religious discourse is how these features of authority come out in interaction and how authority is ultimately constructed and deployed within discourse, something long recognised in Critical Discourse Analysis (Fairclough, 1995, 2001). Because the contexts analysed here are particularly complex, with audiences made up of a range of people with different conceptions of what is authoritative, the speakers must regularly adjust and readjust to what is being said in response to them. Categories of texts might be agreed to be authoritative – few in the discourse presented here would disagree that the word of God is the ultimate authority – but the boundaries of those categories and what constitutes them precisely when they are actually used proved to be extremely problematic in situations where they could be challenged, and surprisingly unproblematic when they were used in ways that suggested mutual agreement. Shabir Ally and David Hunt, for example, went back and forth about whether the Bible and Qur'an should be categorised as the word of God, while the Qur'an verses quoted by the sheikh in answers to questions by other Muslims were accepted without pause as supporting whatever point was being made.

This fluidity in context is in part due to the mediatisation of religious discourse and the emergence of new ways to distribute one's message to a variety of audiences. The speakers analysed have represented a range of backgrounds and experiences, with some like Shabir Ally and the *Bad Christian* podcast host Joey Svenson holding traditional positions of authority in traditional religious institutions, while others, like Ali Dawah, are perhaps more exceptional in their rise to authority as religious figures, given their relative lack of theological training and background. The easy answer to this question is simply that new forms of technologically mediated communication have made it possible for anyone to garner attention. Ali Dawah is the most obvious product of social media, but the others, the *Bad Christian* podcast hosts, and Shabir Ally and his opponents, have more complicated journeys to authority that mix so-called old and new media channels – Ally still appears on television and two of the *Bad Christian* podcast hosts originally were recognised as Christian music artists. In the case of Ally as well, the debate videos were not posted by him or his organisation, but rather by fans and others hoping to get his message out.

Although the concept of micro-celebrity is linked to the rise of social media and internet personalities (Marwick & boyd, 2011; Page, 2012; Raun, 2018), authenticity and intimacy, key features of social media celebrity, are also important in the construction of public persona building, if not exactly celebrity, for religious authorities. Religious authorities in the text can be seen positioning themselves as struggling with the same issues and concerns of laypeople, and connecting one to one with those who approach and question them. This accessibility and authenticity, supported by the authority of the word of God, create conditions where people can feel a connection to podcast hosts or the social media personality. What is perhaps more surprising when looking at the figures in the interaction is how unremarkable they are. Technological changes may facilitate the emergence of these figures in new ways, but their emergence in and of itself is perhaps less surprising than it may appear. Religious authorities throughout history have followed different and often unexpected paths to notoriety; thinking of different public authorities on religion throughout the West, they are not necessarily chosen by institutions with clear criteria for who should be in power. The authority of a televangelist like Joel Olsteen comes from neither his theological prowess nor the backing of a large religious institution. He has power because he connects with his audience and produces something they are willing to consume, the promise of living *Your Best Life Now* (Olsteen, 2004).

The simple description of the market, and the ways in which each of the speakers orients to a market economy, is perhaps the most obvious indication that seeing religious discourse as fundamentally different, that the most important part of interaction around religion is the attempt to speak the ineffable, is problematic. Religious figures and their positions as authorities on religious belief and practice are remarkably natural. At the same time, they produce content which is ultimately a kind of entertainment and orienting towards talk about religion primarily as 'religious' rather than any other element of its production (mediatisation in this case) should be revisited, with the tools of discourse analysis reapplied to sermons and prayers and religious songs. They need to be looked at in the same way we consider any other form of interaction and work to understand their social function.

The analysis has shown the explanatory value of this approach. Authority and power are constructed in the minutia of interaction between people of religious belief and in interaction about those beliefs, as those interactions consider the institutional, doctrinal, and traditional positions on particular issues. The things people say, both individual words or phrases like 'saved' or 'Inshallah' and stories about their own faith and the faith of others, construct and reinforce these authority structures, but they happen in everyday interactions when they are deployed in unmarked ways in interaction. People can draw on this authority by making simple references to stories, and second-order discourses go unnoticed as common sense ways of recounting their experiences, by talking, for example, about the struggle of the Christian life or wrestling with a topic or issue. The analysis of discourse shows how these different elements deployed at the right times in the right ways when interacting with others can create a sense of religious authority – an authority that is not given by an institution, but one that emerges from ways of talking about the world.

This analysis has not focused on institutional talk in religious places of worship, but the findings suggest that similar processes might be observed in those contexts as well. Although religious institutions give power to individuals in processes that are perhaps more systematic than the rise of a YouTube star, the performance of authority in any social context is still a performance. It requires the kind of orientation to context, to audience, and to socio-historical precedent in a way that is perhaps more like social media prominence than before. Considering their constituent elements, Joel Olsteen's performance as a religious authority perhaps doesn't differ as substantially from the *Bad Christian* podcast or Ali Dawah as it might appear.

Of course, the access to wide audiences provided by technology and the ability to quickly rise to prominence should be considered in thinking about how religious discourse is likely to develop. At the same time, mapping a trajectory where the role of institutional religion and authorities is further disregarded and social media celebrities become the spiritual guides of the future based simply on the number of likes they receive is problematic and ignores how historical precedent remains an important part of deciding whom to believe. Even Ali Dawah, posting videos online, knows this and foregrounds his 'offline' credibility with sheikhs and established religious figures. Without them, he runs the risk of being simply another unqualified voice, like the commenters on his videos whom he criticises.

6.2   Challenges and Opportunities

The free market is undoubtedly the driving force in contemporary life in the West, and the relationship between religious belief and practice and market forces is a recurring theme in contemporary life. From the debates to the YouTube videos to the podcasts, the presentation of religious belief and practice has been oriented towards gaining the largest audience possible and engaging with topics in which the audience is interested. The presence of those forces could be seen explicitly in the advertising placed on the *Bad Christian* podcast, by advertisers who were selling religious products. The market forces could be seen implicitly in the support for the debates given by Evangelical and dawah organisations for running the events. The questions of right belief and practice were always, in each context, also about attempting to convince others, particularly those who weren't yet a consumer of the product (in the case of advertising) or an adherent to the faith (in the case of evangelism and dawah) to change their behaviour in light of what was being said.

The market influences first how religious messages are produced in contemporary life. Public debates, podcasts, and YouTube videos exist because they have audiences that are interested in them. The debate as we have seen, for example, does little in terms of resolving disagreements between people or providing clarity about the positions of Christianity or Islam. They are popular both as events in the physical world and in their second lives as YouTube videos because of their entertainment value as drama. The two figures in the debate fight each other rhetorically, and each side can subsequently say that the other side has been 'destroyed', even if the actual tone of the debate focuses on mutual understanding and collegiality. Conflict, simply speaking, sells.

This orientation towards conflict in the discussion of religious discourse is on the face of it quite problematic, particularly if the expressed goal of the events is to bring people together and have a dialogue rather than a debate. If, however, the ultimate function of the debates, as different parts of the analysis have shown, is to give religious spokespeople a platform to present their beliefs, using another belief system as a foil, how these debates can lead to any kind of real mutual understanding is not clear. We have seen this repeatedly in the analysis of the debates in particular. None of the speakers modelled shifts in positions based on the information they heard. Instead, the model for inter-action was to respond and refute, to take the point of the opponent and show how whatever they said is actually further evidence of one's own point. The questions that were asked at the end of the debates showed that this approach to the other was internalised by people in the audience, who often asked disin-genuous, leading questions, crafted to trip up the person with whom they disagreed.

At the same time and perhaps ironically, an unintended consequence of the debates may be their ability to accomplish the thing they have been disingenu-ously billed as – making people rethink what they believe considering others' arguments. Studies of cognition in discourse have shown this: people don't only listen to the factual points of the other; in speaking with someone else, they can take their perspective and empathise with them (Hoffman, 2000; Cameron, 2011a; Richardson, 2017). Although there is no evidence of shifts in opinions within the debates, there is evidence in the work of sociology that the presence of contrasting views presented in online spaces and access to them when they aren't necessarily available in one's day-to-day life can and does affect changes in belief (Smith & Cimino, 2012). Simply hearing the perspec-tive of another when that perspective has been absent in one's own imagination means that a possibility has been opened. That possibility, as I'll discuss in the next section, need not necessarily be positive; indeed, it can be quite negative, but listening to the other, even if it is to refute them, requires in a very basic way listening to what they have to say.

The presence of other faiths, in addition to presenting a chance for religious believers to make an argument for their own faith, may also continue to destabilise their own positions. In the *Bad Christian* podcast, repeated discus-sions about how the hosts and other Christians should respond to the changing world around them came up. The result of this presence of the other, oftentimes within their own in-groups rather than from the outside, created a sense of uneasiness and lack of certainty. Taken to its extreme, this uncertainty leads to the position of someone like American Vice President Mike Pence who speaks of coming persecutions and a changing world where he positions himself as no longer having a place and being violently replaced. In moderation, however, the *Bad Christian* podcast hosts represent how religious change happens in light of the voices of others. They are changes that occur with a lack of certainty, with trepidation and a necessary taking of chances when positions shift. They also, however, appear to lead to a sense of growth and development, that religious faith need not be a prison of fixed ideas and ideals that are adhered to without the possibility for change over time. For the *Bad Christian* podcast hosts, the potential to adapt is a positive one and represents a kind of exercising of faith.

The market for drama and conflict also has an effect on how topics for religious discourse in public spaces are chosen and what gets and doesn't get discussed. Whether the Bible or the Qur'an is the word of God in exclusion of the other clearly makes for a lively debate between Christians and Muslims. However, this framing of the argument and ultimately how it is worked out in the debate orients to less productive ways of interaction. The focus of inter-action becomes winning the debate rather than having a real argument about the topic or empathising with one's opponent. Moreover, topics might be chosen for their entertainment value rather than their actual importance for religious believers. This focus on creating the most interest has consequences, however, for what then becomes important in the interaction between people, both within the same groups and with members of out-groups. Discussions about the deity of Jesus Christ are likely to generate strong opinions in Christians and Muslims, but these discussions have very little potential for drawing people together. The debate does not lead to mutual understanding, but to increased engagement, even if that engagement is not positive. The force driving the emergence of a particular topic or issue as the most important is what will create the most passionate response and get more people to view it. More problematically, these decisions are not necessarily made by individuals plotting to increase viewership and engagement (although in some cases they may be) – the expressed desire for mutual understanding does appear to be the genuine desire of everyone involved. Instead, the surface-level engagement emerges from the interaction of market forces and a structure that favours content which creates, rather than reduces, drama.

These same forces then influence who emerges as an authority in any context. Why Ali Dawah is more popular than others who might be more qualified to speak about Islam and how to live a moral life has to do primarily with his place within the market economy. He is skilled in his use of the platform and also benefits from elements of social media exposure that he doesn't necessarily control, creating him as a figure of authority on YouTube and Instagram, someone who has authority because of their position on the site. The same could be said of any other figure here – they are not speaking because they are the best qualified to speak in any one of the contexts but because they are adept at using a particular platform and the situational circumstances have allowed them to emerge as the key figure.

The *Bad Christian* podcast hosts, in their discussions of megachurch pastors, make clear that the popularisation of religious leaders in the market economy is subject to what is most easily bought and sold. The most religious pastor is not as successful as the pastor who is the most entertaining, and as long as there is choice in where to attend church, as an example, the market forces that are similar to shopping for a car will come to bear on the choice of religious expression as well. Religious expression is a part of everyday life, and the choices that individuals make in relation to religious belief and practice are limited by the social constructs around them, even when they feel that those constructs are being transcended in some way by something supernatural, be it God or anything else. The things people say and the stories they tell each other about their choices show that they are often still very human.

6.3   Diversity and Community

Despite the promises of technology opening worlds of new ideas to individuals, mediatisation and marketisation have had observable restricting effects on who can and can't rise to prominence, stubbornly subject to the same historical forces like ethnicity, class, and gender that have traditionally limited access to power. With the market favouring certain kinds of religious discourse, one consequence can be the narrowing of what religious discourse in public spaces should look like, particularly considering the genres – podcasts, YouTube videos, and debates – represented in this analysis. They tend to attract people, namely men, who are confident and self-assured, confrontational, and argumentative. The nature of public-facing, mediated discourse self-selects for a certain type of speaker. Before rushing to apply the findings from this study more broadly, some consideration should be given again to who is doing the talking.

The exclusion of women's voices in prominent places is a historical, perennial problem in religious discourse and particularly in online spaces, where sexist histories continue to persist. The analysis has shown that discourse around who is and is not able to speak from a position of authority can be understood in relation to positions and storylines, and that positions and storylines, at every level of abstraction, are not ad hoc, novel responses to the conditions of any given interaction. Instead, the positions and storylines can be seen as part and parcel of well-established storylines that can be traced back to sacred texts, in many cases, or to cultural or religious assumptions about relationships among people. These storylines are often implicitly gendered, with the men in positions of power and women either subordinated or ignored entirely. Indeed, of all the disagreements one might track within religious discourse, the clearest point of agreement is that God is 'he', not 'she'.

When gender comes up, the absence of women in the discussions leads to the normalisation of sexist storylines that are told without challenge, like the *Ask the Sheikh* video wherein the sheikh is not pressed on his positioning of all sisters in Islam as needing to focus on their 'real career which is motherhood'. Within men's storylines about the world across all genres of talk and religious categorisations, women consistently played passive or functionary roles and the lack of women in the discourse meant that the possibility for emotional attunement to women's perspectives was also limited. The discourse makes clear that we must highlight that results and findings apply to *men* speaking about religious belief and practice. They are certainly worth studying, but they represent one kind of interaction about religion which must always be recognised as gendered. This is not to say women are entirely absent from the discussions, and Shabir Ally's own terrestrial television show *Let the Qur'an Speak* often features women both as interviewers and as experts. Still, none of the debates that I have viewed on YouTube included Shabir Ally speaking with a woman as an opponent, and the prominent female Muslim vloggers like Dina Tokio are better known for lifestyle and fashion than theology and dawah. The *Bad Christian* podcast's network of podcasts includes some hosted by women, albeit in a significant minority. Men simply and persistently remain the dominant voices.

Lövheim's (2013) call for attention to gender in the analysis of religious discourse should follow in every element of the research process, from the citation of scholars from diverse perspectives to the analysis of diverse texts. The foregrounding of men's voices in religious discourse is a collective choice, and my research methodology – however inadvertent as I'd like to believe it was – has favoured men's voices over women's. Analysts, community members, and religious leaders share in the responsibility of correcting the incomplete picture of religion that emerges from looking only at powerful men speaking loudly. Broadening this focus is not diversity for its own sake; research into only one kind of discourse from a limited set of speakers means that researchers are not seeing the whole picture of religious discourse. Instead, a focus on religious belief and practice being negotiated in other contexts, for example, in intimate community settings, will pay significant dividends in the understanding of how religion functions. Analysis of this discourse, for example in Inge's (2016) study of British Salafi Muslims, can provide more insight into how faith functions in the day-to-day lives of religious believers by working to meet communities where they are and taking time to gain access to the central sites of religious life, where women and men work out the meaning of their faith together, while preparing food or having tea. A realignment in what researchers value as worthy of our attention will foreground these contexts and provide a deeper understanding of what religious belief and practice actually are.

The prominence of self-assured, dominant men in public discourse about religion has consequences for how religious communities are conceived of and spoken about. The *Bad Christian* podcast hosts discuss this most explicitly in relation to megachurches and how churches become known for their pastors. The community structures that emerge around these men are hierarchical and fragile in their reliance on everyone's ability to maintain the necessary ideological purity or avoid serious errors in judgement. The communities around them might be more analogous to fan communities than traditional religious communities, something scholars of religion and mediatisation like Hjarvard (2008, 2013) and Lövheim (2011) have addressed in their work. The celebrity status has consequences beyond simply how leaders are treated and what topics come to prominence, but in the attitudes about religion and how people conceptualise prototypical Christians or Muslims or any other category of belief. Leaders are examples for what religious belief and practice should look like, and their personalities and approaches to day-to-day life have effects on every other arena of social life.

The public, mediated nature of religious discourse appears to be a net positive because public presentation of faith requires taking into account a variety of audiences: those who accept your position, those who oppose you, and those who are uncommitted. Indeed, there are multiple examples of speakers positioning themselves and others in conciliatory ways and allowing for the possibility that those who disagree with them are acting in good faith and are not strictly wrong. Indeed, the very presence of disagreement within religious communities and the interaction between Shabir Ally and his multiple interlocutors are clear evidence that people of differing opinions can and do have civil, rationale conversations about faith, taking into account a wide range of opinions in a respectful way.

At the same time, the contemporary world is full of examples of the failure of moderating effects, particularly in the attacks on religious communities, such as the Tree of Life synagogue shooting in the autumn of 2018 in the United States; another attack on a synagogue in Poway, California; and the attacks on mosques in Christchurch, New Zealand, in the spring of 2019 (Bogost, 2019). All the perpetrators held beliefs fuelled by malignant positionings of religious communities that were not moderated by public discourse about those faiths and showed evidence that the Internet, rather than providing an open forum to experiencing people of different faiths and walks of life in a positive way, instead fuelled these malignant positionings and negative storylines. The abstraction of the storyline to one of good and evil and away from particular people in the particular mosque on a particular day coming for prayer is in part at the root of the problem. Abstraction and categorisation allow for a kind of clarity that specificity always muddies and can allow for violent, dehumanising thinking.

These processes have both positive and negative effects. Individuals understand and model the lives of others and their intentions, and with those models, moral reasoning can show staggering levels of cognitive dissonance. Beliefs can then become more entrenched over time and fuel conspiratorial thinking that goes beyond any reasonable accounting of the world, ending too often now with someone committing heinous, violent acts. At the same time, cognitive dissonance is not always negative. Emotional atunement and the examples of empathy and mutual understanding we've seen suggest that the processes of positioning also allow for communities to accept people with whom they might fundamentally disagree. Cognitive dissonance may create conditions for irrational violence and prejudice, but it also allows people to maintain relationships in spite of what they believe, like the Evangelical Christian parent who both believes in the reality of hell and is also convinced their own atheist son won't be sent there.

The diversity of religious belief and practice and, more importantly, the contact between people of these different faiths in their day-to-day lives are unlikely to subside with the increasing presence of technology. The effects of personalisation and of filter bubbles and echo chambers and isolation are also likely to continue, as they have in the physical world. How these technologies continue to advance and what resistance emerges will likely result in a non-linear development in the future. Other forces, including climate change and political instability on a global scale, could also have a radical effect on how religious discourse develops in the coming years, as uncertainty about the ecological future of the planet changes how humans interact with and around religion or the increased presence of artificial intelligence in day-to-day life leads to humans having less control over their own actions. What will discussion of right belief and practice look like when automated systems become more prominent in surveying behaviours or are used in decision-making about punishment for crimes? What new technologies will begin to augment processes of moral reasoning, and what resistance to those processes might emerge? Whom to believe?

The struggle, if it can be understood as a struggle, of religious belief and practice in the contemporary world, where different voices and perspectives permeate our day-to-day experiences, cannot seem to be avoided. 'Whom to believe' is the great unresolved question, but one that we cannot stop confronting, even if we believe. Baker (1998), it seems, recognises that ultimately we are at the mercy of what we're told and that our attempts to find answers often lead us down a variety of different paths. There are implicit and explicit contradictions built into the reasoning devised to make sense of things that are often inexplicable. The simple answers are unlikely to be satisfying and the uncomfortable truth that our contemporary world, with all of its freedoms, seems to force people to make decisions about what path to choose and whom we will believe in exclusion to others that we might also want to believe. It must be either the Bible or the Qur'an, Jesus or Mohammad, science or faith – you must pick sides.

But people choose sides and then choose other sides. Discourse analysis shows that real interaction is full of contradictions, of positioning that shifts again and again, of storylines that get adopted and adapted, told and retold to any number of contradictory or conciliatory ends. There is no audit trail in real-time interaction; what matters is the last thing said to you and how you will respond to it, a Bakhtinian tension between what new thing might be said and what old thing will reign it in. The future of religious discourse may be uncertain, but the processes that will bring about this future are not. They can be tracked and traced and understood. Religious discourse is not immune to these processes of human interaction – not doctrine, not prayers, not hymns, not sermons. They are all discourse and they can and do and will change when people speak and the world around them changes. What we perceive as right today could very well be perceived as wrong by our children. And the trajectory of belief and practice is ultimately the trajectory of discourse; anything can change if it becomes the topic of discourse. This is neither a good nor a bad thing; it is simply what happens when people talk to each other.

Appendix

Bad Christian Podcast Episodes				
BC	Title	Date	Length hr:min:sec	Word Count
BC 1	#208 Black Lives Matter	2016/7/13	01:18:10	15555
BC 2	#214 Church Shopping vs. Car Shopping	2016/8/10	01:10:27	15305
BC 3	#222 Andy Stanley makes The Wolf List	2016/11/10	01:26:19	18016
BC 4	#244 Everyone is doing it	2017/2/8	01:05:54	14161
BC 5	#251 The Perry Noble Mega church clown show	2017/3/3	01:20:35	17352
BC 6	#266 Male headship	2017/4/1	01:13:22	16261
BC 7	#282 Is Pastor Judah Smith Gay affirming?	2017/5/26	01:35:10	19242
BC 8	#286 Abortion and hell. Our actions don't match beliefs	2017/6/8	01:13:41	16054
Totals			**10:23:38**	**131,946**

All podcasts downloaded from public iTunes feed in July 2017.

Ali Dawah Videos					
A	Title	Date	URL	Length hr:min:sec	Word Count
A1	REACTING TO QUR'AN SURAH BAQARAH VERSE 208	2017/5/31	dvAevse7GVw	00:13:46	2511
A2	IS CAR INSURANCE HARAM? _AskTheSheikh_	2017/5/15	oFg8_4x5Jbw	00:29:24	4892

(*cont.*)

A	Title	Date	URL	Length hr:min:sec	Word Count
			Ali Dawah Videos		
A3	REACTING TO "EX MUSLIM" STORIES	2017/4/24	LlpJ14SH7hg	00:17:24	3738
A4	EMOTIONAL INTERVIEW WITH SISTER IN TWERKING VIDEO …	2017/3/5	fBXN6p58BMg	00:17:51	3652
A5	MARRYING BEHIND MY PARENTS BACK || *AskTheSheikh*	2017/3/12	XranyuVbwI0	00:17:18	2761
A6	THE REALITY 12 || Why marry a divorcee??	2015/12/3	YIxj-RkVbBs	00:19:48	4413
A7	CAN I SELL ALCOHOL & PORK AT WORK? (SPECIFIC FATWA) || *AskTheSheikh*	2017/5/2	r71bhgXIR3E	00:07:19	1070
A8	ARE NASHEEDS REALLY HARAM?? ALI DAWAH	2017/1/10	GACnfqa67Lc	00:17:54	3695
A9	Mufti Menk & Ali Dawah Parents rejecting proposal & Forced marriages	2016/1/14	fQJKl1qqkT8	00:22:04	3859
A10	Ali Dawah & Yusuf Estes || Why we chose islam?	2014/11/4	P0oNnJgg9_I	00:16:00	2981
Totals				**2:58:48**	**33,572**

NB All URLs require the prefix www.youtube.com/watch?v=

				Length hr:min:sec	
D	Name	Date Posted	URL	Length hr:min:sec	Word Count
D1	Debate: Is Jesus the Son of God? (David Wood vs. Shabir Ally)	2015/10/2	of-LkwSC8vE	0:57:39	11,601
D2	Debate: Is Jesus God? Shabir Ally vs. James White	2014/11/12	JUiZ-fyPSHE	2:17:26	25,665
D3	Debate: Numerical Miracles in the Qur'an, Shabir Ally vs. Richard Lucas	2016/11/9	WwHUcth-zzU	1:40:12	18,677
D4	Classic Debate: "The Qur'an or the Bible – which is the Word of God?" Jay Smith vs. Shabir Ally	2016/3/4	cOMWE8ocwKU	2:41:20	30,684
D5	Christianity vs. Islam Debate Dave Hunt vs. Shabir Ally (FULL)	2014/3/29	4WBioHMIQAc	2:40:11	26,233
Totals				**10:16:48**	**112,860**

Shabir Ally Debate Videos

NB: All URLs require the prefix www.youtube.com/watch?v=

References

Abdulla, Rasha A. (2007). Islam, Jihad, and terrorism in post-9/11 Arabic discussion boards. *Journal of Computer-Mediated Communication*, *12*(3), 1063–1081. DOI:10.1111/j.1083-6101.2007.00363.x

Agrama, Hussein Ali. (2010). Ethics, tradition, authority: Toward an anthropology of the fatwa. *American Ethnologist*, *37*(1), 2–18. DOI:10.1111/j.1548-1425.2010.01238.x

Ahmed, S. (2015). The voices of young British Muslims: Identity, belonging and citizenship. In M. K. Smith, N. Stanton, & T. Wylie (Eds.), *Youth Work and Faith: Debates, Delights and Dilemmas* (pp. 37–51). Lyme Regis: Russell House.

Ali Dawah. (n.d.). alidawah (@alidawah) Instagram photos and videos. Retrieved from www.instagram.com/alidawah/ (Accessed on 26 June 2017).

Allington, Daniel, & Swann, Joan. (2009). Researching literary reading as social practice. *Language and Literature*, *18*(3), 219–230.

Ammerman, Nancy T. (2013). Spiritual but not religious? Beyond binary choices in the study of religion. *Journal for the Scientific Study of Religion*, *52*(2), 258–278. DOI:10.1111/jssr.12024

Anthony, Laurence. (2014). AntPConc [Computer Software]. Tokyo, Japan: Waseda University. Available from www.laurenceanthony.net/software.

Ariarajah, S. Wesley. (2017). Religion and violence: A Protestant Christian perspective. *Journal of Ecumenical Studies*, *52*(1), 56–66.

Ashour, Omar. (2010). Online de-radicalization? Countering violent extremist narratives: Message, messenger and media strategy. *Perspectives on Terrorism*, *4*(6), 15–19.

Atkinson, Harley T. (2018). *The Power of Small Groups in Christian Formation*. Eugene: Wipf and Stock Publishers.

Austin, John Langshaw. (1975). *How to Do Things with Words*. Oxford: Oxford University Press.

Bad Christian Podcast. (n.d.). Retrieved from http://badchristianmedia.com/badchristian-podcast (Accessed on 26 June 2017).

Baker, David. (1998). *The Truth about Small Towns*. Fayetteville: The University of Arkansas Press.

Baker, Paul, Gabrielatos, Costas, & McEnery, Tony. (2013). *Discourse Analysis and Media Attitudes: The Representation of Islam in the British Press*. Cambridge: Cambridge University Press.

Bakhtin, Mikhail. (1981). *The Dialogic Imagination*. Austin: University of Texas Press. (1986). *Speech Genres and Other Late Essays*. Austin: University of Texas Press.

Bakir, Vian, & McStay, Andrew. (2018). Fake news and the economy of emotions: Problems, causes, solutions. *Digital Journalism, 6*(2), 154–175.

Bakshy, Eytan, Hofman, Jake M., Mason, Winter A., & Watts, Duncan J. (2011, February). *Everyone's an influencer: Quantifying influence on Twitter*. Paper presented at the Proceedings of the Fourth International Conference on Web Search and Web Data Mining, WSDM 2011, Hong Kong, China.

Bamberg, Michael. (1997). Positioning between structure and performance. *Journal of Narrative and Life History, 7*(1–4), 335–342.

    (2004). Considering counter narratives. In Michael Bamberg & Molly Andrews (Eds.), *Considering Counter Narratives: Narrating, Resisting, Making Sense* (pp. 351–371). Amersterdam: John Benjamins.

Bamberg, Michael, & Georgakopoulou, Alexandra. (2008). Small stories as a new perspective in narrative and identity analysis. *Text & Talk, 28*, 377–396.

Bartkowski, J. (1996). Beyond biblical literalism and inerrancy: Conservative Protestants and the hermeneutic interpretation of scripture. *Sociology of Religion, 57*(3), 259–272.

Bebbington, David W. (1989). *Evangelicalism in Modern Britain: A History from the 1730s to the 1980s*. London: Routledge.

Bentrcia, Rahima, Zidat, Samir, & Marir, Farhi. (2018). An analytic study on the Holy Quran based on the order of words in Arabic and conjunction. *Malaysian Journal of Computer Science* (1), 1–16. DOI:10.22452/mjcs.vol31no1.1

Besecke, Kelly. (2007). Beyond literalism: Reflexive spirituality and religious meaning. In Nancy T. Ammerman (Ed.), *Everyday Religion: Observing Modern Religious Lives* (pp. 169–186). Oxford: Oxford University Press.

Bielo, James. (2008). On the failure of 'meaning': Bible reading in the anthropology of Christianity. *Culture and Religion, 9*(1), 1–21. DOI:10.1080/14755610801954839

    (2009). *Words upon the Word: An Ethnography of Evangelical Group Bible Study*. New York: New York University Press.

    (2019). 'Particles-to-people ... molecules-to-man': Creationist poetics in public debates. *Journal of Linguistic Anthropology, 29*(1), 4–26.

Billig, Michael. (1996). *Arguing and Thinking: A Rhetorical Approach to Social Psychology*. Cambridge: Cambridge University Press.

Billig, Michael, & Tajfel, Henri. (1973). Social categorization and similarity in intergroup behaviour. *European Journal of Social Psychology, 3*(1), 27–52.

Bleich, Erik, & Maxwell, Rahsaan. (2013). Assessing Islamophobia in Britain: Where do Muslims really stand? In Marc Helbling (Ed.), *Islamophobia in the West: Measuring and Explaining Individual Attitudes* (pp. 39–55). London: Routledge.

Bogost, Ian. (2019). The meme terrorists: Violence in synagogues and mosques is kindling for a larger inferno of distrust online. *The Atlantic*. Retrieved from www.theatlantic.com/technology/archive/2019/04/california-synagogue-shooting-worse-you-thought/588352/ (Accessed on 20 May 2019).

boyd, danah. (2011). Social network sites as networked publics: Affordances, dynamics, and implications. In Z. Papacharissi (Ed.), *A Networked Self. Identity, Community, and Culture on Social Network Sites* (pp. 39–58). London: Routledge.

Brown, Penelope, & Levinson, Stephen C. (1987). *Politeness: Some Universals in Language Usage*. Cambridge: Cambridge University Press.

Browse, Sam [@SamBrowse]. (30 April 2019). I think that's unfair. One of my bugbears is the evocation of 'context' as a deus ex machina that miraculously solves all meaning-making issues (what even counts as context?). It seems to me that your author is more systematically describing what's often a very fuzzy concept! [Twitter Post]. Retrieved from https://twitter.com/SamBrowse/status/1123182131 671392256?s=20 (Accessed on 10 May 2019).

Bruce, Tayyiba. (2017). New technologies, continuing ideologies: Online reader comments as a support for media perspectives of minority religions. *Discourse, Context & Media.*

Bullock, Josh. (2018). *The Sociology of the Sunday Assembly: 'Belonging without Believing' in a Post-Christian Context.* London: Kingston University. Retrieved from http://eprints.kingston.ac.uk/id/eprint/41775

Burgess, Jean, & Green, Joshua. (2008, 15–18 October). *Agency and controversy in the YouTube community.* Paper presented at the Internet Research 9.0: Rethinking Community, Rethinking Place, Copenhagen.

Cameron, Lynne. (2011). Metaphors and discourse activity. In Lynne Cameron & Rob Maslen (Eds.), *Metaphor Analysis: Research Practice in Applied Linguistics, Social Sciences and the Humanities* (pp. 147–160). London: Equinox.

(2012). *Metaphor and Reconciliation: The Discourse Dynamics of Empathy in Post-Conflict Conversations.* London: Routledge.

(2015). Embracing connectedness and change: A complex dynamic systems perspective for applied linguistic research. *Association Internationale de Linguistique Appliqué (AILA) Review, 28*(1), 28–48.

Campbell, Heidi A. (2017). Surveying theoretical approaches within digital religion studies. *New Media & Society, 19*(1), 15–24. DOI:10.1177/1461444816649912

Campbell, Heidi A., Joiner, Lane, & Lawrence, Samantha. (2018). Responding to the meme-ing of the religious other. *Journal of Communication & Religion, 41*(2), 27–42.

Caraway, Brett. (2011). Audience labor in the new media environment: A Marxian revisiting of the audience commodity. *Media, Culture & Society, 33*(5), 693–708. DOI:10.1177/0163443711404463

Carrette, Jeremy, & King, Richard. (2004). *Selling Spirituality: The Silent Takeover of Religion.* London: Routledge.

Casasanto, Daniel. (2009). Embodiment of abstract concepts: Good and bad in right- and left-handers. *Journal of Experimental Psychology: General, 138*(3), 351.

Castelli, Elizabeth A. (2005). Praying for the persecuted church: US Christian activism in the global arena. *Journal of Human Rights, 4*(3), 321–351. DOI:10.1080/14754830500257554

Chafe, Wallace. (1988). Punctuation and the prosody of written language. *Written Communication, 5*(4), 395–426.

Charteris-Black, Jonathan. (2016). *Fire Metaphors: Discourses of Awe and Authority.* London: Bloomsbury Publishing.

Chaves, Mark, & Gorski, Philip S. (2001). Religious pluralism and religious participation. *Annual Review of Sociology, 27*(1), 261–281.

Chilton, Paul, & Kopytowska, Monika. (2018). *Religion, Language, and the Human Mind.* Oxford: Oxford University Press.

Cimino, Richard, & Smith, Christopher. (2007). Secular humanism and atheism beyond progressive secularism. *Sociology of Religion, 68*(4), 407–424.

Cimino, Richard, & Smith, Christopher. (2011). The new atheism and the formation of the imagined secularist community. *Journal of Media and Religion*, *10*(1), 24–38. DOI:10.1080/15348423.2011.549391

(2014). *Atheist Awakening: Secular Activism and Community in America*. Oxford: Oxford University Press.

Clack, Beverley. (2018). Lived religion: Rethinking human nature in a neoliberal age. *International Journal of Philosophy and Theology*, *79*(4), 355–369.

Clark, Billy. (2013). *Relevance Theory*. Cambridge: Cambridge University Press.

Clift, Rebecca, & Helani, Fadi. (2010). Inshallah: Religious invocations in Arabic topic transition. *Language in Society*, *39*(03), 357–382.

Coleman, Simon. (2000). *The Globalisation of Charismatic Christianity* (Vol. 12). Cambridge: Cambridge University Press.

Cook, Michael. (2000). *The Koran: A very Short Introduction*. Oxford: Oxford University Press.

Creese, Angela. (2008). Linguistic ethnography. In Stephen May (Ed.), *Encyclopedia of Language and Education* (pp. 229–241). Bakingstoke: Springer.

Crenshaw, Kimberle. (1989). Demarginalizing the intersection of race and sex: A black feminist critique of antidiscrimination doctrine, feminist theory and antiracist politics. *University of Chicago Legal Forum*, 1, Article 8.

Crystal, David. (1965). *Linguistics, Language, and Religion*. Philadelphia: Hawthorn Books.

(2008). *A Dictionary of Linguistics and Phonetics*. Oxford: Blackwell.

Darquennes, Jeroen, & Vandenbussche, Wim. (2011). Language and religion as a sociolinguistic field of study: Some introductory notes. *Sociolinguistica*, *25*, 1–11.

Davies, Bronwyn, & Harré, Rom. (1990). Positioning: The discursive production of selves. *Journal for the Theory of Social Behaviour*, *20*(1), 43–63.

De Fina, Anna, & Georgakopoulou, Alexandra. (2011). *Analyzing Narrative: Discourse and Sociolinguistic Perspectives*. Cambridge: Cambridge University Press.

DeYoung, Kevin. (2014). *Taking God at His Word: Why the Bible Is Knowable, Necessary, and Enough, and What That Means for You and Me*. Wheaton, IL: Crossway.

Dictionary of Christianese. (2013). God said it, I believe it, that settles it. Retrieved from www.dictionaryofchristianese.com/god-said-it-i-believe-it-that-settles-it/ (Accessed 3 February 2019).

Dorst, Aletta, & Klop, Marry-Loïse. (2017). Not a holy father: Dutch Muslim teenagers' metaphors for Allah. *Metaphor and the Social World*, *7*(1), 65–85.

Downes, William. (2011). *Language and Religion: A Journey into the Human Mind*. Cambridge: Cambridge University Press.

(2018). Linguistics and the scientific study of religion: Prayer as a cognitive register. In Paul Chilton & Monika Kopytowska (Eds.), *Religion, Language, and the Human Mind* (pp. 89–114). New York: Oxford University Press.

Durkheim, Emile. (2008 [1915]). *The Elementary Forms of the Religious Life*. Oxford: Oxford University Press.

Eagle, David E. (2015). Historicizing the megachurch. *Journal of Social History*, *48*(3), 589–604. DOI:10.1093/jsh/shu109

Edwards, Derek. (2008). Intentionality and mens rea in police interrogations: The production of actions as crimes. *Intercultural Pragmatics*, *5*(2), 177–199.

Eglin, Peter, & Hester, Stephen. (2003). *The Montreal Massacre: A Story of Membership Categorization Analysis*. Waterloo: Wilfrid Laurier University Press.

Eickelman, Dale F., & Anderson, Jon W. (2003). *New Media in the Muslim World: The Emerging Public Sphere*. Bloomington: Indiana University Press.

Einstein, Mara. (2007). *Brands of Faith: Marketing Religion in a Commercial Age*. London: Routledge.

Eisenstein, Elizabeth L. (1980). *The Printing Press as an Agent of Change*. Cambridge: Cambridge University Press.

El-Nawawy, Mohammed. (2009). *Islam dot com: Contemporary Islamic Discourses in Cyberspace*. London: Springer.

El-Sharif, Ahmad. (2018). The Muslim prophetic tradition: Spatial source domains for metaphorical expressions. In Paul Chilton & Monika Kopytowska (Eds.), *Religion, Language, and the Human Mind* (pp. 263–293). New York: Oxford University Press.

El Naggar, Shaimaa. (2018). 'But I did not do anything!' – analysing the YouTube videos of the American Muslim televangelist Baba Ali: Delineating the complexity of a novel genre. *Critical Discourse Studies*, *15*(3), 303–319.

Engelke, Matthew. (2014). Christianity and the anthropology of secular humanism. *Current Anthropology*, *55*(S10), S292–S301. DOI:10.1086/677738

Etling, Bruce, Kelly, John, Faris, Robert, & Palfrey, John. (2010). Mapping the Arabic blogosphere: Politics and dissent online. *New Media & Society*, *12*(8), 1225–1243. DOI:10.1177/1461444810385096

Fairclough, Norman. (1995). *Critical Discourse Analysis: The Critical Study of Language*. Harlow: Pearson.

(2001). *Language and Power*. Harlow: Pearson.

Fairclough, Norman, & Wodak, Ruth. (1997). Discourse analysis: A multidisciplinary introduction. In Teun A. van Dijk (Ed.), *Discourse as Social Interaction* (pp. 258–284). London: Sage.

Fauconnier, Gilles. (1984). *Mental Spaces: Aspects of Meaning Construction in Natural Language*. Cambridge: Cambridge University Press.

Ferguson, Charles A. (1985). The study of religious discourse. In D. Tannen & J. E. Alatis (Eds.), *Language and Linguistics: The Interdependence of Theory, Data, and Application* (pp. 205–213). Washington, DC: Georgetown University Press.

Fernando, Mayanthi. (2009). Exceptional citizens: Secular Muslim women and the politics of difference in France. *Social Anthropology*, *17*(4), 379–392. DOI:10.1111/j.1469-8676.2009.00081.x

Foucault, Michel. (1971). The orders of discourse. *Social Science Information*, *10*(2), 7–30.

Freund, Katharina. (2014). 'Fair use is legal use': Copyright negotiations and strategies in the fan-vidding community. *New Media & Society*, *18*(7), 1347–1363. DOI:10.1177/1461444814555952

Fuller, Robert C. (2001). *Spiritual, but not Religious: Understanding Unchurched America*. Oxford: Oxford University Press.

Gao, Xiuping, Lan, Chun, Chilton, Paul, & Kopytowska, Monika. (2018). Buddhist metaphors in the Diamond Sutra and the Heart Sutra: A cognitive perspective. In Paul Chilton & Monika Kopytowska (Eds.), *Religion, Language, and the Human Mind* (pp. 229–262). New York: Oxford University Press.

Gavins, Joanna. (2007). *Text World Theory: An Introduction*. Edinburgh: Edinburgh University Press.

Ghadbian, Najib. (2000). Political Islam and violence. *New Political Science*, *22*(1), 77–88. DOI:10.1080/713687889

Gholami, Reza. (2017). The art of self-making: Identity and citizenship education in late-modernity. *British Journal of Sociology of Education*, *38*(6), 798–811. DOI:10.1080/01425692.2016.1182006

Gibbs, Raymond. (1994). *The Poetics of Mind: Figurative Thought, Language and Understanding*. Cambridge: Cambridge University Press.

(2006). *Embodiment and Cognitive Science*. Cambridge: Cambridge University Press.

Gibbs, Raymond, & Franks, Heather. (2002). Embodied metaphor in women's narratives about their experiences with cancer. *Health Communication*, *14*(2), 139–165.

Goffman, Erving. (1959). *The Presentation of Self in Everyday Life*. New York: Doublesday.

Gramby-Sobukwe, Sharon, & Hoiland, Tim. (2009). The rise of mega-church efforts in international development: A brief analysis and areas for further research. *Transformation*, *26*(2), 104–117. DOI:10.1177/0265378809103386

Gumperz, John J. (1982). *Language and Social Identity*. Cambridge: Cambridge University Press.

Hamilton, Adam. (2014). *Making Sense of the Bible: Rediscovering the Power of Scripture Today*. New York: HarperOne.

Hannan, Jason. (2018). Trolling ourselves to death? Social media and post-truth politics. *European Journal of Communication*, *33*(2), 214–226.

Harré, Rom. (2000). The social construction of terrorism. In F. M. Moghaddam & A. J. Marsella (Eds.), *Understanding Terrorism* (pp. 91–102). Washington, DC: APA Press.

Harré, Rom, Moghaddam, F. M., Cairnie, T. P., Rothbart, D., & Sabat, S. R. (2009). Recent advances in positioning theory. *Theory & Psychology*, *19*(1), 5–31.

Harré, Rom, & van Langenhove, Luk. (1998). *Positioning Theory: Moral Contexts of Intentional Action*. London: Blackwell Publishers.

Harrison, Victoria S. (2006). The pragmatics of defining religion in a multi-cultural world. *International Journal for Philosophy of Religion*, *59*(3), 133–152.

Harvey, David. (2007). *A Brief History of Neoliberalism*. Oxford: Oxford University Press.

Herring, Susan. (2004). Slouching toward the ordinary: Current trends in computer-mediated communication. *New Media and Society*, *6*(1), 26–36.

Hinch, Jim. (2016). Evangelicals are losing the battle for the Bible. And they're just fine with that. *LA Review of Books*. https://lareviewofbooks.org/article/evangelicals-are-losing-the-battle-for-the-bible-and-theyre-just-fine-with-that/

Hjarvard, Stig. (2008). The mediatization of religion: A theory of the media as agents of religious change. *Northern Lights: Film & Media Studies Yearbook*, *6*(1), 9–26.

(2013). *The Mediatization of Culture and Society*. London: Routledge.

Hoffman, Martin L. (2000). *Empathy and Moral Development: Implications for Caring and Justice*. Cambridge: Cambridge University Press.

Hopkins, Nick, & Greenwood, Ronni Michelle. (2013). Hijab, visibility and the performance of identity. *European Journal of Social Psychology*, *43*(5), 438–447. DOI:10.1002/ejsp.1955

Housley, William, & Fitzgerald, Richard. (2002). The reconsidered model of membership categorization analysis. *Qualitative Research*, *2*(1), 59–83.

(2009). Membership categorization, culture and norms in action. *Discourse & Society*, *20*(3), 345–362.

Hunter, Andrea. (2016). Monetizing the mommy: Mommy blogs and the audience commodity. *Information, Communication & Society*, *19*(9), 1306–1320. DOI:10.1080/1369118X.2016.1187642

Hutchings, Timothy. (2007). Creating church online: A case-study approach to religious experience. *Studies in World Christianity*, *13*(3), 243–260.

(2017). *Creating Church Online: Ritual, Community and New Media*. London: Routledge.

Inge, Anabel. (2016). *The Making of a Salafi Muslim Woman: Paths to Conversion*. Oxford: Oxford University Press.

Jacobson, Jessica. (2006). *Islam in Transition: Religion and Identity among British Pakistani Youth*. London: Routledge.

Jayyusi, Lena. (1984). *Categorization and the Moral Order*. London: Routledge/Kegan & Paul.

Johnson, Mark. (1987). *The Body in the Mind: The Bodily Basis of Meaning, Imagination, and Reason*. Chicago: University of Chicago Press.

Keach, Benjamin. (1975). *Preaching from the Types and Metaphors of the Bible*. Grand Rapids: Kregel.

Khamis, Susie, Ang, Lawrence, & Welling, Raymond. (2017). Self-branding, 'micro-celebrity' and the rise of social media influencers. *Celebrity Studies*, *8*(2), 191–208. DOI:10.1080/19392397.2016.1218292

Knott, Kim. (2015). *The Location of Religion: A Spatial Analysis*. London: Routledge.

Koller, Veronika. (2017). The light within: Metaphor consistency in Quaker pamphlets, 1659–2010. *Metaphor and the Social World*, *7*(1), 5–24.

Labov, William. (1972). *Language in the Inner City*. Philadelphia: University of Pennsylvania Press.

Labov, William, & Waletzky, Joshua. (1997). Narrative analysis: Oral versions of personal experience. *Journal of Narrative and Life History*, *7*(1), 3–38.

Lakoff, George. (1987). *Women, Fire, and Dangerous Things: What Categories Reveal about the Mind*. Chicago: University of Chicago Press.

Lakoff, George, & Johnson, Mark. (1980). *Metaphors We Live By*. Chicago: University of Chicago Press.

(1999). *Philosophy in the Flesh: The Embodied Mind and Its Challenge to Western Thought*. New York: Basic Books.

Larsen-Freeman, Diane, & Cameron, Lynne. (2008). *Complex Systems and Applied Linguistics*. Oxford: Oxford University Press.

Lave, Jean, & Wenger, Etienne. (1991). *Situated Learning: Legitimate Peripheral Participation*. Cambridge: Cambridge University Press.

Lazareth, William Henry. (2001). *Christians in Society: Luther, the Bible, and Social Ethics*. Minneapolis: Fortress Press.

Lee, Lois. (2015). *Recognizing the Non-religious: Reimagining the Secular*. Oxford: Oxford University Press.

(2017). Vehicles of new atheism: The atheist bus campaign, non-religious represen-
tations and material culture. In Christopher R. Cotter, Philip Andrew Quadrio, &
Jonathan Tuckett (Eds.), *New Atheism: Critical Perspectives and Contemporary
Debates* (pp. 69–86). Cham: Springer International Publishing.

Lieber, Paul S., & Reiley, Peter J. (2016). Countering ISIS's social media influence.
Special Operations Journal, 2(1), 47–57. DOI:10.1080/23296151.2016.1165580

Lövheim, Mia. (2011). Mediatisation of religion: A critical appraisal. *Culture and
Religion, 12*(2), 153–166. DOI:10.1080/14755610.2011.579738

(2013). *Media, Religion and Gender: Key Issues and New Challenges*. London:
Routledge.

Lytra, Vally, Volk, Dinah, & Gregory, Eve. (2016). *Navigating Languages, Literacies
and Identities: Religion in Young Lives*. London: Routledge.

Malley, B. (2004). *How the Bible Works: An Anthropological Study of Evangelical
Biblicism*. Walnut Creek, CA: AltaMira Press.

Mamdani, Mahmood. (2002). Good Muslim, bad Muslim: A political perspective on
culture and terrorism. *American Anthropologist, 104*(3), 766–775. DOI:10.1525/
aa.2002.104.3.766

Marsden, George M. (2006). *Fundamentalism and American Culture*. Oxford: Oxford
University Press.

Marwick, Alice, & boyd, danah. (2011). To see and be seen: Celebrity practice on
Twitter. *Convergence, 17*(2), 139–158. DOI:10.1177/1354856510394539

McGrenere, Joanna, & Ho, Wayne. (2000). Affordances: Clarifying and evolving a
concept. *Graphics Interface, 2000*, 179–186.

McNamara, Patrick, & Giordano, Magda. (2018). Cognitive neuroscience and religious
language: A working hypothesis. In Paul Chilton & Monika Kopytowska (Eds.),
Religion, Language, and the Human Mind (pp. 115–134). New York: Oxford
University Press.

Moon, Dawne. (2004). *God, Sex, and Politics: Homosexuality and Everyday
Theologies*. Chicago: University of Chicago Press.

Mukherjee, Sipra. (2013). Reading language and religion together. *International
Journal of the Sociology of Language, 220*, 1–6.

Neary, Clara. (2017). Truth is like a vast tree. *Metaphor and the Social World, 7*(1), 103–121.

Neill, Stephen Charles. (1964). *A History of Christian Missions*. London: Penguin Books.

Nuttall, G. F. (1992). *The Holy Spirit in Puritan Faith and Experience*. Chicago:
University of Chicago Press.

Obaidi, Milan, Kunst, Jonas R., Kteily, Nour, Thomsen, Lotte, & Sidanius, James.
(2018). Living under threat: Mutual threat perception drives anti-Muslim and
anti-Western hostility in the age of terrorism. *European Journal of Social
Psychology, 48*(5), 567–584. DOI:10.1002/ejsp.2362

Oberlin, Kathleen C., & Scheitle, Christopher P. (2019). Biblical literalism influences
perceptions of history as a scientific discipline. *Socius, 5*. DOI:10.1177/
2378023119826425

Ochs, Elinor, & Capps, Lisa. (2011). *Living Narrative*. Cambridge: Harvard University
Press.

Olsteen, Joel. (2004). *Your Best Life Now*. New York: Hachette Book Group.

Omoniyi, Tope, & Fishman, Joshua A. (2006). *Explorations in the Sociology of
Language and Religion*. Amsterdam: John Benjamins Publishing Company.

Packer, James Innell. (1973). *Knowing God.* London: Hodder and Stoughton.

(1978). *The Evangelical Anglican Identity Problem: An Analysis.* Oxford: Latimer.

Page, Ruth. (2012). The linguistics of self-branding and micro-celebrity in Twitter: The role of hashtags. *Discourse & Communication*, *6*(2), 181–201. DOI:10.1177/ 1750481312437441

Pariser, Eli. (2011). *The Filter Bubble: What the Internet Is Hiding from You.* New York: Penguin UK.

Parker, Christopher S., & Barreto, Matt A. (2014). *Change They Can't Believe in: The Tea Party and Reactionary Politics in America.* Princeton: Princeton University Press.

Peplow, David. (2011). 'Oh, I've known a lot of Irish people': Reading groups and the negotiation of literary interpretation. *Language and Literature*, *20*(4), 295–315.

(2016). *Talk about Books: A Study of Reading Groups.* London: Bloomsbury.

Peplow, David, Swann, Joan, Trimarco, Paola, & Whiteley, Sara. (2015). *The Discourse of Reading Groups: Integrating Cognitive and Sociocultural Perspectives.* London: Routledge.

Pigott, Robert. (2013). Doing church without God. Retrieved from www.bbc.co.uk/ne ws/uk-24766314 (Accessed on 20 August 2018)

Pihlaja, Stephen. (2013). 'It's all red ink': The interpretation of biblical metaphor among Evangelical Christian YouTube users. *Language and Literature*, *22*(2), 103–117.

(2014a). *Antagonism on YouTube: Metaphor in Online Discourse.* London: Bloomsbury.

(2014b). 'Christians' and 'bad Christians': Categorization in atheist user talk on YouTube. *Text & Talk*, *34*(5), 623–639.

(2016). 'What about the wolves?': The use of scripture in YouTube arguments. *Language and Literature*, *25*(3), 226–238.

(2017a). More than fifty shades of grey: Copyright on social network sites. *Applied Linguistics Review*, *8*(2–3), 213–228.

(2017b). 'When Noah built the ark . . . ': Metaphor and biblical stories in Facebook preaching. *Metaphor and the Social World*, *5*(1), 86–101.

(2018). *Religious Talk Online: The Evangelical Discourse of Muslims, Christians, and Atheists.* Cambridge: Cambridge University Press.

Pihlaja, Stephen, & Thompson, Naomi. (2017). 'I love the Queen': Positioning in young British Muslim discourse. *Discourse, Context & Media*, *20* (Supplement C), 52–58. https://DOI.org/10.1016/j.dcm.2017.08.002

Piper, John, Taylor, Justin, & Helseth, Paul Kjoss. (2003). *Beyond the Bounds: Open Theism and the Undermining of Biblical Christianity.* Wheaton: Crossway.

Puckett, Lily. (13 May 2019). Christians should prepare to be 'shunned' for their beliefs, Mike Pence warns as he reaffirms Trump administration's anti-abortion stance. Retrieved from www.independent.co.uk/news/world/americas/us-politics/mike-pence -abortion-christian-liberty-university-a8910916.html (Accessed on 13 May 2019)

Quranspeaks.com. (n.d.). About us | QuarnSpeaks.com. Retrieved from www .quranspeaks.com/about (Accessed on 26 June 2017)

Rampton, Ben, Tusting, Karin, Maybin, Janet, et al. (2004). UK linguistic ethnography: A discussion paper. Retrieved from Linguistic Ethnography Forum website: www .ling-ethnog.org.uk (Accessed 14 August 2012)

Raun, Tobias. (2018). Capitalizing intimacy: New subcultural forms of micro-celebrity strategies and affective labour on YouTube. *Convergence*, *24*(1), 99–113.

Richardson, Peter. (2012). A closer walk: A study of the interaction between meta-phors related to movement and proximity and presuppositions about the reality of belief in Christian and Muslim testimonials. *Metaphor and the Social World, 2* (2), 233–261.

(2017). An investigation of the blocking and development of empathy in discussions between Muslim and Christian believers. *Metaphor and the Social World, 7*(1), 47–65.

Richardson, Peter, & Pihlaja, Stephen. (2018). Killing in the name: Contemporary Evangelical Christian interpretations of the Jericho Massacre in the context of anti-immigration and anti-Muslim trends. *Postscripts: The Journal of Sacred Texts and Contemporary Worlds, 9*(1), 27–49.

Ringrow, Helen. (2020). 'Beautiful masterpieces': Metaphors of the female body in modest fashion blogs. In Helen Ringrow & Stephen Pihlaja (Eds.), *Contemporary Media Stylistics* (pp. 15–34). London: Bloomsbury.

Robin, Corey. (2011). *The Reactionary Mind: Conservatism from Edmund Burke to Sarah Palin*. Oxford: Oxford University Press.

Rosch, Eleanor, & Lloyd, Barbara B. (Eds.) (1978). *Cognition and Categorization*. Hillsdale: Lawrence Erlbaum Associates.

Rosowsky, Andrey (Ed.) (2017). *Faith and Language Practices in Digital Spaces*. Bristol: Multilingual Matters.

Sabat, Steven R. (2003). Malignant positioning and the predicament of people with Alzheimer's disease. In Rom Harré & Fathali Moghaddam (Eds.), *The Self and Others Positioning Individuals and Groups in Personal, Political, and Cultural Contexts*. Westport: Praeger.

Sacks, Harvey. (1992). *Lectures on Conversation*. Oxford: Blackwell.

Sacks, Harvey, Schegloff, Emanuel, & Jefferson, Gail. (1974). A simplest system-atics for the organization of turn-taking for conversation. *Language, 50*(4), 696–735.

Sargeant, Kimon Howland. (2000). *Seeker Churches: Promoting Traditional Religion in a Nontraditional Way*. New Brunswick: Rutgers University Press.

Saunders, Nathan Joseph. (2015). *Crabgrass Piety: The Rise of Megachurches and the Suburban Social Religion, 1960–2000*. Columbia: University of South Carolina Press.

Schegloff, Emanuel. (1972). Notes on a conversational practice: Formulating place. In D. N. Sudnow (Ed.), *Studies in Social Interaction* (pp. 75–119). New York: The Free Press.

Schmidt, Jan-Hinrik. (2014). Twitter and the rise of personal publics. In Katrin Weller, Axel Bruns, Jean Burgess, Merja Mahrt, & Cornelius Puschmann (Eds.), *Twitter and Society* (pp. 3–14). New York: Peter Lang.

Schultze, Quentin J. (2003). *Televangelism and American Culture: The Business of Popular Religion*. Eugene: Wipf and Stock Publishers.

Seib, Philip, & Janbek, Dana M. (2010). *Global Terrorism and New Media: The Post–Al Qaeda Generation*. London: Routledge.

Semino, Elena, & Culpeper, Jonathan. (2002). *Cognitive Stylistics: Language and Cognition in Text Analysis* (Vol. 1). Amsterdam: John Benjamins.

Sherkat, Darren E., Powell-Williams, Melissa, Maddox, Gregory, & de Vries, Kylan Mattias. (2011). Religion, politics, and support for same-sex marriage in the United

States, 1988–2008. *Social Science Research*, *40*(1), 167–180. https://DOI.org/10.1016/j.ssresearch.2010.08.009

Shrikant, Natasha. (2018). 'There's no such thing as Asian': A membership categorization analysis of cross-cultural adaptation in an Asian American business community. *Journal of International and Intercultural Communication*, *11*, 1–18.

Sider, John W. (1995). *Interpreting the Parables: A Hermeneutical Guide to Their Meaning*. Grand Rapids: Zondervan.

Silvestre-López, Antonio-José, & Ferrando, Ignasi Navarro i. (2017). Metaphors in the conceptualisation of meditative practices. *Metaphor and the Social World*, *7*(1), 26–46. DOI:10.1075/msw.7.1.03sil

Smith, Christopher, & Cimino, Richard. (2012). Atheisms unbound: The role of the new media in the formation of a secularist identity. *Secularism and Nonreligion*, *1*(0), 17–31. http://DOI.org/10.5334/snr.ab

Smith, Greg, Cooperman, Alan, Mohamed, B., et al. (2015). America's changing religious landscape. Washington, DC: Pew Research Center.

Smith, Wilfred Cantwell. (1994). *What Is Scripture?: A Comparative Approach*. Minneapolis: Fortress Press.

Social Bluebook. (n.d.). Socialbluebook.com. Retrieved from https://socialbluebook.com/ (Accessed 26 September 2018).

Southern Baptist Convention. (n.d.). The Baptist Faith and Message. *Southern Baptist Convention Statement of Faith*. Retrieved from Southern Baptist Convention website: www.sbc.net/bfm/bfm2000.asp#i (Accessed 13 October 2010)

Souza, Ana. (2016). Language and faith encounters: Bridging language-ethnicity and language-religion studies. *International Journal of Multilingualism*, *13*(1), 134–148. DOI:10.1080/14790718.2015.1040023

Spencer, Robert. (2006). *The Truth about Muhammad: Founder of the World's Most Intolerant Religion*. New York: Simon and Schuster.

Sperber, Dan, & Wilson, Deirdre. (1986). *Relevance: Communication and Cognition*. London: Blackwell Publishers.

Spilioti, Tereza, & Tagg, Caroline. (2017). The ethics of online research methods in applied linguistics: Challenges, opportunities, and directions in ethical decision-making. *Applied Linguistics Review*, *8*(2–3), 163–167.

Spolsky, Bernard. (2003). Religion as a site of language contact. *Annual Review of Applied Linguistics*, *23*, 81–94.

(2006). Introduction, Part II. In Tope Omoniyi & Joshua A. Fishman (Eds.), *Explorations in the Sociology of Language and Religion* (pp. 4–8). Amsterdam: John Benjamins.

Steger, Manfred B. (2017). *Globalization: A very Short Introduction* (Vol. 86). Oxford: Oxford University Press.

Stockwell, Peter. (2005). *Cognitive Poetics: An Introduction*. London: Routledge.

Szuchewycz, Bohdan. (1994). Evidentiality in ritual discourse: The social construction of religious meaning. *Language in Society*, *23*(3), 389–410. DOI:10.1017/S0047404500018030

Tagg, Caroline, Seargeant, Philip, & Brown, Amy Aisha. (2017). *Taking Offence on Social Media: Conviviality and Communication on Facebook*. London: Springer.

Tajfel, Henri. (1983). *Social Identity and Intergroup Relations*. Cambridge: Cambridge University Press.

208   References

Tajfel, Henri, Billig, Michael, Bundy, Robert, & Flament, Claude. (1971). Social categorization and intergroup behaviour. *European Journal of Social Psychology*, *1*(2), 149–178.

Thompson, Mark D. (2006). *A Clear and Present Word: The Clarity of Scripture*. London: Intervarsity Press.

Thumma, Scott. (1991). Negotiating a religious identity: The case of the gay Evangelical. *Sociology of Religion*, *52*(4), 333–347. DOI:10.2307/3710850

Trammell, Jim. (2015). Jesus? There's an app for that! Tablet media in the 'new' electronic church. In Mark Ward (Ed.), *The Electronic Church in the Digital Age: Cultural Impacts of Evangelical Mass Media*. Westport: Praeger pp. 219–237.

Tsur, Reuven. (2003). Deixis and abstractions: Adventures in space and time: Editors' preface. *Cognitive Poetics in Practice* (pp. 53–66). London: Routledge.

Turner, Mark, & Fauconnier, Gilles. (1995). Conceptual integration and formal expression. *Metaphor and Symbol*, *10*(3), 183–204.

Limitations on exclusive rights: Fair use, 17 USC § 107 Stat. (1976).

US Copyright Office. (2006). Fair use. Retrieved from www.copyright.gov/fls/fl102 .html (Accessed 12 November 2008).

van Noppen, Jean-Pierre. (1981). *Theolinguistics*. Brussels: Studiereeks Tijdschrift Vrije Universiteit Brussel.

(1983). *Metaphor and Religion (Theolinguistics 2)*. Brussels: Vrije Universiteit Brussel.

(2006). From theolinguistics to critical theolinguistics: The case for communicative probity. *ARC, The Journal of the Faculty of Religious Studies, McGill University*, *34*, 47–65.

(2011). Critical theolinguistics vs. the literalist paradigm. *Sprache und Religion/ Language and Religion/Langue et Religion (Sociolinguistica 25)*. Berlin/ New York: de Gruyter, 28–40.

(2012). God in George W. Bush's Rhetoric. Retrieved from www.o-re-la.org/index .php/analyses/item/175-god-in-george-w-bush%E2%80%99s-rhetoric (Accessed 21 August 2018).

Walls, N. Eugene. (2010). Religion and support for same-sex marriage: Implications from the literature. *Journal of Gay & Lesbian Social Services*, *22*(1–2), 112–131. DOI:10.1080/10538720903332420

Werth, Paul. (1994). Extended metaphor – A text-world account. *Language and Literature*, *3*(2), 79–103.

(1999). *Text Worlds: Representing Conceptual Space in Discourse*. London: Longman.

Whiteley, Sara. (2011). Text world theory, real readers and emotional responses to *The Remains of the Day*. *Language and Literature*, *20*(1), 23–42.

Wierzbicka, Anna. (2018). Speaking about God in universal words, thinking about God outside English. In Paul Chilton & Monika Kopytowska (Eds.), *Religion, Language, and the Human Mind* (pp. 19–51). New York: Oxford University Press.

Winchester, Daniel, & Guhin, Jeffrey. (2018). Praying 'Straight from the Heart': Evangelical sincerity and the normative frames of culture in action. *Poetics*, *72*, 32–42. https://DOI.org/10.1016/j.poetic.2018.10.003

Wong, Janelle S. (2018). *Immigrants, Evangelicals, and Politics in an Era of Demographic Change*. New York: Russell Sage Foundation.

Wuthnow, Robert. (1985). The growth of religious reform movements. *The ANNALS of the American Academy of Political and Social Science*, *480*(1), 106–116. DOI:10.1177/0002716285480001009

(2011). *America and the Challenges of Religious Diversity*. Princeton: Princeton University Press.

Yandell, Keith E. (2002). *Philosophy of Religion: A Contemporary Introduction*. London: Routledge.

Yates, Timothy. (1996). *Christian Mission in the Twentieth Century*. Cambridge: Cambridge University Press.

Yelle, Robert, Handman, Courtney, & Lehrich, Christopher (Eds.). (2019). *Language and Religion*. Berlin: De Gruyter.

Index

Key Concepts, Terms, and People